ANGLING AND THE LAW

Angling and the Law

MICHAEL GREGORY

LL.B. of the Middle Temple, Barrister-at-Law

2nd Edition

Charles Knight
London and Tonbridge
1974

Charles Knight & Co. Ltd.
11—12 Bury Street, London, EC3A 5AP
Dowgate Works, Douglas Road, Tonbridge

ISBN 0 85314 211 4

Typeset in Great Britain by
Specialised Printing Services Ltd, London
and printed by
Lewis Reprints Ltd, Tonbridge

CONTENTS

PREFACE TO THE SECOND EDITION

Angling law has taken a wash-and-brush-up since 1967, and so therefore has this book. The new Salmon and Freshwater Fisheries Act, 1972, has reformed some aspects of the law the angler meets face to face (close seasons, fishing licences, prohibited methods of taking fish) and others he hopes never to be on the receiving end of — trial and punishment of offenders and powers of bailiffs. The Act also tinkers with topics such as stocking, fish passes, catch returns and byelaws.

The Theft Act, 1968, and the Criminal Damage Act, 1971, in abolishing the time-dishonoured crimes of larceny and malicious damage, have pupped new laws against poachers and vandals. Other young legislation, especially the Countryside Act, 1968, and the Part of the Transport Act, 1968, dealing with inland waters, is designed to organise our enjoyment of the open-air, "including fishing" as the latter measure keeps saying. New bodies have been conceived or spawned, others condemned to death.

Recent fishy court decisions have on the whole demonstrated the strong legal hand held by owners and occupiers of fishing — especially *Burgess* v. *Gwynedd River Authority* (1972) (£7,000 damages for injury to a fishery by drainage works) and *Rawson* v. *Peters* (successful trespass claim by an angling club against a canoeist).

These and other novelties have made inroads into most pages of the first edition. The book has been re-shaped somewhat, and sea fishing, with its considerable new legislation, given a chapter to itself.

The Government plans for water reorganisation are foreshadowed and explained — especially in Chapter 22. It is important for the indulgent reader to note that if and when the projected laws are passed, river authorities will die a death and the proposed regional water authorities will take over all things wet and watery.

I must acknowledge again the ever-ready help of the Fisheries Department of the Ministry of Agriculture, Fisheries and Food, and of the skilful publishers of this work.

MICHAEL GREGORY
Fleet Farm House, Fleet

November, 1972

PREFACE TO THE FIRST EDITION

This book gathers together in one place the law concerning angling at a time when great and Governmental interest is being taken in the problem of providing leisure in the countryside for our teeming millions. It is a time when Countryside Conferences have disclosed that angling, with its own three million and more teeming devotees, has far and away more practitioners than any other active recreation in this country – a time when we have a Minister of Sport ready and willing to see angling benefit from grants under the Physical Training and Recreation Acts, 1937 and 1958, when a Countryside Commission is about to be appointed, when landowners, overshadowed by multifarious taxmen, are more and more developing and leasing fisheries, and when the Water Resources Act, 1963, has radically altered the law of waters but has done so with a proper regard to angling interests.

Anglers and owners of fishing rights are strongly armed by the law to repel boarders but angling clubs and associations, as well as the angler himself, will need to be vigilant to protect the interests of those three million adherents against gathering hazards imperilling their pastime. It is hoped the recent formation of the National Anglers Council will help to see to this. Appendices to this book deal in detail with two of the most formidable of these enemies of angling, namely pollution and water abstraction, against which the owners of fishing have a shield if they care to use it.

It is appreciated that most who are concerned with angling and the administration of fisheries are not lawyers and will have no love for the pomposities of a legal textbook. It is hoped that these have been suitably avoided. At the same time it is believed that there is a place on the legal bookshelf for a work on this subject. The legal phrase and technicality has therefore not been shunned, but the policy has been adopted of explaining them as they occur. Recognising that the word of the law comes alive when clothed with real-life cases, the text is amply illustrated with examples from the courtroom.

Proper attention is paid to the owner of fishing and to the angling club in the chapters ahead, as well of course to the angler whether he be after salmon, trout, coarse or sea fish. Appendices therefore include a model fishing lease, model rules for angling clubs, typical fishery byelaws and a list of waters where no licence is required for freshwater fishing. The Sea Fisheries Regulation Act, 1966, incommodiously passed through Parliament during the course of printing but nevertheless the changes made by it are included in this book.

Enough of groundbaiting the swim! Before casting ahead, contemplative reader, permit me however to acknowledge my indebtedness and gratitude to the most helpful and skilful publishers and printers of this book, and also to the many other guides whose advice has been invaluable, especially the Fisheries Department of the Ministry of Agriculture, Fisheries and Food, Mr J.E.Maher of the Country Landowners' Association, an incomparable expert on watery subjects, Mr Charles Wade, Director of the Anglers' Co-operative Association, which has a proud record of saving waters from the menace of pollution, and the Avon and Dorset River Authority who have kindly allowed their Fishery Byelaws to be reproduced.

MICHAEL GREGORY
Fleet Farm House, Fleet

July, 1967

TABLE OF CASES

TABLE OF STATUTES

CHAPTER 1

FISHING LAW AND ITS ORIGINS

In 1175 a Scottish statute of Richard the Lionhearted laid down that so much of the mid-stream channel of a river must be kept free of obstruction that a well-fed three-year-old pig, sideways on to the stream, would not touch either side. It also forbade fishing at week-ends between Saturday sunset and Monday sunrise. This was the first positive intervention we know of by the law to protect fishing. A century later came the first known English statutes, the *Placita Coronae* for Cumberland in 1278, orders regulating salmon fisheries in the Eden and Esk and requiring obstructions placed in these rivers to have a free gap large enough for a sow and her piglets to pass through. In view of man's propensity for destroying what he values, such laws have been life-giving to fisheries, and during the last one hundred years the law's contribution to angling has certainly been life-*saving*. The law is by no means perfect, but the contemplative angler reading the "dos" and "don'ts" on his 25p day ticket, and hazarding a gesture for the law and its restrictions, would do his conscience no harm by giving it a polite salute — for it is undoubtedly the angler's greatest ally.

Three Million "Well-governed" Anglers

Those who seem to have a mystic knowledge of how many do what, without counting them, have disclosed that Great Britain has three million anglers. Imagine the result if each of these was a "law unto himself" and his pastime subject to the unbridled whim of any others who wanted, or thought they wanted, to use or destroy this country's waters as they saw fit. History ancient and modern has shown that uncontrolled exploitation of natural resources or assets by the few, is sufficient to destroy them for the many. That great Public Relations Officer for anglers, Izaak Walton, came out with this lyrical flow:

> "No life so happy and so pleasant, as the life of a well-governed angler; for when the lawyer is swallowed up with business, and the statesman is preventing or contriving plots, then we sit on cowslip-banks, hear the birds sing, and possess ourselves in as much quietness as these silent silver streams . . . "[1]

---

[1] *Compleat Angler* Chapter V, Fourth Day.

Today he might comment that it was just as well the lawyer and the lawmaker were about their business, and that the angler has been "well-governed" because if they had not been there would now be precious little, if any, angling, cowslip-banks, birds, silver streams or fish.

At times the law may have been slow to step to the fisherman's aid, but it has always been there or thereabouts since they measured things by the girth of pigs. The public can fish free of charge from the sea-shore and in tidal rivers today, because Magna Carta gave them the right in 1215 and the law has preserved it ever since. At the same time Magna Carta freed rivers from weirs which obstructed not only navigation but the passage of migratory fish. Seven hundred and fifty years later these ancient laws still hold good, and we find the Salmon and Freshwater Fisheries Act, 1965, striking a modern blow for the legitimate angler by barring unauthorised electric fishing.

The Modern Law

It is only in the last one hundred years or so, however, that Parliament has made a national effort to prevent harmful exploitation of fisheries. In 1861, following a report of a Royal Commission the legislature started on a course of drastic activity for the welfare of fishing interests, starting with the passing of the Salmon Fishery Act, 1861. The law's restrictions at that time were insufficient to prevent man's avarice from ruling the waters, and man, if he was suitably positioned in a river could and did fill his fishery with devices of any number or design with the object of getting every passing salmon by hook or by crook — preferably crook.

This led James Paterson in the Preface of his book *The Fishery Laws including the Laws of Angling* published in 1863 to include this castigating passage (hardly likely to endear him to much of his potential readership):

"The riparian owners have exclusive access to most of the waters. Holding the key of the situation, they monopolise the means of capture. As between themselves, they have been distinguished for unneighbourly cupidity. The common law undoubtedly was too easy in its tenets, for it allowed each to catch all the fish he could, by whatever means he pleased, provided these were not such as to destroy and annihilate the neighbour's shares of the common subject matter, and even this check there was no effective machinery for enforcing. Each accordingly sought to do what he liked with his own part of the river, and often selfishly resorted to weirs, dams and fixed engines with the object of driving every living inhabitant of the waters into his own net, regardless of the impoverishment of his neighbour."

The 1861 Act repealed thirty-three statutes and got down to the task of well-governing the ungoverned fisherman. In 1865 the English Commissioners for Fisheries were appointed to investigate what fixed devices there were in each fishery for taking salmon, certifying those which were legal and condemning the others. Fishery Statutes followed every few years and began to protect both trout and coarse fishing as well as salmon.

The Salmon and Freshwater Fisheries Act, 1923. By 1923 this spate of legislation had produced eighteen statutes, and the Salmon and Freshwater Fisheries Act, 1923, repealed them all and consolidated their provisions with amendments in this single measure. This Act is still the main Act regulating angling and protecting salmon and freshwater fisheries. It has been added to and amended by the following further Acts:

> The Salmon and Freshwater Fisheries (Amendment) Act, 1929;
> The Salmon and Freshwater Fisheries Act, 1935;
> The Salmon and Freshwater Fisheries Act, 1923 (Amendment) Act, 1964;
> The Salmon and Freshwater Fisheries Act, 1965;
> The Salmon and Freshwater Fisheries Act, 1972.

These later Acts (all short ones, except for the 1972 Act) have tinkered with the law. The 1964 and 1965 Acts, both "one section Acts"[1], made an over-modest start on implementing the many important recommendations of the Bledisloe Committee on "Salmon and Freshwater Fisheries" (1961).[2] The 1972 Act, with sixteen sections and three schedules, has made a belated effort to get on with it.

In addition the Diseases of Fish Act, 1937, was passed for preventing the spreading of disease among salmon and freshwater fish. The Water Resources Act, 1963, though not primarily a fishing statute, has played an important part on the angling scene, not least because in handing over to the new-born river authorities the duties of the river boards, which it exterminated, it gave them the added duty of controlling water abstraction. The river authorities are also the authorities responsible for inland fisheries. All this is soon to be changed when the proposed regional water authorities take over the responsibilities of river authorities (see Chapter 22).

Sea Angling

In contrast, sea angling is practically untrammelled by Acts of Parliament, though the many statutes dealing with commercial harvesting of the sea, and with shipping, can impinge on the sport.

The Common Law

In the chapters ahead the common law is frequently mentioned. By the common law is meant the law which is not statute law, not written in Acts of Parliament. Some of our most cherished rights are not to be found laid down in any statute, but are in the common law. This is the law which is derived largely from custom and the decisions of the Courts. It is sometimes said to be the unwritten law, but this is a bad description because it is recorded through being repeated by the judges in their judgments, a sufficient number

---

[1] "One Section Acts" in fact have two sections, but only one has any meat in it.
[2] HMSO, Command Paper 1350 (1961).

of which are preserved in law reports. It is also expounded in the writings of the great jurists. Furthermore, the common law is constantly developing by judges deciding, in the cases they try, how it applies in many varied circumstances.

Nearly all the law concerning ownership of fishing rights is in the common law and, although statute law prevails over and can repeal any part of it, the common law is a powerful ruler. Its power will be seen, for example, in Chapter 20 on pollution. For all the armoury given to river authorities by statute, none of it is so powerful in combating pollution as the common law rights of the riparian land owners who own the fishing.

England and Wales

Scottish law is based on a different system from that of England and Wales, although much of it is the same and the ultimate Court of Appeal for all is the House of Lords. The statutes mentioned above extend only to England and Wales, except where any provision is said by the Act to apply to Scotland or Northern Ireland. The 1923 and 1972 Acts make special provision for rivers which cross the England/Scotland border and also for the Solway Firth.[1] An exception is the Diseases of Fish Act, 1937, which applies to Scotland with certain modifications.

Abbreviations in this book

A book on angling law must make frequent reference to the Salmon and Freshwater Fisheries Acts, and the Minister of Agriculture, Fisheries and Food. Both are quite a mouthful. For this reason, unless the context indicates otherwise, the following abbreviations are used:

> "The 1923 Act", means the Salmon and Freshwater Fisheries Act, 1923.

> "The 1972 Act", means the Salmon and Freshwater Fisheries Act, 1972.

> "The Minister", means the Minister of Agriculture, Fisheries and Food.[2]

---

[1] See the Salmon and Freshwater Fisheries Act, 1923, ss. 82–85, and Salmon and Freshwater Fisheries Act, 1972, s. 15. See also *Gibson* v. *Ryan* [1967] 3 All E.R. 184 – prosecutions in England under the Salmon and Freshwater Fisheries (Protection) (Scotland) Act 1951 for offences committed on 'so much of the river Tweed as is situated outwith Scotland'.

[2] These abbreviations (except "1972 Act") have the same meanings in the Salmon and Freshwater Fisheries Acts – see 1923 Act, s. 92(1); and 1972 Act, s. 14.

CHAPTER 2

THE FISH

Four Categories of Fish

Much of the law for the angler is found in the six Salmon and Freshwater Fisheries Acts, 1923–72. These divide fish into three main groups which it calls freshwater fish, salmon and trout. There is a fourth group dealt with by separate legislation, namely, sea fish. The law also makes special rules for certain fish which fall into these categories such as rainbow trout, sturgeon and oysters, and also for eels and elvers which do not quite fit into any neat legal compartment. Except for sea fish, fish are divided into these categories mainly because of differences in the time of their spawning season. Different close seasons are therefore laid down for each category.[1] Rules are also made regarding methods which may be used to capture the members of each category.

Salmon are given special attention by the law because, being of regal status among fish and having an enhanced financial value compared with their lesser brethren, they require greater protection against unscrupulous exploitation and poaching.

Freshwater fish. This is a poor description, because as far as the 1923 Act is concerned:

" 'Freshwater fish' means fish living in fresh water exclusive of salmon and trout and of any kinds of fish which migrate to and from tidal waters and of eels."[2]

In other words these are what are generally called "coarse fish". Those the angler will be interested in principally are barbel, bleak, bream, carp, chub, dace, grayling, gudgeon, perch, pike, roach, rudd, tench, combinations of these such as pike-perch, and possibly such lesser fellows as the loaches, minnows or pope.

Salmon are defined simply.

---

[1] River authorities may now dispense with a close season for freshwater fish and rainbow trout – Salmon and Freshwater Fisheries Act, 1972, s. 4. See Chapter 3.

[2] Salmon and Freshwater Fisheries Act, 1923, s. 92(1). "Eels include elvers and the fry of eels (Salmon and Freshwater Fisheries Act, 1972, s. 14(3). For purposes of the Diseases of Fish Act, 1937, eels would be included in the definition of freshwater fish (s. 10(1)).

"The expression 'salmon' means all fish of the salmon species."[1]

Trout call for three interpretations in the 1923 Act. First:

"The expression 'trout' means any fish of the salmon family commonly known as trout and includes 'migratory trout' as hereinafter defined."[1]

Then the promised definition:

"The expression 'migratory trout' means trout which migrate to and from the sea."[1]

Then the Act tells us:

"This Act shall apply to char in like manner as to trout as if in this Act the expression trout included char."

In short, "trout" when referred to in the Acts includes two groups of the family *salmonidae*, namely the *salmones* (trout) and the *salvelini* (char).

Sea Fish generally means fish of any kind found in the sea except for fish of the salmon species and migratory trout.[2] This includes shell fish and other crustaceans.

Royal Fish

Should an angler catch a sturgeon, porpoise or whale, and survive, he will usually be obliged to "offer it to the Sovereign", for these are "royal fish" (even though the last two named are not fish at all but mammals). A statute of Edward II made in 1324[3] lays down that whales and sturgeons taken within the King's dominion shall belong to the King. Sir Matthew Hale (1609–76) in his historical *De Jure Maris* wrote that the royal fish were "sturgeon, grampuses, or great fish".

A royal patent granting certain privileges to the High Admiral of the United Kingdom was more graphic, conveying to him the right to "all royal fishes, such as sturgeons, grampuses, whales, porpoises, dolphins, riggs, and generally all other fishes of very large bulk or fatness".[4]

According to Hale, royal fish "taken in the wide sea" belong to the taker, and it is thought the Crown's privilege relates to "fish" taken in territorial waters. The Crown's prerogative does not, however, extend to fish

---

[1] Salmon and Freshwater Fisheries Act, 1923, s. 92(1); but for purposes of the Diseases of Fish Act, 1937, salmon includes all *salmonidae* (s. 10(1)), which brings in trout. Rainbow trout are not included in close seasons for trout, see p.11 below.
[2] See Sea Fisheries Regulation Act, 1966, s. 20; Sea Fish (Conservation) Act, 1967, s. 22(1); and see further Chapter 6.
[3] De Prerogativa Regis 17 Ed. 2 st. 2, c. 11.
[4] See *Lord Warden of Cinque Ports* v. *R.* (1831) 2 Hag. Ad. 438.

taken from waters where the Crown's right has been relinquished. It was decided in 1831 that the Lord Warden was entitled to royal fish within the jurisdiction of the Cinque Ports.[1] Haggard's Admiralty Reports quaintly relate how "in 1829 the Master and crew of seven oyster smacks discovered a whale three miles from the shore and towed it onto Whitstable beach". The Admiralty Court issued a warrant for "the arrest of the whale, oil, blubber and bones" as these were claimed as "perquisites of the Lord Warden". The "smacksmen" and the Crown also laid claim to them. The Court decided in favour of the Lord Warden who during "time whereof the memory of man runneth not to the contrary" had been entitled to all the perquisites of the sea within the jurisdiction of the Cinque Ports. It is therefore doubtful also whether the royal privilege extends to non-tidal waters, so that if the whales which in 1967 caused excitement by entering the Thames estuary had managed to penetrate above Teddington Lock, an interesting point of law would have arisen for the advisers of the circus proprietor who was only dissuaded from capturing them by the advice that they were "royal fish".

Eels

Although expressly omitted from the definition of freshwater fish, these maligned creatures receive a measure of protection in the coarse fish close season,[2] and the Salmon and Freshwater Fisheries Acts enable Ministerial Orders to be made for the benefit of eel fisheries. Orders may apply the laws for freshwater fish to eels.[3] For example, an order came into operation on February 22, 1965, enabling the Essex River Authority to make byelaws in its area extending to eel and elver fisheries its powers under the 1923 Act regarding the acquisition and use of fisheries, fishing rights and fish rearing establishments, the need for rod licences, and prohibition of fishing by methods illegal for other fish, and in particular prohibiting the use of fish roe for bait.[4] Restrictions are also made on the use of eel baskets, but these are for the protection not of eels but salmon and trout.[5]

---

[1] See *Lord Warden of Cinque Ports* v. *R.* (1831) 2 Hag. Ad. 438.
[2] See Chapter 3.
[3] S. 1 of 1935 Act.
[4] Essex River Board Area (Eels and Elvers) Order, 1964 (S. 1 1965 No. 337).
[5] 1923 Act, s. 36, and see p.11.

CHAPTER 3

CLOSE SEASONS

At present there are standard close seasons for freshwater fish, salmon and trout laid down by Parliament. There is no close season for sea fish. In some close seasons it is forbidden to fish for the protected fish by any means whatsoever. Other close seasons prohibit for certain periods specified methods of fishing. River authorities may, however, make byelaws to alter in their areas the standard close seasons within limits specified by the 1923 Act and the 1972 Act. This can be awkward for the angler, especially as many river authorities specify different close seasons in different parts of their areas, and often for different reaches of the same rivers. Usually the close season for migratory trout is different from that for other trout.[1]

Any person breaking the rules for close seasons commits an offence, for which the maximum penalty is a fine of £100, or, on a second or subsequent conviction, £200.[2]

Duty of River Authorities to Make Close Season Byelaws

The 1972 Act has introduced a code making for even more flexibility. The scheme is for all close seasons and close times for salmon and trout (but not necessarily freshwater fish, rainbow trout or eels) to be dealt with in local byelaws by June 29, 1975 — i.e. three years from the passing of the Act. River authorities are required to make the necessary byelaws (if they do not already exist) by that date.[3] In making the byelaws they have more freedom than before the 1972 Act as to when the close seasons shall be, but they must still keep to the minimum periods laid down in the 1923 Act. Once the byelaws are made for any river authority area, the standard close seasons cease to have effect in that area. Until byelaws take over in any area the standard close seasons continue to apply. It looks, therefore, as though the standard close seasons for salmon and trout will be dead and buried before June 29, 1975. For the sake of accuracy, however, two reservations must be expressed.

---

[1] Details of all close seasons are given in the biennial publication *Where to Fish* (Harmsworth Press Ltd).

[2] Salmon and Freshwater Fisheries Act, 1972, s. 12 and Sched. 2. See also p.169 below for other possible penalties.

[3] *Ibid.*, s. 3(1).

Firstly, although it is well known the intention behind section 3 of the 1972 Act is to require river authorities within three years to make byelaws for every kind of salmon and trout close season, the section does not say so. It states that every river authority must within three years make byelaws fixing the annual close season and weekly close time for salmon and trout (other than rainbow trout). The annual close season and weekly close time do not apply to fishing by rod and line, or by putts and putchers, because the 1923 Act says so.[1] It would appear therefore that there is no duty to fix any rod and line and putts and putchers close seasons by byelaws. The river authorities are, however, charged by the 1972 Act with making the byelaws "under section 59(1)(a) to (d) of the 1923 Act". As section 59(1)(b) and (d) empower the making of byelaws to fix close seasons for rod and line (and a new para (bb) to fix close seasons for putts and putchers), it is left to implication that the obligation to fix close seasons by byelaws within three years extends to close seasons for rod and line and putts and putchers. It is also left to implication that when such byelaws are made the standard close seasons for rod and line and putts and putchers will cease to have effect, though here the implication is stronger because a schedule to the 1972 Act lists these among "Repeals of the 1923 Act taking effect on the coming into force of byelaws".[2] This is hardly good enough for those who must try to understand the Act. It remains to be seen whether the Courts think it good enough at law.

Secondly, if a river authority defaults in making the necessary byelaws by June 29, 1975, the Minister may make the byelaws.[3] As it is left to the Minister's discretion whether to do so, it is conceivable that for some areas no byelaws will be made. Presumably this will be the case where salmon or trout are unknown — in which case the standard close seasons would in effect lie dormant but capable of leaping to life should trout or salmon introduce themselves, or be introduced, to pastures new.

Close Seasons for Freshwater Fish

The 1972 Act states "the annual close season for freshwater fish shall be the period between 14th March and 16th June except in relation to waters for which such a season is dispensed with or a different period is substituted by byelaws".[4] This means that the angler may fish for coarse fish up to midnight on March 14 and during the whole of June 16, but not in between. By making byelaws the river authorities may alter the dates for their own areas, or dispense with the close season altogether. The power to dispense with the close season is a novelty of the 1972 Act. It is also an oddity, because if the close season· is not dispensed with it must be at least

---

[1] See Salmon and Freshwater Fisheries Act, 1923, ss. 26(1) and 27(1); and s. 31(1) which does not refer to putts and putchers.
[2] Salmon and Freshwater Fisheries Act, 1972, Sched. 3, Part II.
[3] *Ibid.*, s. 3(2).
[4] *Ibid.*, s. 4(5).

ninety-three days. This stems from a policy of trying to please opposite camps at the same time. It is generally acknowledged that a close season for coarse fish cannot be justified on scientific grounds[1], but certain angling bodies are vehemently opposed to its abolition. Others do not want unnecessary restrictions — hence the logic defying compromise, all ninety-three days or nothing.

During the close season no person may fish for, take or kill, or attempt to take or kill any freshwater fish "in any inland water".[2] By bringing in the phrase "inland water", the 1972 Act has extended the close season to some waters previously exempt — such as waters not connected with or communicating with any river, but within a river authority area. "Inland water" here has the same meaning as in the Water Resources Act, 1963, s.135.[3] It is an important definition, and runs as follows:

' "inland water" means any of the following, that is to say —
(a) so much of any river, stream or other watercourse, whether natural or artificial and whether tidal or not, as is within any of the river authority areas;
(b) any lake or pond, whether natural or artificial, and any reservoir or dock, in so far as any such lake, pond, reservoir or dock does not fall within the preceding paragraph and is within any of the river authority areas; and
(c) so much of any channel, creek, bay, estuary or arm of the sea as does not fall within the preceding paragraphs and is within any of the river authority areas.'

Any reference to an inland water includes a reference to part of an inland water.[3]

The restrictions do not apply (a) to the removal of freshwater fish by the owner or occupier from any "several fishery"[4] where salmon or trout are specially preserved; (b) to any person fishing with rod and line, and with written permission of the owner or occupier of the fishery, in any several fishery where salmon or trout are specially preserved; (c) to any person with written permission taking fish for scientific purposes or for bait in a several fishery — or, so long as it does not contravene a byelaw, in any other fishery.[5]

---

[1] Cf. Bledisloe Committee Report "Salmon and Freshwater Fisheries" (1961) Cmnd. Paper 1350, para. 69.
[2] Salmon and Freshwater Fisheries Act, 1972, s. 4(3).
[3] Ibid., s. 14(1).
[4] See p.72 below for meaning of several fishery.
[5] Salmon and Freshwater Fisheries Act, 1972, s. 4(4).

The former provisions against selling freshwater fish have been repealed by the 1972 Act.[1]

Rainbow Trout

The 1972 Act introduces a power to lay down an annual close season for rainbow trout. No standard close season is specified. Instead there is an optional power to fix the close season by byelaws. As with freshwater fish, if a close season is fixed, it must be for not less than ninety-three days.[2] It is an offence to fish for, take or kill, or attempt to take or kill, rainbow trout in any inland water[3] during the close season for rainbow trout.[4] The same exemptions from these restrictions apply as for freshwater fish.[5]

Eels and Lamperns

There is no close season for eels or lamperns, but during the close season for freshwater fish, it is illegal to fish for eels by rod and line[4], except in waters where this method is authorised by byelaws. Also the same exemptions apply as in the case of freshwater fish.[5]

It is also illegal between December 31 and June 25 following to hang, fix or use in any water frequented by salmon or migratory trout any baskets, nets, traps or devices for catching eels. It is forbidden during the same period to place in any inland water any device whatsoever to catch or obstruct any fish descending the river. At no time in the year is it permissible to place upon the apron of a weir any basket, trap or device for taking fish. In spite of these restrictions, however, eel baskets not exceeding ten inches in diameter in any part may be used, if they are constructed to be fished with bait and are not used at a dam or other obstruction, or in any conduit or artificial channel by which water is deviated from a river. Devices for catching eels which are forbidden by these rules may, however, be authorised by the river authority or the Minister of Agriculture, Fisheries and Food.

Wheels or traps for taking lamperns may be placed on the apron of a weir between August 1 and March 1 following.[6]

Close Season for Salmon

By the 1923 Act salmon have an annual close season, during which they may only be fished for with rod and line or putts and putchers, but there are also separate close seasons for rod and line and for putts and putchers, and a weekly close time. Putts and putchers are basket traps, and it is usually irrelevant that they may be used during the annual close season, because the close season for putts and putchers normally covers the whole of the annual close season and more.

---

[1] *Ibid.*, s. 16(3) and Sched. 3.
[2] *Ibid.*, s. 4(1) and (6).
[3] See p.10 above for meaning of "inland water".
[4] Salmon and Freshwater Fisheries Act, 1972, s. 4(3).
[5] Salmon and Freshwater Fisheries Act, 1972, s. 4(4).
[6] Salmon and Freshwater Fisheries Act, 1923, s. 36.

As explained above (p.8) the standard close seasons and close time apply until superseded by byelaws which river authorities have a duty to make by June 28, 1975. In making the byelaws, the river authorities are no longer bound to fix the close seasons to commence by any particular dates, and they are no longer bound by a maximum period for the close time.[1] They are still bound by the minimum periods specified in the 1923 Act.

(1) *The standard annual close season* for salmon (usually known as the close season for nets) is between August 31 and February 1 following (i.e. they may be taken on the days mentioned, but not in between). When fixed by byelaws the annual close season must be at least 153 days.

(2) *The standard close season for rod and line* is between October 31 and February 1 following. When fixed by byelaws this close season must be at least ninety-two days.

(3) *The standard close season for putts and putchers* is between the commencement of the annual close season and May 1 following. The 1972 Act now enables this close season to be fixed by byelaws, with a minimum period of 242 days.[2]

(4) *The standard weekly close time* is between 6 a.m. on Saturday and 6 a.m. on Monday. When fixed by byelaws the close time must be at least forty-two hours.

No person may fish for, take, kill or attempt to take or kill, salmon (1) during the annual close season, except with a rod and line, or with putts and putchers; (2) with rod and line during the close season for rod and line; (3) with putts and putchers during the close season for putts and putchers; and (4) during the weekly close time, except with rod and line, or with putts and putchers unless (in all these cases) it is done with the written permission of the river authority or Ministry of Agriculture, Fisheries and Food, for the purpose of artificial propagation of fish, or for some scientific purpose.[3]

Removal of "Fixed Engines"

As soon as the annual close season for salmon starts the 1923 Act requires the occupier to remove "fixed engines" for taking salmon, or else to render them incapable of taking or obstructing the passage of salmon, and the same applies during the weekly close time. Putts and putchers may remain in use except during the close season for them.[4]

"Fixed engines" are defined in the 1923 Act to include a variety of contrivances such as anchored or floating nets of many descriptions and also putts and putchers, but not fishing weirs or fishing mill dams.[5]

---

[1] Salmon and Freshwater Fisheries Act, 1972, s. 3(3).
[2] *Ibid.*, s. 3(4).
[3] Salmon and Freshwater Fisheries Act, 1923, ss. 26 and 27. The minimum periods are given in s. 59(1)(*a*)-(*c*), as amended by Salmon and Freshwater Fisheries Act, 1972, s. 3(4).
[4] Salmon and Freshwater Fisheries Act, 1923, s. 28.
[5] *Ibid.*, s. 92(1) – defined in Chapter 8.

The 1923 Act also makes it an offence to do *anything* to deter salmon from passing up a river during the annual close season or weekly close time, whether it be by placing obstructions in the river or otherwise. This provision does not prevent the angler from fishing for other kinds of fish which may legally be caught nor, again, does it apply to putts and putchers in the weekly close time.[1]

Sale of Salmon

It is an offence to buy, sell, expose for sale, or have in one's possession for sale any salmon, or part of a salmon, between August 31 and February 1 following, or have in one's possession the whole or part of a salmon to sell between those dates,[2] unless it has been canned, frozen, cured, salted, pickled, dried or preserved in some other way outside Great Britain or Ireland or so preserved within Great Britain and Ireland after February 1 and before August 31 in any year. Nor is it an offence if the fish was caught as a clean salmon outside Great Britain and Ireland, or if it was caught as a clean and mature fish within Great Britain and Ireland lawfully by some means other than by rod and line.

The usual rule that an accused person is innocent until proved guilty does not apply to anyone buying, selling and so on, salmon out of season.[3]

Close Season for Trout

By the 1923 Act trout (other than rainbow trout) have an annual close season during which they may only be fished for with rod and line, a close season for rod and line, and a weekly close time. Because of their different breeding habits — or lack of them — rainbow trout are not subject to the trout close seasons and weekly close time, but are separately provided for (see p.11 above).

By a new provision of the 1972 Act, byelaws are now to be made fixing a close season for putts and putchers.[4] As noted above (p.8) river authorities have a duty to fix close seasons and a weekly close time for trout by byelaws. In doing so, as in the case of salmon (see p.12 above), they are freed from some of the time and date limitations formerly imposed on them.[5]

The standard annual close season for trout is between August 31 and March 1 following. When fixed by byelaws the annual close season must be at least 181 days.

The standard close season for rod and line is between September 30 and March 1 following. When fixed by byelaws this close season must be at least 153 days.

The standard weekly close time is between 6 a.m. on Saturday and 6 a.m. on Monday. When fixed by byelaws the close time must be at least

[1] *Ibid.*, s. 29.
[2] *Birkett* v. *McGlassons Ltd* [1957]1 All E.R. 369.
[3] Salmon and Freshwater Fisheries Act, 1923, s. 30.
[4] Salmon and Freshwater Fisheries Act, 1972, s. 3(4).
[5] *Ibid.*, s. 3(3).

forty-two hours.

Putts and putchers. There is no standard close season. When fixed by byelaws the close season must be at least 242 days.

During the annual close season, the close season for rod and line, and weekly close time it is forbidden to fish for, take, kill or attempt to take or kill trout, except that rod and line may be used for these purposes in the weekly close time and the part of the annual close season which is open to rod and line. It is not an offence to do any of these things for the purpose of the artificial propagation of fish, the stocking or re-stocking of waters, or for some scientific purpose, provided written permission has first been obtained from the river authority or Ministry of Agriculture, Fisheries and Food.

The effect of permitting, or requiring, river authorities to make byelaws fixing a close season for putts and putchers for trout is obscure. Unlike the other close seasons and close times, there is no provision making it an offence to fish for, take or kill trout (or to attempt to) by putts and putchers in the putts and putchers close season. On the other hand (unlike the salmon annual close season and weekly close time) putts and putchers clearly may not be used for trout in the annual close season and weekly close time for trout. It is therefore doubtful what penal byelaw can be made against putts and putchers for trout unless it is by way of fixing the annual close season.

The rules for obstruction of salmon during the annual close season and close time apply to the obstruction of migratory trout during the close season and weekly close time for trout.[1]

Sale of Trout

As with salmon, it is an offence to buy, sell or expose for sale any trout except rainbow trout during the statutory close season, i.e. between August 31 and March 1 following, or have them in one's possession for sale between those dates.[2] The exceptions to this rule are the same as for salmon (see p.13) except that the season during which it is permissible to have canned, frozen, etc., fish within Great Britain and Ireland is, of course, between March 1 and August 31, and again the burden of proving innocence falls on the person buying, selling, etc., the fish.[3] A further exception allows trout to be bought or sold, etc., for the purpose of the artificial propagation of fish, or the stocking or re-stocking of waters, or for some scientific purpose.[4]

Seizure of Fish

If any salmon, trout or freshwater fish are bought, sold, exposed for sale or in possession for sale in contravention of the 1923 Act, they may be

---

[1] Salmon and Freshwater Fisheries Act, 1923, s. 31. The minimum periods are given in s. 59(1)(*d*), as amended by Salmon and Freshwater Fisheries Act, 1972, s. 3(4).
[2] *Ibid.*, s. 32, see *Birkett* v. *McGlassons Ltd* [1957]1 All E.R. 369.
[3] Salmon and Freshwater Fisheries Act, 1929, s. 1.
[4] Salmon and Freshwater Fisheries Act, 1923, s. 32.

seized by any of the following officers: an officer of a river authority acting within the river authority area; or an officer of a marketing authority within his authority's area; or a person appointed by the Minister for the purpose; or any police officer.[1]

---

[1]*Ibid.*, s. 78.   S. 78 has not been amended although the prohibition against selling freshwater fish has been repealed by the 1972 Act.   For disposal of seized fish, see p.170.

CHAPTER 4

PERMISSIONS AND FISHING LICENCES

The general rule is that the angler may not fish until he has obtained two kinds of permissions — (1) the right to fish — e.g. by permission of the owner of the fishing rights — and (2) an official fishing licence from the river authority (called in angling vernacular a "rod licence"). The official fishing licence is obtainable from the Fisheries Officer at the river authority offices, but it can often be obtained more conveniently from local fishing tackle shops, post offices, riverside inns or angling club secretaries.

The Owner's Permission

All waters are owned by somebody — except for the high seas. Possession of a river authority licence to fish does not mean the holder can fish anywhere he likes without permission of the owner of the fishing rights.[1] Equally, having the owner's permission does not mean that the angler may fish without an official licence. As will be seen in Chapter 5 in most *tidal* waters the public have the right to fish. In non-tidal waters they have not, although in some places the owners tolerate public fishing. By joining an Angling Club the angler obtains the right to fish in the waters owned or leased by the Club and this is often the best and cheapest way of obtaining permission to fish. "Day tickets" giving permission to fish are, however, obtainable on many private or Club waters, and it is common for inns to hold fishing rights and to grant permission to fish for the day or longer periods.

Official Fishing Licences

Fishing licences for salmon and trout. A river authority fishing licence is required before an angler may lawfully fish for salmon or trout in any water in a river authority area. A licence for salmon and trout is therefore needed everywhere in England and Wales, except in the Metropolitan area and the Thames and Lee catchment areas, where in any case these fish at present are virtually non-existent. A licence for salmon fishing also covers trout fishing.[2]

---

[1] *Cf.* Salmon and Freshwater Fisheries Act, 1972, Sched. 1, para. 16.
[2] *Ibid.*, s. 6(6).

Fishing licences for freshwater fish and eels. The 1972 Act has reversed the policy regarding fishing licences for freshwater fish. Formerly no licence was needed except in an area where the Minister had made an order requiring one. Now river authorities are required to bring fishing for freshwater fish or eels into the licensing system, "except so far as excused by the Minister".[1] Drastic though this reversal may appear, in practice it should make little difference because licences to fish for freshwater fish were already required by orders covering most of England and Wales. Bringing eel fishing into the licensing system is a new departure. Again, no licence will be needed in the Metropolitan, Lee and Thames areas, because these areas are not governed by river authorities.

If a licence is held to fish for salmon and trout, the same licence is sufficient for fishing for freshwater fish and eels by the same means authorised by the licence.[2]

Licence requirements. A licence duty is payable for a fishing licence, but the river authority may grant exemption from payment "in special cases".[3] The fishing licence must state the period for which it is valid, the area for which it is valid, the description of fish authorised to be fished for (i.e. salmon, trout, freshwater fish or eels) and the "instruments" the holder is allowed to use.[4] By "instruments" is meant the tackle or device which may be used to catch the fish — e.g. rod and line, or putts and putchers.

The duty payable is fixed by the river authority. A different licence duty may be charged for different periods, or for different parts of the area, or for different kinds of fish, or for different "instruments" to be used, and now, by a new provision, for "different classes of licence holder" (e.g. small boys and girls, or aged ones).[5] This is often done. For instance, at the time of writing the Devon River Authority charge a substantial sum for a salmon and trout season licence over its whole area, a lesser sum for any one of its principal fishing rivers, and less again for any one of certain other rivers. At the same time it has separate rates for weekly and daily licences, separate rates for general trout fishing, separate rates for non-migratory trout fishing, and again a different scale of rates for juvenile anglers under sixteen years. By no means all river authorities go in for these elaborate permutations.[6]

Anyone likely to want a licence (which is probably what is meant by the term used, "an interested person") has a chance to object before a river authority fixes or alters a licence duty. At least one month in advance the river authority must publish in one or more local papers a notice of its intention. If "any interested person" puts in a written objection to the

---

[1] *Ibid.*, s. 6(2).
[2] *Ibid.*, s. 6(7).
[3] *Ibid.*, Sched.1, para.1.
[4] *Ibid.*, s. 6(3).
[5] *Ibid.*, Sched. 1, para. 2.
[6] It would appear that a temporary licence must not be for more than 14 days (*ibid.* Sched. 1, para. 7). Details of charges and other useful details are given in the biennial publication *Where to Fish*, Harmsworth Press Ltd.

Minister during the month following publication of the notice, the river authority must not fix or alter the duty without the Minister's approval. The Minister may approve, refuse or modify the proposed duty. The duty must not take effect until the beginning of the year after it is fixed by the river authority, or approved by the Minister.[1]

Who may use the licence

Usually a fishing licence is issued to an individual and a licence to fish by rod and line may not be used by anyone else.[2] An angler cannot, for example, lend his licence to a friend.

General licences. It is possible for a person or association having the *exclusive* right to fish on any waters to obtain a *general licence* to fish on those waters.[3] Under the general licence not only the holder but also any person authorised by him in writing may fish the waters concerned in any legal manner without an individual licence.[4] The Secretary of a fishing association may therefore obtain a general licence for its private waters and issue authorisations to members. The river authority is allowed to attach conditions to a general licence. The conditions (if any) and also the charge for a general licence are agreed between the river authority and the person or association getting it.[5] In *Mills* v. *Avon and Dorset River Board*[6] the Court decided that a general licence may not be withheld without good reason. The river board had decided on a policy of issuing general licences to no-one for 1954 because the majority of owners had commercialised their fishing and the board were thereby losing revenue. Mr Justice Vaisey said:

"To withhold the issue of general licences in a wholesale and indiscriminate manner strikes me as being very inequitable, and I cannot understand why an owner, who by commercialisation or otherwise deprives the board of income which they would otherwise receive, should not be charged an appropriate higher fee for a general licence, instead of having his general licence refused altogether. Still less can I understand why what I may call an innocent owner should be penalised, and the conclusion I have reached in this case is that a fishery owner is entitled to a general licence unless the board can adduce some good reason for withholding it referable to the applicant himself, or to the conditions under which his own fishery is being used."

A licence to use an instrument other than rod and line for catching salmon or trout (e.g. salmon baskets) may be used not only by the person to

---

[1] *Ibid.*, Sched. 1, paras. 3 to 6.
[2] *Ibid.*, s.6(3).
[3] *Ibid.*, s. 6(8).
[4] A person disqualified from holding a fishing licence may not be authorised (*Ibid.*, s. 12(7)).
[5] *Ibid.*, s. 6(8) and Sched. 1, para. 8.
[6] [1955] 1 All E.R. 382.

whom it is granted, but also by his duly authorised agents or servants provided their names are entered on the licence. A fee of 20p is to be paid for every name endorsed on the licence. The 1972 Act makes provision for limiting the number to be entered, and makes it an offence to resort to certain deceitful tricks regarding such entries.[1]

Granting and Refusing Licences. A person who commits offences against the fishing laws may be disqualified by the Court from holding a fishing licence (or from fishing under a general licence) for up to one year, provided he is not a first offender.[2] A disqualified person may therefore be refused a licence. No other person may be refused a licence to fish with rod and line if he tenders the proper licence duty.[3]

River authorities may make orders, confirmed by the Minister, limiting for a period not exceeding ten years the number of licences that may be issued during the year for fishing in public waters for salmon or trout (other than rainbow trout) with any instrument other than rod or line. The order also should state how to select who are to be given licences, if too many people apply. The 1972 Act lays down a procedure for making these orders, which gives an opportunity to any person opposed to the proposal to object before a decision is made, and includes safeguards for previous licence holders dependent on fishing for their livelihood.[4]

Offences. In all cases where licences to fish are needed, it is an offence to fish for or take, without a licence, fish for which a licence is needed. If a licence is held, it is an offence to employ a method of fishing not authorised by the licence or to fish for or take fish otherwise than in accordance with the conditions of the licence. It is also an offence for a person to have in his possession, with the intention of using it, an "instrument" he is not authorised by a fishing licence to use.[5] In *Gibson* v. *Ryan*[6] the English Divisional Court, interpreting the equivalent Scottish statute, decided that neither a basket, nor a rubber dinghy (both containing scales and blood of salmon) were "instruments". The accused was charged with, and acquitted of, being found in possession of an instrument which could be used in the taking of salmon or trout, contrary to the Salmon and Freshwater Fisheries (Protection) (Scotland) Act, 1951.

The maximum penalty for any of these offences is a £50 fine for a first offence, and £100 fine for subsequent offences. If the offender acts together with another offender to commit the offence higher penalties can be imposed.[7]

Any taking of live fish except by means authorised by a licence would be an offence, *but not dead fish.* In 1890[8] a passer-by had the good fortune

---

[1] *Ibid.*, s. 6(4) and Sched. 1, paras. 9 to 14.
[2] *Ibid.*, s. 12(7).
[3] *Ibid.*, Sched. 1, para. 15.
[4] *Ibid.*, s. 7.
[5] *Ibid.*, s. 8.
[6] [1967]3 All E.R. 184.
[7] 1972 Act, s. 12(4).
[8] *Gazard* v. *Cook* (1890) 55 J.P. 102.

to find a 27 lb. salmon "left by the receding tide on the sands in the River Severn", but had the misfortune to be charged with taking it without a licence. As the fish had been attacked by gulls, and there was no evidence that it was alive when picked up, the justices assumed it was dead and dismissed the summons. The appeal court upheld the justices saying a licence was not needed to take dead fish. In *Stead* v. *Tillotson*[1] though, the appeal court directed the justices to convict where the accused picked dying trout out of the water with their hands. The fish had been poisoned but there was nothing to show that the accused had poisoned them. The court added "if the justices are satisfied that the respondents had nothing to do with rendering the fish in their condition, and merely removed the dying fish from the river, they can dismiss the summons."

But what if the angler without a licence fishes for a kind of fish for which a licence is not needed in waters where he might catch a fish for which a licence is necessary? This came up for decision in a number of nineteenth century cases, and the answer the Court gave was that if the angler's intention was to fish for authorised fish, it was no offence to fish for these even though it was possible to catch unauthorised fish. Where an angler without a licence was fishing with worm bait in waters where a trout licence was needed, it was no offence,[2] nor was it an offence where nets were used to catch mullet in the Frome where a licence was needed for netting salmon.[3] In both cases the fisherman was believed to have lawful intentions – but he would be an optimistic angler today who expected to have such luck in similar circumstances!

A licence to fish by rod and line, unless otherwise stated, is a licence to fish with a single rod and line only. In *Combridge* v. *Harrison*[4], where an angler who held a licence was fined for fishing for trout with three rods and lines simultaneously, Mr Justice Wright on dismissing his appeal said "It should however be clearly understood that our decision does not go to the extent of saying that a man should not go to fish with more than one rod and line; all we say is that he must not use more than one rod or line at a time when he has only one licence". On some waters there is a rule that only one rod and line may be tackled up at a time.

Where a licence is held to fish only by rod and line, the angler may, however, use a gaff with a plain unbarbed metal hook, or a tailer or landing net for landing fish.[5]

Production of Licence. Any person holding a fishing licence for the area, or any member of a river authority, or any official water bailiff (appointed under the Water Resources Act, 1963), or any constable, may

[1] (1900) 64 J.P. 343.
[2] *Marshall* v. *Richardson* (1889) 60 L.T. 605.
[3] *Watts* v. *Lucas* (1871) 24 L.T. 128.
[4] (1895) 72 L.T. 592.
[5] 1972 Act, s. 6(5).

require anybody found fishing, in waters where a licence is required, to produce his licence or authority and to give his name and address. Any of these persons, except the mere licence holder, may do the same if they reasonably suspect somebody to be about to fish, or to have fished within the past half hour. Failure to produce the licence or authority, or to state correctly the name or address, is an offence, but if within seven days the licence or authority is produced at the river authority office, the holder cannot be convicted of failing to produce it. Anyone, with the exception of a constable, exercising this power must first produce evidence of his authority or his licence.[1]

In the case of *Wharton* v. *Taylor*[2] an angler fishing without a licence in September, 1964, was acquitted by the Magistrates, because after he was spoken to by a water bailiff he obtained a licence for the whole of 1964. On appeal by the prosecution the Divisional Court directed the Magistrates to convict the angler, because it was no defence to the charge to obtain a licence after the offence had been committed.

---

[1] *Ibid.*, s. 9.
[2] *The Times*, May 14, 1965.

CHAPTER 5

RIGHTS OF THE PUBLIC TO FISH

Tidal Waters. The public has no right to fish in any non-tidal waters. On the other hand, the public has the right to fish in all tidal waters, except where their right was lost before Magna Carta, 1215, by the King granting the fishing rights to a subject. For example, all rights in the tidal Arun and the River Beaulieu were granted away before 1215, the latter by King John in 1204.[1] Magna Carta stopped the King depriving the public of its fishing rights. The tidal waters in which the public may fish as of right include, as Hale[2] said, "the sea and creeks or arms thereof" and also estuaries and tidal rivers.

Where does a river become non-tidal? The Courts have had to decide on a number of occasions how to tell where a river ceases to be tidal and becomes non-tidal. In *Horne* v. *Mackenzie*[3] the Court said the deciding test was whether fresh water prevailed over salt water. Later in *Reece* v. *Miller*[4] the Court decided a river was not tidal where it was not usually salt and the river was not affected by ordinary tides, even though it was affected by exceptional tides. The point came up neatly for decision in *West Riding of Yorks. River Board* v. *Tadcaster U.D.C.*[5] when the Court refuted the suggestion that there must be horizontal ebb and flow of the water for it to be tidal. By a local statute it was an offence to discharge sewage into Yorkshire rivers, except "tidal waters". The U.D.C. had an outfall at a place where water rose and fell with the ordinary sea tide, but there was no discernible horizontal tidal movement. The appeal court held that it was tidal water, and the Chief Justice, Lord Alverstone, quoted with approval the statement in Stuart Moore's *History and Law of Fisheries*[6] — "the point at issue is clearly decided on the principle that the limit of tidalty is to be measured by the fluctuation of the water in its rise and fall at ordinary tides up and down the banks".

The answer, then, is that public fishing ceases at the point in the river where ordinary sea tides cease to cause the water to fluctuate both horizontally along the banks and vertically up and down them.

---

[1] See also *Stephens* v. *Snell* (1939) All E.R. 622. Axmouth p.93 below.
[2] *De Jure Maris.*
[3] (1839) 6 Cl. and Fin. 628.
[4] (1882) 8 Q.B.D. 626.
[5] (1907) 97 L.T. 436.
[6] *History and Law of Fisheries* (1903) p.102.

Non-tidal Waters. Although the general public can obtain certain legal rights, for example rights of way or rights of navigation, by custom, long use, or dedication, the public cannot obtain the right to fish in non-tidal waters by these or any other means.[1] Even though the public has fished without objection or hindrance for centuries in a reach of a non-tidal river, they do so without any legal right. This was vividly illustrated in *Wells* v. *Hardy*[2] where an angler who was a responsible officer of an angling Club was prosecuted for illegally fishing in the Thames in a place where he had himself been in the habit of fishing for over twenty years, and the public for as long as anyone could remember, without any objection from the riparian (i.e. the river bank) owners. He was found guilty and fined 5s. In many non-tidal waters public fishing is tolerated but this does not signify the right to fish.

Nor does the right of public navigation carry with it the right to fish.

These points were cleared up by two earlier Thames cases both reported in 1891 — one as a footnote to the other — and both concerning the same reach of the river. One need look no further than the lucid judgments in these cases for the answers to most questions which arise regarding members of the public fishing in non-tidal rivers. Nothing could be clearer than this:

> "There is another most important matter to be recollected as regards such streams as the Thames — namely that although the public have been in the habit, as long as we can recollect, and as long as our fathers can recollect, of fishing in the Thames, the public have no right to fish there — I mean they have no right as members of the public to fish there. That is certain law. Of course they may fish by the licence of the lord or owner of the particular part of the bed of the river, or they may fish by the indulgence, or owing to the carelessness or good nature, of the person who is entitled to the soil, but right to fish themselves as the public they have none."[3]

Then Mr Justice North, in the course of his lengthy judgment in *Smith* v. *Andrews*[4] said:

> "The idea is sometimes entertained that the right to pass along a public navigable river carries with it the right to fish in it, but so far as regards non-tidal rivers this is not so . . . Persons using a navigable highway no more acquire thereby a right to fish there than persons passing along a public highway on land acquire a right to shoot upon it."

He added that though some reported cases might seem to indicate the contrary, they were all dealing with tidal rivers, where of course the public

---

[1] *Smith* v. *Andrews* (1891) 2 Ch. 678.
[2] [1964] 2 Q.B. 447.
[3] *Per* Bowen L. J., *Blount* v. *Layard* (1891) Ch. 681 at p.689.
[4] [1891] 2 Ch. 678 at pp.695-6.

have the right to fish. In both of these Thames cases the riparian landowner claimed that a member of the public, fishing without permission, was trespassing. Of the landowner in his case, Mr Justice North said:

> "She and her agents have also from time to time given leave to fish to very numerous persons who applied for it, and it is only fair to say she has always expressed her willingness to permit fishing in her water so long as it is done by her leave, and not in express defiance of her rights."[1]

He added, later in his judgment, after deciding that she had proved her ownership of the fishing rights and that the public could not acquire them:

> "Every country, every district, furnishes numerous instances in which privileges are permitted to the public which could not be claimed and would not be tolerated for one moment as of right. It would be very unfair and unjust to a proprietor that any unfavourable inferences should be drawn from such concessions, or that they should be used against him as evidence of an adverse right; and I will add that it is very much against the interest of the public that attempts to use them should be made, as the result necessarily is to check the giving or continuance of facilities for public enjoyment liable to be thus misconstrued or abused."

These apposite comments echo Lord Justice Bowen in the earlier case (it had been heard in 1888 but not reported until Mr Justice North referred to it in his judgment in 1891):

> "I can conceive nothing more unfortunate than that the owners of the right of fishing on large streams should be driven to prevent the successors and followers of Izaak Walton from dropping their lines for fish, for fear that their doing so should crystallise into a right. It would be a most unfortunate thing for the public if that should ever happen."

The Foreshore. The right of public fishing in tidal waters permits the public to fish in the sea on the foreshore. The foreshore is the land between the high and low water marks of ordinary tides. These marks are not easy to ascertain because the high tide mark is taken as the point of the medium high tide between the spring and neaps taking an average over the whole year. The Court said in *Attorney-Gen.* v. *Chambers* (1854)[2] of the high tide boundary "for about three days it is exceeded and for about three days it is left short and on one day of the week is reached. This point of the shore therefore is for about four days in every week reached and covered by the tides." They might have added, too, that the mark was by no means stationary. As Kent

---

[1] At p.699.
[2] (1854) 23 L. J. Ch. 662.

sea anglers will know, for example, the one-time seashore town of Sandwich is now two miles from the sea, the boundary of the foreshore having receded two miles since Roman times.

The foreshore is mostly owned by the Crown, though in places other persons have obtained the ownership by charter, statute or other means. Whether it is owned by the Crown, a public authority or a private individual, the public right of fishing remains unless, as we have seen, the fishing rights were granted away before Magna Carta.

It may be that the need to identify the limits of the foreshore does not arise for sea anglers, except where the right of public fishing has been lost, because when the sea flows above high water mark it is still tidal water, and below low water mark the high seas begin.[1]

The only use the public can lawfully make of the foreshore is fishing and navigation.[2] There must be some doubt whether the fisherman may go onto the beach or seashore to exercise his right, because recently, in *Alfred F. Beckett Ltd.* v. *Lyons*[3], Lord Justice Harman said, "The only clear right of the public on the foreshore is the right to pass over it in boats when it is covered with water for the purpose of fishing." However, activities on the foreshore incidental to the public right of fishing or navigation are lawful.[2] Incidental rights to fishing which the courts have recognised on the foreshore have been the right to fixed moorings, which also may be established above high water by custom[4], and the right to collect and deposit shell fish.[5] In *Truro Corporation* v. *Rowe*[6], however, it was decided that fishermen had no right to set aside part of the seashore exclusively for themselves to store oysters. It is clear, therefore, that the sea fisherman's right is not confined to floating over the foreshore to fish, and it is suggested that where the public right of fishing remains, beach fishing on the foreshore is included, and digging for, or otherwise collecting, bait.

The public right to go onto the foreshore for the purposes of fishing or navigation does not extend above mean high water mark. This land is presumed by law to belong to the owner of the land adjoining the seashore, or estuary.[7] The angler may therefore obtain access to the foreshore from the land side by public rights of way only, or by permission of the adjoining occupiers. Rights connected with fishing may, however, be acquired above high water mark by immemorial custom. The right to land nets was presumed by the Court in *Gray* v. *Bond*[8], and a customary right to dry them above high water may be established even though the kinds of nets and the manner of

---

[1] *R.* v. *Keyn* (1876) 2 Ex. D. 63.

[2] *Fitzhardinge* (Lord) v. *Purcell* [1908] 2 Ch. 139.

[3] [1967] 1 All E.R. 833.

[4] *A.-G.* v. *Wright* [1897] 2 Q.B. 318.

[5] *Bagott* v. *Orr* (1801) Bos. & Pul. 472.

[6] [1901] 2 K.B. 870.

[7] *Baird* v. *Fortune* (1861) 5 L.T. 2.

[8] (1821) 2 B. & B. 667.

drying them has varied from time to time.[1] A right to ground boats above high water has been recognised,[2] but there is no such right for fishermen in the absence of custom.[3]

Oddly enough, the public has not even a right to bathe[4], let alone sunbathe, build sandcastles, play cricket or otherwise frolic on the beach (though normally, of course, the owners of the soil tolerate these uses), and in *Llandudno U.D.C.* v. *Woods*[5] it was held that a clergyman was not entitled to hold religious services on the beach. The public may not take seaweed from the beach, but floating seaweed may be taken in connection with the rights of fishing or navigation.[6] Nor is there any right to gather seacoal on the seashore.[7]

If the public right of fishing should conflict with the public right of navigation, navigation prevails over fishing (see Chapter 19) but the public having no further rights over the foreshore, the fisherman's right prevails in all other cases.

Access to the Water. The right to use river banks does not go automatically with the public right of fishing in tidal waters.[8] Here again it must be remembered that all land belongs to somebody. Often there are public rights of way along river banks. If there are not, the angler will require the permission of the landowner to go on the river bank, and also to get to the water if it cannot be done by a right of way. A public right of way, however, only gives the public a right to pass to and fro, and not to stay and fish from it.

The right to use river banks is dealt with more fully in Chapter 15.

Boats. Where the public have fishing rights in tidal rivers, they may fish from boats if the river is suitable for navigation. This is an ancient right given by the common law of the country. A tidal navigable river may be looked upon as a public highway, as may the sea, but as with a public road it may be used only in a reasonable manner and a boat user must not cause an obstruction – nor navigate without due care and attention!

There is no common law right for the public to navigate non-tidal waters, but, unlike fishing rights, the public may obtain this right. It may be given by statute[9], or by dedication of the landowners, or be presumed if the public have navigated since time immemorial[10] – but the right of fishing does not go with the right of navigation.[11]

See further Chapter 19 for the conflict between fishing and navigation rights.

[1] *Mercer* v. *Denne* [1905] 2 Ch. 538.
[2] *Aiton* v. *Stephen* (1876) 1 App. Cas. 456.
[3] *Ilchester (Lord)* v. *Raishley* (1889) 5 T.L.R. 739.
[4] *Brinckman* v. *Matley* [1904] 2 Ch. 313, following *Blundell* v. *Catterall* (1821) 5 B. & A. 268.
[5] [1899] 2 Ch. 705.
[6] *Baird* v. *Fortune* (1861) 5 L.T. 2.
[7] *Alfred F. Beckett Ltd.* v. *Lyons* [1967] 1 All E.R. 833.
[8] *Ball* v. *Herbert* (1789) 3 T.R. 253.
[9] E.g. Thames Conservancy Act, 1932, s. 79.
[10] *Bower* v. *Hill* (1835) 2 Scott 535.
[11] *Smith* v. *Andrews* (1891) 2 Ch. 678.

CHAPTER 6

SEA FISHING

The law for the sea-fishing industry, and for navigation at sea, is not within the scope of this book. It is a large subject with its own hefty statute law and a mass of statutory instruments (Orders made by Ministers).[1] The sea angler, however, needs to know something about this system of law, because although it is designed for his commercial brethren it affects everybody who fishes in the sea.

The High Seas and Territorial Waters

The right to fish on the high seas is open to all people of all nations. The right to fish in territorial waters of a country is by international law the exclusive right of the subjects of the country, so that foreign nationals may only fish in British territorial waters by licence of the Crown. By international law the high seas commence at the limit of territorial waters.[2] By a treaty or convention a nation can bind itself in favour of another nation not to fish in specified places on the high seas.

The extent of territorial waters varies from place to place. The Territorial Waters Jurisdiction Act, 1878, set the territorial waters for the British Isles to extend three nautical miles seaward from low water mark.[3] Now the Fishery Limits Act, 1964, as a result of an international convention, has extended the fishery limits of the British Islands to twelve miles from low water (i.e. beyond the normal limit of territorial waters), and divided this into two sectors, "the exclusive fishery limits" and "the outer belt". The "exclusive fishery limits" are the inner six miles, and foreign fishing vessels are not allowed to fish in this sector. They are only allowed to fish in "the outer belt" if they are registered in a country to whom this privilege is extended by Orders of the Minister to give effect to Conventions. In spite of

---

[1] Happily, much of the statute law has been consolidated in the Sea Fisheries Regulation Act, 1966, the Sea Fish (Conservation) Act, 1967, and the Sea Fisheries Act, 1968.
[2] But see *R.* v. *Keyn* (1876) 2 Ex. D. 63 – by English law the high seas commence at low water mark. For the extent of high seas, see *R.* v. *Liverpool Justices, ex p. Molyneux* [1972] 2 All E.R. 471.
[3] The Territorial Waters Order in Council, 1964, qualifies this basic rule by including in the base line the coast of islands and of low tide elevations. The validity of this Order was challenged unsuccessfully in the "pirate" radio station case *R.* v. *St. Augustine, Kent, Justices* (Times December 14, 1966).

the twelve mile rule, the British fishery limits are not to extend more than halfway between England and the Channel Isles and France.[1]

The right of the public to fish the foreshore is dealt with in Chapter 5 above.

Administration of Sea Fisheries. The Minister of Agriculture, Fisheries and Food has the overall responsibility for sea fisheries, and he may set up sea fisheries districts in any parts of the exclusive fishing limits, together with parts of the adjoining coast if wanted, and local fisheries committees to regulate the sea fishing within each district.[2]

The local fisheries committees regulate the sea fisheries in their districts by way of byelaws and by appointing fishery officers to enforce the byelaws. The byelaws must be displayed in prominent places in the fishery districts, and copies must be available for purchase.[3] The byelaws may do any of the following things:

(1) Restrict or prohibit specified methods of fishing for sea fish, and make rules regarding the tackle that may be used — for example by specifying the size of mesh for nets.[4]

(2) Make rules for crab or lobster fishing, and for regulating shell fisheries.[4]

(3) Prohibit or regulate the deposit or discharge of solid or liquid substances harmful to sea-fish[4], but cannot stop local authorities discharging sewerage under statutory powers.[5]

(4) Restrict or prohibit the fishing for or taking of all or any specified kinds of sea-fish during specified periods.[4]

No byelaw may be made which conflicts with river authority byelaws, or which "prejudicially affects any several fishery[6], or any right on, to or over any portion of the seashore" established by law, except with the consent of the person having the right.[5]

In *Denithorne* v. *Davies*[7], the Court refused to declare a byelaw unreasonable (and thereby invalid) which prohibited the use of edible crab for bait. Though it was thought to be drastic it was not patently oppressive.

The Minister can under various Acts of Parliament make Orders doing much the same kind of things as the local fishery committees can do by byelaws.

"Sea-fish" means here fish of all kinds found in the sea (including crustaceans and shell fish) but not including fish of the salmon species or

---

[1] Fishery Limits Act, 1964, s. 1(4) — See Sea Fisheries Act, 1968, for enforcement of the fishery limits.

[2] Sea Fisheries Regulation Act, 1966, s. 1. Where the district is part of or adjacent to the coast of Wales the Minister acts jointly with the Secretary of State for Wales (Wales (Transfer of Functions) Order 1969, S.I. 1969 No. 388). Shell Fisheries are regulated under the Sea Fisheries (Shellfish) Act, 1967.

[3] Sea Fisheries Regulation Act, 1966, s. 9.

[4] *Ibid.*, s. 5(1).

[5] *Ibid.*, s. 6.

[6] See p.72 below for meaning of "several fishery".

[7] [1967] 2 Lloyds Rep. 489.

migratory trout. Salmon and migratory trout are included for the purposes of certain sections of the Sea Fish (Conservation) Act, 1967.[1]

Sea Fishery Officers (not to be confused with fishery officers of local fisheries committees) also have powers to enforce sea fishery laws. These officers are "a motley crew" consisting not only of officers especially appointed, but also, among others, commissioned officers of any of H.M. Ships, Customs Officers, Coastguards, and Officers of the Minister's sea fishery inspectorate. They have wide powers of boarding boats, mustering the crew, and examining all manner of things from the ship's log book to the ship's lights, and any fish or fishing gear on the boat.[2]

Close Seasons. There are no close seasons for sea fish, though it is possible for byelaws to prohibit fishing in specified places for all or specified kinds of sea-fish for a period. The close seasons for salmon and trout must be observed as dealt with in Chapter 3 above. Parts of the sea are within river authority areas and may be covered by close season byelaws. Where there are no byelaws the standard close seasons for salmon and trout will apply.

Ministerial Orders may be made prohibiting the landing, selling, or exposing, offering or having in one's possession for sale, in Great Britain, any lobster carrying spawn attached to its tail or other part of its exterior, or which from its condition can be shown to have been carrying spawn when it was taken. It is an offence in any event (without an Order being made) to do similar acts to spawning edible crabs or to any that have recently cast their shells, unless they are intended for bait for fishing.[3]

Size Limits. Ministerial Orders may be made imposing size limits for any species of sea-fish. It is an offence to land, sell, or expose, offer or have in one's possession for sale, in Great Britain, any sea-fish smaller than the size prescribed for the species by an Order. The size limits under the current order[4], measuring the fish from tip of snout to extreme end of tail fin, are:

Cod, 30 cms; haddock, 27 cms; hake, 30 cms; plaice, 25 cms; witches, 28 cms; lemon soles, 25 cms; soles (solea solea), 24 cms; turbot, 30 cms; brill, 30 cms; megrims, 25 cms; whitings, 25 cms; dabs, 15 cms.

The offence is committed if part of a fish is landed only, and the part is smaller than the size laid down for the species.[5]

Fishery officers, police officers and certain others are given power to board boats or enter premises to enforce the size limit rules, and may search for and examine sea-fish in any place and in any receptacle in which they might be. An authorised officer detecting a contravention of the rules may confiscate the under-size fish.[6]

---

[1] *Ibid.*, s. 20; Sea Fish (Conservation) Act, 1967, s. 22(1).
[2] Sea Fisheries Act, 1968, ss. 7–10.
[3] Sea Fisheries (Shellfish) Act, 1967, s. 17.
[4] The Immature Sea-Fish Order, 1968, S.I. 1968 No. 1618.
[5] Sea Fish (Conservation) Act, 1967, s. 1(2).
[6] *Ibid.*, s. 16.

Illegal Methods of Fishing. Section 9 of the Salmon and Freshwater Fisheries Act, 1923[1], which prohibits the use of explosives, poisons, and electrical devices with the intention of taking or destroying fish (see p.37 below), is not confined to salmon, trout or freshwater fish. In this case the 1923 Act protects fish in "waters adjoining the coast of England and Wales and within the exclusive fishery limits of the British Islands" as well as fish in inland waters. The river authority can give permission to use these methods for special purposes, and in this connection it should be noted that for the purposes of its functions relating to fisheries, a river authority area extends out to sea to the extent of the exclusive fishing limits.[2]

The other methods of fishing made illegal by the 1923 Act and 1972 Act do not apply to sea-fish[3], and in general there are no restrictions on the gear or tackle that may be used to fish for sea-fish. The Minister may, however, (and does) make Orders laying down rules for the construction, size mesh and use of nets and may do so for other fishing gear. Sea fishery officers have power of enforcement and seizure of illegal gear.[4] Byelaws of local fisheries committees, as we have seen above, may make stipulations about the manner of fishing and the tackle that may be used in their areas. Failure to comply with Orders or byelaws is a punishable offence.

Jurisdiction of Magistrates. If an offence is committed against the sea fishing laws, the offender might technically be outside the boundaries of any court's jurisdiction. To get over this laws have been passed to bring the offender within the jurisdiction of the Magistrates for the nearest adjacent area on land. If an offence is committed on the sea coast or at sea (not on board ship) it is taken as committed within the county abutting on the sea coast or sea at that place.[5] Should an offence be committed on board ship the usual rule of law applies, that the accused may be tried at any port he is brought into.[6]

Sea-Fishing Boats. There is much law concerning sea-fishing boats, which must be registered in a fishing boat register and be lettered and numbered. A "fishing boat" generally is a vessel of whatever size, and in whatever way propelled, which is used by any person in sea fishing or in carrying on the business of a sea fisherman.[7] This would not be applied to a boat used for recreation, even if sea angling was carried on from it, and so further details are not given here.

---

[1] As repealed and replaced by the Salmon and Freshwater Fisheries Act, 1965.
[2] Water Resources Act, 1963, s. 9.
[3] See Chapter 7 below. The illegal methods may not be used for salmon or trout in the sea.
[4] Sea Fish (Conservation) Act, 1967, ss. 3 and 15.
[5] Sea Fisheries Acts and see 1923 Act, s. 75 dealt with on p.170 below.
[6] Cf. *R.* v. *Liverpool Justices, ex p. Molyneux* [1972] 2 All E.R. 471.
[7] Sea Fisheries Act, 1868, s. 5.

Pier Fishing

The owners of piers (who may be the local authority or Harbour authority) usually allow public access to them, and also angling from them. What may or may not be done on the pier is usually laid down in byelaws.

Litter. The besetting sin of pier anglers is to make a mess, and in too many cases to leave a mess. As much of the mess is, or has recently been, alive and sticky (e.g. fish, lugworm) there is a constant danger of this conduct leading to the closing of piers to angling, if not permanently, at least during seasons when other members of the public are likely to be about. This unhappily has already happened in certain places.

Where no payment is made to go on the pier, and the public have free access, litter-leavers may be prosecuted under the Litter Act 1958 (see p.62 below). Most piers are not open to the public free of charge, and in these cases the position is governed by the byelaws, which it is believed normally make it an offence to leave litter.

Accidents on the pier. Every man has a legal duty to take care that he causes no injury to his fellow men. If through carelessness he does an injury to another or to his property he may be held liable to pay him compensation. This, of course, is what one would expect. The angler on the pier must take care to see that his weights and hooks do no harm to others on, under, or near the pier.

Likewise the pier owners must maintain it in a safe condition, and if somebody who is allowed on the pier is injured by reason of the defective condition of the pier, he would normally be entitled to compensation unless all reasonable steps had been taken to prevent the accident.[1] But what if the angler on paying to go on the pier receives a ticket which states on the back that he goes on it at his own risk, and that the owners shall not be liable for any injury received by him even if caused by the defective condition of the pier or the negligence of themselves or their servants or agents?

This self-exoneration from negligence will be effective to protect the pier owners provided that the person given the ticket either knows of the condition on the back when he receives it, or sufficient steps are taken to bring it to his attention. If, on the other hand, the pier angler does what most of us do, and puts the ticket in his pocket without reading it, provided there is nothing to draw his attention to them, the words on the back of the ticket will avail the pier owners little when part of the pier gives way and the angler falls into the sea, injuring himself or damaging or losing his tackle.[2]

In a number of cases, however, small print on the back of tickets (for example cloakroom or railway tickets) has effectively exonerated the issuers from liability for negligence. In one case, for example, an illiterate lady bought a railway excursion ticket which had on the face of it "Excursion. For conditions, see back". The back of the ticket told anyone given to reading the

---

[1] See note on Occupiers' Liability Act, 1957, in Chapter 9.
[2] *Chapleton* v. *Barry U.D.C.* (1940) 1 K.B. 532.

backs of tickets that the conditions could be found in the Company's timetables (which cost 6d.). The timetable excluded liability for injury however caused. The lady was injured on the journey and the Court of Appeal held that she could not claim damages, and should have known about the Company's conditions.[1] It is interesting to note, therefore, that the Law Commissioners recently appointed to put forward necessary law reforms have recommended in their First Programme an examination of "The desirability of prohibiting, invalidating or restricting the effects of clauses giving exemption from, or limiting liability for, negligence".

---

[1] *Thompson* v. *L.M.S. Railway Co.* [1930] 1 K.B. 41.

CHAPTER 7

ILLEGAL METHODS OF FISHING AND KINDRED OFFENCES

Rules for fair fishing are usually laid down by angling clubs, and also by the owners of fishing rights and by local byelaws. These must, of course, be observed by the anglers concerned. The general law (mainly the 1923 Act as amended by the 1972 Act) also prohibits certain forms of fishing, or perhaps we should say of taking fish. Few anglers would describe as fishing, for instance, the killing of fish by hurling a hand grenade into the water – an illegal method known to have been tried on occasion (without much success) by bored soldiery.

Prohibited "Instruments"

The 1972 Act has refurbished the law against cheating fish out of the water, leaving it simpler, more extensive, and generally offering less joy to the trickster and poacher. It says:

"No person shall –
(a)   use any of the following instruments, that is to say –
   (i)   a firearm within the meaning of the Firearms Act 1968;
   (ii)   an otter lath or jack, wire or snare;
   (iii)   a crossline or setline;
   (iv)   a spear, gaff, stroke-haul, snatch or other like instrument;
   (v)   a light;
    for the purpose of taking or killing salmon, trout or freshwater fish;
(b)   have in his possession any instrument mentioned in paragraph (a) above intending to use it to take or kill salmon, trout or freshwater fish; or
(c)   throw or discharge any stone or other missile for the purpose of taking or killing, or facilitating the taking, or killing of any salmon, trout or freshwater fish."[1]

It will be seen that the prohibitions do not apply to taking or killing eels or sea fish.

---

[1] Salmon and Freshwater Fisheries Act, 1923, s. 1(1) as amended by the 1972 Act, s.1(1)

It is an offence to do any of the forbidden things, unless the accused can prove that it was done for the purpose of preservation or development of a private fishery and with the previous permission of the river authority, or of the Minister where no river authority exists.[1] A private fishery is one where the public have no right to fish.

Heavier penalties may be imposed if the offence is committed by a person "acting together with another".[2]

"A Firearm". In the first edition of this book we pointed out the anomaly that shooting at fish was not prohibited (unless the rule about explosives, p.37 below, could be stretched). The 1972 Act fills the gap. The meaning of "firearm" in the Firearms Act, 1968, is complex and ramified. Basically it is "a lethal barrelled weapon of any description from which any shot, bullet or other missile can be discharged" and it includes machine guns and other repeaters and weapons which discharge noxious liquid or gas. Component parts, certain accessories and ammunition are counted as firearms too, so anyone found in possession of these intending to use them in connection with the taking or killing of fish commits the offence.[3]

"Otter Lath or Jack". Some guidance is given by the 1923 Act to the meaning of these ambiguous words, by stating that "the expression otter lath or jack includes any small boat or vessel, board, stick, or other instrument, whether used with a hand line, or as auxiliary to a rod or line, or otherwise for the purpose of running out lures, artificial or otherwise".[4] The otter used for angling was a float from which lines ran out with a number of baited hooks or flies attached. It was moored or trailed to a boat.[5] It is devices of this kind which it is thought the expression "otter, lath or jack" describes. The Irish case of *Alton* v. *Parker*[6] decided that otter in this connection did not mean the animal. The defendant fished on Lough Derg by a line extended from a boat to a floating wooden implement. This was one of a number of contrivances known as an otter. The defendant contended that the prohibition only applied to live otters − a good try, but unsuccessful.

"Wire or Snare", "Gaff". The 1923 Act expressly allows the use of a "gaff (consisting of a plain metal hook without a barb) or tailer as auxiliary to angling with a rod and line". Nor is it an offence to have possession of a gaff or tailer intending to use it this way.[7]

"A Crossline or Setline". These have been brought into the rogue's gallery by the 1972 Act. Both are conveniently defined: ' "crossline" means a fishing line reaching from bank to bank across water and having attached to it one or more lures or baited hooks; "setline" means a fishing line left

---

[1] 1923 Act, s. 1(2).

[2] 1972 Act, s. 12(3) and Sched. 2.

[3] See definitions of "firearm" and "prohibited weapon", Firearms Act, 1968.

[4] 1923 Act, s. 1(3)(a).

[5] See Lloyd's Encyclopaedic Dictionary (1895).

[6] (1891) L.R.Ir. 87.

[7] 1923 Act, s. 1(4) as amended by 1972 Act, s. 1(3).

unattended in water and having attached to it one or more lures or baited hooks'.[1]

"Stroke-haul", "Snatch". The 1923 Act also sheds light on the expression "stroke-haul or snatch" by stating that it "includes any instrument or device, whether used with a rod and line or otherwise, for the purpose of foul hooking any fish".[2] The snatch was vividly described in the "Standard" of October 21, 1878.

"Snatching" it said "is a form of illicit piscicapture. A large triangle is attached to a line of fine gut well weighted with swan-shot or a small plummet. Some 'snatchers' will use two, three or even four triangles; but the mode of operation is, of course, the same. The line is then dropped into some quiet place where fish are plentiful − a deep corner pool, on the outfall of a drain, or the mouth of a small affluent − and, as soon as the plummet has touched the bottom, it is twitched violently up. It is almost a certainty that on some one or other of the hooks, and possibly on more than one, will be a fish foul-hooked."

Stroke-haul is an apparatus (used for illegal capture of fish) formed of three hooks joined back to back, and weighted with lead.[3]

"Other Like Instrument". *Jones* v. *Davies*[4] decided that a net with an illegally close mesh is not a "like instrument" to a snare, so that its use is not an offence under s. 1 of the 1923 Act − though it may be an offence under s. 7, or byelaws.

"A Light". What use of a light is supposed to be illegal is something the 1972 Act might have cleared up but has not. It is suggested that what is intended to be forbidden is the resort to poachers' tricks with lights − shining them into the water to facilitate the capture of fish in a way respectable authors are not supposed to know about. Presumably the use and possession of a light by the angler to enable him to see what he is doing in the dark is allowed, and likewise the practice of many reputable anglers of beaming a spotlight onto their floats after dark.

"Stone or Missile". The 1972 Act now extends protection from stone and missile throwing to freshwater fish. Previously the wording forbade throwing or discharging the projectile "into any water". This has been changed presumably to protect leaping fish and to catch the offender whose aim is too bad to hit the water.

Fish Roe and Fish Spawn. It is illegal to use fish roe of any kind for the purpose of fishing for salmon, trout or freshwater fish. It is also illegal to buy, sell, expose for sale or have in one's possession any roe of salmon or trout. Presumably, if the roe is inside the fish, the law is not broken, unless it is being kept with the object of breaking the law.

---

[1] 1972 Act, s. 1(2).
[2] 1923 Act, s. 1(3)(*b*) and see *Prescott* v. *Hutchin* (The Times November 16, 1966).
[3] See Shorter Oxford English Dictionary, 2nd ed., 1936, p.2046.
[4] [1898] 1 Q.B. 405.

It is convenient to deal with spawn here, following the example of the 1923 Act, which makes it an offence for any person wilfully to "disturb any spawn or spawning fish, or any bed, bank, or shallow on which any spawn or spawning fish may be". "Wilfully" is the key word here, so that the offence could not be committed inadvertently. Any person who has a right to take materials from any water is not prejudiced in the exercise of his right.[1] Likewise, where there is a right to dredge, scour, cleanse or improve any navigable river, canal or other inland navigation, the exercise of the right is not prejudiced.[2] The Usk River Board's final report before becoming the Usk River Authority, disclosed seven prosecutions for "unlawfully disturbing a shallow". It could, of course, only be an offence in the spawning season.

An important exception as regards both the use of fish roe, and the disturbance of spawning is laid down by the Act. No offence is committed if the previous written permission of the river authority (if there is one, otherwise the Minister) has first been obtained, and the act was done for the purpose of the artificial propagation of salmon, trout or freshwater fish, or for some scientific purpose, or for the purpose of the preservation or development of a private fishery.[3]

It is now an offence to introduce spawn into an inland water without official consent.[4]

Nets. Nothing is said in the Salmon and Freshwater Fisheries Acts about the use of nets to catch freshwater fish. This is left to byelaws and local rules. The acts do, however, control the use of nets for taking salmon and migratory trout, and for sea fishing.

It is forbidden to "shoot or work any seine or draft net for salmon or migratory trout" in a river authority area across more than three-quarters of the width of any water[5], contravention being an offence.

A seine net is a long movable net with a buoyed headline and a weighted ground rope. It is usually paid out from a boat and hauled in to shore by land lines.

It is also an offence to take or attempt to take salmon or migratory trout anywhere with a net having a mesh of less than two inches from knot to knot (the measurement to be made on each side of the square), or eight inches measured round each mesh when wet. This rule does not apply to the use of a landing net as auxiliary to angling with rod and line.[6]

This law cannot be circumvented by doubling up nets because it is also an offence to place two nets one behind the other, or so near to each other as to have the practical effect of diminishing the mesh of the nets. *Dodd* v. *Armor*[7] decided that a trammel net is not a single net but two or more placed

---

[1] 1923 Act, s. 4.
[2] *Ibid.*, s. 89.
[3] *Ibid.*, s. 5.
[4] 1972 Act, s. 10, and see p.39 below.
[5] Salmon and Freshwater Fisheries Act, 1923, s. 6. (amended by 1964 Act).
[6] *Ibid.*, s. 7.
[7] (1867) 31 J.P. 773.

one behind the other, and therefore it is illegal in a river authority area. Nets may not be covered with canvas, nor may "any other artifice" be resorted to, in order to get round the rules regarding the size of mesh which may be used. Byelaws may be made allowing smaller mesh dimensions in any place[1], and may lay down lawful specifications for nets and the manner in which they may and may not be used.[2]

Sea Fishing Nets. As regards sea-fishing, regulations may be, and have been, made giving a specification for nets which may lawfully be used.[3]

Poison, Explosives and Electric Fishing. The law against pollution is dealt with fully in Chapter 20 but it must be noted here that nothing may be put into any water containing fish (of any kind) which would make the water poisonous or injurious to the fish, or to the food of fish, or to spawning grounds, or to the spawn of fish.[4]

In addition to this general anti-pollution law to protect fisheries, a recent statute[5] has brought in a modernised version of a prohibition which was in s. 9 of the 1923 Act. It says that no person may use "any explosive substance, any poison or other noxious substance, or any electrical device" with the intention of taking or destroying fish. This applies "in or near any waters", including coastal waters within the territorial limits of the British Islands. It is also an offence to have in one's possession any explosive or noxious substance or any electrical device for the purpose of illegal fishing.[6]

An important qualification is that no offence is committed if any of these things are done for a scientific purpose, or for the purpose of protecting, improving or replacing stocks of fish, provided that official permission is obtained in writing. The permission is to be obtained from the river authority in a river authority area, from the Thames Conservancy in their area, from the Lee Conservancy Catchment Board in their area, and from the Minister in the London area. No permission may be given by these authorities to use noxious substances, however, except with the approval of the Minister. This qualification is also extended to the general anti-pollution prohibition mentioned above.[7]

A person convicted of any of these offences may be fined or imprisoned and the Court may order the forfeiture of any fish illegally taken or in his possession at the time of the offence, and of any instrument, substance or device used in the commission of the offence. If the conviction is on indictment (that is, before a judge and jury, instead of the magistrates) any vessel or vehicle used in or in connection with the offence, or in which any substance or device unlawfully in the offender's possession was contained at the time of the offence, may be forfeited.[8]

---

[1] *Ibid.*, s. 7(3).
[2] *Ibid.*, s. 59(1)(f) as amended by 1972 Act, s. 5(2) and see Chapter 22 for byelaws.
[3] See Chapter 6.
[4] Salmon and Freshwater Fisheries Act, 1923, s. 8.
[5] Salmon and Freshwater Fisheries Act, 1965.
[6] See the 1965 Act which repeals and re-enacts a new s. 9 to the 1923 Act.
[7] The same qualification applies to byelaws made under the 1923 Act, s. 59(1)(p), and to Rivers (Prevention of Pollution) Act, 1951, s. 2(1)(a).
[8] 1972 Act, s. 12 and Sched. 2.

It need hardly be said that this should be a severe deterrent to anyone going on an unlawful expedition by boat or motor-car.

"Electric fishing" may therefore only be carried out with official permission, and if done from a boat without permission, the offender is liable to lose not only the apparatus, but the boat as well. He may also lose the apparatus, the boat, and possibly his motor-car if he is found with electric fishing equipment or other proscribed equipment, and the Court is satisfied that he intended to use them for illegal fishing.

The expression "poison or other noxious substance" could include anything injurious to the life or health of fish or which, if put in the water, would make their capture easier.[1] In the Irish case of *R.* v. *Antrim Justices* (1906)[2] it was also said, by Chief Baron Palles, that

> "the time at which the deleterious character of the matter is to be ascertained is the moment it enters the river. The effect of the action upon it of the water of the river, which necessarily must be *after* it has entered it, is in my view absolutely immaterial."

Interference with Dams, Floodgates or Sluices. It is an offence without lawful excuse to destroy or damage any dam, floodgate or sluice with the intention of taking or destroying fish.[3] A dam includes any weir or other kind of fixed obstruction for damming up water.[4] It is also illegal to fix traps, eel baskets, etc. to weirs at certain times of the year (see p.11 above).

Size Limits. River authorities and the Ministry of Agriculture, Fisheries and Food have the power to lay down the size limits for the sundry species of freshwater fish and trout by byelaw[5], and where fishing licences are required, the size limits are usually printed on the licence and also how they are to be measured. Club rules may also specify size limits. Fish taken below the permitted size limit must be immediately returned to the water, though in some waters it is permissible when a match is fished to retain them in a keep net until they have been weighed in. An example of size limits is given in the extract from the Avon and Dorset River Authority Byelaws in Appendix C.

Immature and Unclean Fish. No person may knowingly take, kill or injure, or attempt to take, kill or injure any salmon, trout or freshwater fish which is unclean or immature, but it is not an offence if it is done accidentally and the fish is returned to the water with the least possible injury. It is also an offence to buy, sell, expose for sale or have in one's possession such fish.[6] These prohibited acts may be done, however, by a

---

[1]*Cf. R.* v. *Cramp* (1880) 5 Q.B. 307 — an abortion case.
[2](1906) 2 I.R. 298 at p.329.
[3]Salmon and Freshwater Fisheries Act, 1923, s. 9 as amended by the 1965 Act and the Criminal Damage Act, 1971, s. 11(5).
[4]1923 Act, s. 92(1).
[5]*Ibid.*, s. 59(1)(*m*).
[6]*Ibid.*, s. 3.

person with official written permission, if done for the purpose of artificial propagation of fish, or for some scientific purpose, or for the preservation or development of a private fishery.[1]

In law an unclean fish is one about to spawn, or which has recently spawned and not recovered from it. An immature salmon is one less than twelve inches in length measured from the tip of the snout to the fork or cleft of the tail.[2]

These offences of taking immature and unclean fish can only be committed "knowingly". In *Hopton* v. *Thirlwall*[3] in 1863 an angler was charged under the Salmon Fishery Act, 1861, which made it an offence for a person "wilfully to take or destroy the young of salmon, or have in his possession the young of salmon." The accused had taken both trout and young salmon from the River Ilton and was found with them in his creel. The Justices were satisfied that he did not know the difference between samlets and trout and that he honestly believed they were trout. The appeal court held that in the circumstances he was rightly acquitted.

Illegal Stocking. By a new provision of the 1972 Act, a person commits an offence if he introduces any fish or spawn of fish into an inland water[4], or has any fish or spawn in his possession intending to introduce them into an inland water, unless he first obtains the written consent of the appropriate river authority.[5]

Obstructing Passage of Fish and Use of Fixed Engines. This is dealt with in Chapter 8.

Byelaws. The "illicit forms of piscicapture" referred to in this chapter are banned throughout the country[6], but, as ever, byelaws may lay down additional rules locally. Byelaws have the same force as other laws and may regulate for any area the size of the trout or any freshwater fish which may be taken, and make rules regarding nets, tackle, lines, bait, and night fishing, and prohibit fishing in any waters.[7] Thus, for example some waters are "fly only", and on some a limit is placed on the catch.

---

[1] *Ibid.*, s. 5.
[2] *Ibid.*, s. 92(1).
[3] (1863) 9 L.T. 327.
[4] See p.10 above for meaning of "inland water".
[5] 1972 Act, s. 10.
[6] The Salmon and Freshwater Fisheries Acts apply in England and Wales. See *Gibson* v. *Ryan* [1967] 3 All E.R. 184 and p.4 above for Scottish laws applying to the Tweed south of the border.
[7] Salmon and Freshwater Fisheries Act, 1923, s. 59 and see Chapter 22.

CHAPTER 8

OBSTRUCTIONS TO PASSAGE OF SALMON AND TROUT

Part II of the Salmon and Freshwater Fisheries Act, 1923, lays down rules to ensure that fish are not unduly impeded in migrating. The fish it is concerned about are salmon and migratory trout. This is of course important for anglers. Most of the terms given to the obstructions it is concerned about are *featured* in the definition section of the Act, s. 92, as set out on pp.44—45 below. This being an Act of Parliament the terms are usually not defined and it is as well to note when the Act says a term *"means"* something, and when it just says it *"includes"* something.

Fixed Engines

The 1923 Act provides that no new fixed engine for taking or facilitating the taking of salmon or migratory trout or for detaining, or obstructing their free passage may be erected or used in any inland or tidal water except by river authorities which have been given the power to do so by what are known as "Part IV orders".[1] Contravention is an offence[2], and the offending fixed engine may be taken over or destroyed by any person authorised by the river authority, or by the Minister. In *Ingram* v. *Percival*[3] the Court decided the offence can be committed below low water mark where there is a perceptible ebb and flow of the tide.

If the fisherman's intention is not to catch salmon or trout, no offence is committed[4], but the Court may infer such an intention even though the fixed engine usually caught other fish.[5]

What is a "fixed engine"? This dated term has come down from the old Salmon Fishery Acts, living on as they died off. The 1923 Act is (among other things) consolidating, its "definition" embodying all the ingredients from the "definitions" of the term in the earlier Salmon Fishery Acts of 1861, 1865 and 1873 — and this is how it comes out in s. 92(1) of the 1923 Act:

"The expression fixed engine includes:
    (*a*)   stake net, bag net, putt, putcher; and

---

[1] See Chapter 22.
[2] Salmon and Freshwater Fisheries Act, 1923, s. 11.
[3] [1968] 3 All E.R. 657.
[4] *Watts* v. *Lucas* (1871) 24 L.T. 128.
[5] *Davies* v. *Evans* (1902) 86 L.T. 819.

(*b*) any fixed implement or engine for taking or facilitating the taking of fish; and

(*c*) any net secured by anchors and any net or other implement for taking fish fixed to the soil, or made stationary in any other way, not being a fishing weir or fishing mill dam; and

(*d*) any net placed or suspended in any inland or tidal waters unattended by the owner or a person duly authorised by the owner to use the same for taking salmon or trout, and any engine, device, machine, or contrivance, whether floating or otherwise, for placing or suspending such last-mentioned net or maintaining it in working order or making it stationary."

" . . . *Or made stationary in any other way*". These words were added as a result of the decision in the case of *Thomas* v. *Jones* in 1864[1], a prosecution under the 1861 Act. The late Lord Chief Justice Goddard related the story in his inimitably forthright fashion, giving judgment in the case of *Percival* v. *Stanton.*[2] He said:

> "*Thomas* v. *Jones* came before a court of the Queen's Bench Division. In that case a net was used on the River Tivy, near Cardigan, by a fisherman who had got his net secured at one end but the Court held that it was not a 'fixed engine' because, being unsecured at the other end, directly the salmon hit the net the net rolled round the salmon and therefore, because it could roll around the salmon, it was not a fixed net. Whether I should have decided the case in the same way as the Court of Queen's Bench decided it in 1864, if I had been alive and sitting in 1864, I do not know. I have a strong suspicion that I should not. So . . . the Legislature stepped in and put an amending definition of 'fixed equipment' in s. 39 of the Salmon Fishery Act, 1865."

The addition of the words "or made stationary in any other way" still left room for doubt. In *Olding* v. *Wild*[3] the Justices acquitted the fisherman who used a net secured at one end to a pole which was driven into the soil. Half of the net was stretched across the channel of the tidal estuary from a boat anchored to a buoy. The fisherman let out the rest of the net and made a sweep of the channel. On appeal from the Justices the Divisional Court held that as the net was fixed to a pole it was within the description "made stationary in any other way" and as such was a fixed engine.

In *Gore* v. *Special Commissioners for English Fisheries*[4] the Divisional Court held that a stop net was a fixed engine. This was indeed a border-line case, because the human hand played a part in holding the device stationary. The Court decided that this device was "made stationary" because it was used

---

[1] (1864) 5 B. & S. 916.
[2] [1954] 1 All E.R. 392.
[3] (1866) 14 L.T. 402.
[4] (1871) 24 L.T. 702.

from an anchored boat, and the poles holding the net rested on the side of
the boat by their own weight, even though a man's hand was kept on them.
The Court added, however, that a net held by hand would not always be a
"fixed engine", for example, a casting net would not.

   "*Secured by Anchors.*" These words seem plain enough but they were
not plain enough to prevent the prosecution of two Northumberland
fishermen for using a net in the sea near Alnmouth in a way they thought
legal and had practised for over thirty years without a challenge from the law.
They attached light anchors to the net to act as a brake or drag, but allowing
the net to drift with the tide. They were charged with using a fixed engine
illegally (under s. 11 of the 1923 Act). The Justices did not think the net was
a "fixed engine" and dismissed the charge. On appeal by the River Board the
Divisional Court agreed with the Justices. A quotation from Lord Goddard's
judgment in this case, *Percival* v. *Stanton*[1] has already been given above. What
he said about when anchors do and do not render a net a "fixed engine"
might well be the last word on the subject:

   "The first thing I should say with regard to a 'fixed engine' is that it
must be fixed . . . If a thing is fixed, it seems to me it must be stationary" he
declared at the beginning of his judgment, and summing up at the end he said,
with further Goddardian forthrightness:

> "It seems to me that in all cases of this kind to some extent it must
> be a question of degree . . . I do not want it to be said that, if it is shown
> that a net has been let down with anchors attached to it, the net ceases to
> be a 'fixed engine' merely because the anchors have dragged as they might
> do in a storm. If they are put down with the intention of anchoring the
> net to the sea-bed, then I think the net becomes 'secured by anchors'. But
> if, as the justices found in this case, these little light anchors were used,
> not for that purpose but merely to act as a brake or drag on a net which
> was intended to drift with the tide, it seems to me that one cannot say
> that the net is a 'fixed engine'. First, it is not 'fixed', and secondly, it is
> not 'secured by anchors'. It has got anchors on it but they do not secure it.
> Nor is it 'made stationary in any other way' because it is not stationary, it
> moves."

   "*Unattended by the owner.*" Strict proof of the offender's ownership
of the net is not needed. In *Vance* v. *Frost*[2] the Appeal Court said that if
there was evidence of fishermen using a net in their possession, the obvious
inference was that they owned it.

Exceptions for 1861 Fixtures

   The Royal Commission which reported in 1860 recommended that *all*
fixed engines should be abolished, and this recommendation was at first

---

[1] [1954] 1 All E.R. 392.
[2] (1894) 58 J.P. 398.

accepted by the Government of the day. This brought forth protests from the vested interests, such as those who had the right to place putts and putchers in tidal rivers for taking salmon — rights which had in many cases been operated from ancient times. The Salmon Fishery Act, 1861, therefore, in making illegal the use of fixed engines for taking salmon, excluded those used in the lawful exercise of an ancient right. Then by the Salmon Fishery Act, 1865, Commissioners for English Fisheries were appointed to look into the legality of all fixed engines for taking salmon in England and Wales. They were given the powers to remove or suppress those which were not legalised by being excluded from the 1861 Act, and those they found to be legal because of their ancient pedigree were certified as "privileged fixed engines". By the time the Commissioners were wound up under the Salmon Fishery Act, 1873, they had done a fairly thorough job of certifying lawful "fixed engines".

The 1923 Act preserves the right to use fixed engines which lawfully existed in 1861 because of their ancient lineage.[1]

By s. 80(1) of the 1923 Act it is sufficient proof of certification as a privileged fixed engine to produce the certificate sealed with the seal of the Commissioners and signed. A copy of an order of the Commissioners or of any plan or map accompanying the order is sufficient evidence of it if it is sealed with their seal (s. 80(2)).

There were plenty of disputes while the Commissioners were at work and the following important points about the exceptions were brought out by the Courts:

(1) *The "ancient right or mode of fishing" must be a private one.* A fisherman using fixed engines in exercise of his public right of fishing is not excused even though there has been a public right since time immemorial. In the case of *Bevins* v. *Bird*[2], the Divisional Court held that the use of stake nets by a fisherman to catch salmon in Morecambe Bay, though practised for many years in exercise of the *public* right of fishing, was unlawful.

(2) *The use must have been lawful in* 1861. This rule defeated the owner of 480 putchers and three stake nets in the River Severn in the case of *Holford* v.*George.*[3] In order to establish the legality of the stake nets it was necessary to prove that stake nets were operated there at the time of a statute of Henry VI, and the legality of the putchers depended on their use before Edward I's Magna Carta. The owner could prove the use of these devices for forty-five years, but the Commissioners would not presume earlier use and they refused to certify them as privileged fixed engines. An appeal to the Divisional Court failed. Oke[4] states that in two other appeals from the Commissions which are not reported — *Waite* v. *George* and *Cadogan* v. *George* — the Court indicated that on proof of uninterrupted use of fixed

---

[1] Salmon and Freshwater Fisheries Act, 1923, s. 11(4).
[2] (1865) 12 L.T. 306.
[3] (1868) 18 L.T. 817.
[4] *Salmon and Freshwater Fisheries Act, 1923* (4th Edition).

engines for sixty years, without evidence of non-use before that, the Court was bound to draw the inference of immemorial usage.

Obstruction of Salmon in Close Season. The 1923 Act makes special provision prohibiting the obstruction of salmon or doing anything to deter their migration during the annual close season and weekly close time, and requiring fixed engines to be removed or rendered incapable of taking, or obstructing the passage of, salmon. This is dealt with above in Chapter 3.

Dams and Weirs. King Edward I's Magna Carta[1] still has in force this law:

> "Chapter 23. Wears. All wears from henceforth shall be utterly put down by Thames and Medway, and through all England, but only by the sea-coasts."

— an old fashioned way of saying "Down with inland weirs!"

A later statute, of Edward III[2], made lawful all weirs in existence before the reign of Edward I, but ordered the destruction of any erected during or after the reign of Edward I. These statutes were not enacted in order to ensure that salmon and trout could migrate up and down rivers. Their object was to prevent hindrances to navigation, and the Courts have held in modern times that the prohibition in Magna Carta quoted above only related to navigable rivers.[3]

The Commissioners for English Fisheries appointed in 1865 (see p.43 above) did not have to certify weirs or dams in lawful use. They were enjoined, however, to remove illegal "fishing weirs" and to render incapable of taking fish any illegal "fishing mill dams". The 1923 Act, s. 12 makes it an offence to use any fishing weir or fishing mill dam for taking or facilitating the taking of salmon or migratory trout, unless they were lawfully in use on August 6, 1861 (the date on which the Salmon Fishery Act, 1861, became law).

By section 92(1) of the 1923 Act:

> " '*Dam*' includes any weir or other fixed obstruction used for the purpose of damming up water."
>
> " '*Fishing mill dam*' means a dam used or intended to be used partly for the purpose of taking or facilitating the taking of fish, and partly for the purpose of supplying water for milling or other purposes."
>
> " '*Fishing weir*' means any erection, structure or obstruction fixed to the soil either temporarily or permanently across, or partly across, a river or branch of a river, and used for the exclusive purpose of taking or facilitating the taking of fish."

---

[1] 25 Ed. I c. 1 (General Confirmation of the Charters, 1297) re-enacting 9 Hen. III c. 26 (Magna Carta, 1225).
[2] 25 Ed. III st. 4, c. 4, (1350).
[3] *Leconfield* v. *Lonsdale* (1870) 23 L.T. 155.

" *'Mill'* includes any erection for the purpose of developing water power, and the expression 'milling' has a corresponding meaning."

It may be noted that a dam having no device for catching fish does not become a fishing mill dam merely because the owner *occasionally* takes the opportunity to catch fish – e.g. by netting fish in a pool below the dam. The purpose of the dam must partly be for catching fish if it is to fall within the definition.[1]

When the owner of a dam abandons beyond question the use of it for fishing, it then ceases to be a fishing mill dam.[2]

Free Gaps and Fish Passes

Free gaps in weirs. A fishing weir which extends more than halfway across any river at its lowest state of water, must not be used for taking salmon or migratory trout unless it has a free gap or opening to enable fish to pass through. The free gap must be in the deepest part of the river between the points where it is intercepted by the weir. The sides of the gap must be in line with and parallel to the direction of the stream at the weir. The bottom of the gap must be level with the natural bed of the river above and below the gap. The width of the gap in its narrowest part must be not less than one-tenth of the width of the river, provided that it need not be more than forty feet wide however wide the river, and it must never be narrower than three feet.[3]

It is an offence to break any of these rules about free gaps, or to make any alteration in the bed of a river in such a manner as to reduce the flow of water through a free gap.[4]

If the deepest part of the river changes, for example by the river changing its course, the position of its free gap will need changing also if the fishing weir is to be used for taking salmon or trout.

"River" is defined to include a stream[5], and so a weir across a stream or an arm of a river containing salmon or migratory trout must have a free gap, if it extends more than halfway across. Chief Justice Cockburn said in *Rolle v. Whyte*[6] that water flowing between an island and a river bank was not a stream (nor a river) but his argument is so odd that it is hard to believe that it would be followed. If he is to be believed, a weir extending more than halfway between the bank and an island in a river containing salmon or migratory trout, would not need a fish pass – unless it extended more than halfway across the total width of the river at that point.

---

[1] *Garnett* v. *Backhouse* (1867) 17 L.T. 170.
[2] *Rossiter* v. *Pike* (1878) 4 Q.B.D. 24.
[3] Salmon and Freshwater Fisheries Act, 1923, s. 13(1).
[4] *Ibid.*, s. 13(2).
[5] *Ibid.*, s. 92(1).
[6] (1868) L.R. 3 Q.B. 286 at p.304.

Fish Passes

In fishing mill dams. A fishing mill dam may not be used for taking salmon or migratory trout unless it has attached to it a fish pass. The fish pass must be of a form and dimensions approved by the Minister of Agriculture, Fisheries and Food, and kept so. A fishing mill dam may not be used for taking salmon or migratory trout unless a constant flow of water is kept running through it sufficient to enable these fish to pass up and down it.[1] The Minister can now make his approval provisional until the fish pass is functioning to his satisfaction, and, after giving at least 90 days notice, may revoke a provisional approval.[2]

Any use of a dam, or attempt to use it, in contravention of these rules is an offence.[3]

A lawful fishing mill dam (even of ancient legal ancestry) automatically becomes illegal for all time for the purposes of taking fish if at any time it fails to comply with the laws for fish passes, and any device attached to it for trapping fish may thereafter be removed by the river authority.[4]

Fish passes needed for new dam works since 1873. The owner or occupier must within a reasonable time notified by the river authority, or the Minister, make and thereafter maintain in efficient state a fish pass in any waters frequented by salmon or migratory trout, of such form and dimensions as the Minister may approve (if no such fish pass already exists) where a new dam is constructed, or an existing one altered, or any other obstruction is created, which obstructs or increases the obstruction to the passage of salmon or migratory trout, since August 31, 1873.[5]

The Minister can make his approval provisional until it is functioning to his satisfaction, and, after giving at least 90 days notice, may revoke a provisional approval. On revoking it, however, he may grant an extension of time for making an approved fish pass.[2]

Failure by the owner or occupier to make, or to keep in an efficient state, such a fish pass, is an offence.[6] If the owner or occupier, after receiving a notice, does not construct the fish pass as required, the river authority, or Minister as the case may be, may have the work done and recover the expense of doing it from the defaulter.[7] It is an offence to obstruct "any authorised person whilst doing any such works".[8]

An alteration of a dam or other obstruction does not make the owner or occupier liable to be required to make a fish pass, if the dam or obstruction when altered causes no more obstruction to the passage of salmon or migratory trout than was caused by it as lawfully constructed or

---

[1] Salmon and Freshwater Fisheries Act, 1923, s. 14(1).
[2] 1972 Act, s. 2.
[3] 1923 Act, s. 14(2).
[4] *Ibid.,* s. 14(3).
[5] *Ibid.,* s. 19(1).
[6] *Ibid.,* s. 19(2).
[7] *Ibid.,* s. 19(3).
[8] *Ibid.,* s. 19(4).

maintained at any previous date, unless the alteration is a rebuilding or reinstatement of at least half its length.[1]

A notice requiring the making and maintenance of a fish pass does not authorise:

"The doing of anything that may injuriously affect any public waterworks or navigable river, canal or inland navigation, or any dock, the supply of water to which is obtained from any navigable river, canal or inland navigation, under the provisions of any Act of Parliament."[2]

There is no direction to pay compensation for any loss or damage, or expense, suffered by anyone through complying with the requirements of s. 19, except that the owners of fishing rights cannot be prosecuted for fishing near dams (under s. 17) unless they have been compensated (see p.50 below).

Supply of Water to Dams and Fish Passes. Sluices for drawing off water which would otherwise flow over a dam in waters frequented by salmon or migratory trout must be kept shut on Sundays and at all times when the water is not required for milling purposes, so that the water will flow over the dam, or over the fish pass if there is one, unless excused by the river authority or the Minister[3], otherwise an offence is committed.[4]

No offence is committed, however, if a sluice is opened to let off flood water, or for milling, or when necessary for navigation, or after notice in writing to the river authority, or the Minister, for cleaning or repairing any dam or mill or its appurtenances.[5]

Power of River Authorities to Construct and Alter Fish Passes. By s. 20 of the 1923 Act a river authority may "construct and maintain in any dam or in connexion[6] therewith a fish pass of such form and dimension as the Minister may approve", but, in doing so must do no injury "to the milling power, or to the supply of water of or to any navigable river, canal or other inland navigation".[7] The Minister may make his consent or approval provisional until it is functioning to his satisfaction, and, after giving at least 90 days notice, may revoke a provisional consent or approval.[8]

Also with the Minister's consent a river authority may abolish, alter, or restore to its former state of efficiency, any existing fish pass or free gap, or substitute another fish pass or free gap. Again, no injury may be done to the milling power, or to the supply of water of or to any navigable river, canal or other inland navigation.[9] Anybody who injures such a new or existing fish

---

[1] Salmon and Freshwater Fisheries Act, 1923, s. 19(5)(c).
[2] *Ibid.*, s. 19(5)(a).
[3] *Ibid.*, s. 18(1).
[4] *Ibid.*, s. 18(2).
[5] *Ibid.*, s. 18(3).
[6] It is irrelevant but interesting to note that the Act sometimes spells this word "connexion" and sometimes "connection".
[7] Salmon and Freshwater Fisheries Act, 1923, s. 20(1).
[8] 1972 Act, s. 2(1) and (2).
[9] 1923 Act, s. 20(2).

pass can be made to pay for repairs[1], and it is an offence to obstruct authorised works under s. 20.[2]

Compensation. If a river authority in exercising its powers under s. 20 of the Act, causes injury "to any dam" by constructing, abolishing or altering a fish pass, or by abolishing or altering a free gap, any person sustaining loss thereby may recover compensation for the injury sustained. If agreement cannot be reached regarding the amount of the compensation to be paid, it is to be settled by an arbitrator appointed by the Minister.[3] This is a very limited liability upon river authorities to pay compensation, because it is confined to injury "caused to any dam". If no injury is caused to a dam, a person suffering loss from the river authority's work is entitled to no compensation in the absence of negligence by the river authority.

Proceedings to obtain compensation must be commenced within two years of the completion of the work giving rise to the claim.[4]

Procedure for Minister's Consent and Objections. Before the Minister may give a river authority consent to construct, abolish, or alter a fish pass, or to abolish or alter a free gap under s. 20 reasonable notice must be given to the owner and occupier of the dam, fish pass or free gap, with a plan and specification of the proposed work and the Minister must take into consideration any objections by the owner or occupier.[5]

Compulsory purchase of bank. A river authority is given power to purchase compulsorily "so much of the bank adjoining a dam as may be necessary for making or maintaining a fish pass" under s. 20.[6] If the river authority resorts to compulsory purchase it must go through the compulsory purchase procedure referred to below at pp.51–52 and pay for the property purchased at its open market price.

Approval of fish passes by Minister. Where the 1923 Act requires fish passes to be "of such form and dimensions as the Minister may approve", once the Minister's approval is given (and not revoked)[7], it is open to nobody to say that the fish pass does not conform with the requirements of the Act — even if it does not. This is because s. 21(1) says so, and it is a convenient example of the omnipotence of English Statute Law. When a statute says something is deemed to be something — it is.

Offences Against Fish Passes and Free Gaps. Section 22 of the 1923 Act makes it an offence to do any of the following:

(1) Wilfully alter or injure a fish pass.

(2) Do any act whereby salmon or trout are obstructed or liable to be obstructed in using a fish pass, or whereby a fish pass is rendered less efficient.

---

[1] *Ibid.*, s. 20(3).
[2] *Ibid.*, s. 20(4).
[3] *Ibid.*, s. 20(5).
[4] *Ibid.*, s. 25.
[5] *Ibid.*, s. 20(6).
[6] *Ibid.*, s. 20(7).
[7] 1972 Act, s. 2(4).

(3) Alter a dam or the bed or banks of a river so as to render a fish pass less efficient.

(4) Use any contrivance or do any act whereby salmon or trout are in any way liable to be scared, hindered or prevented from passing through a fish pass.

If any of those offences are committed the offender shall "in every case" pay any expense which may be incurred in restoring the fish pass to its former state of efficiency, and the expense may be recovered in a summary manner.[1] The expenses may be incurred by the owner or occupier of the fish pass, or by the river authority exercising its powers under s. 20 of the Act (see p.47). The same does not apply to the remaining offences under s. 22 given below, but before listing them it should be noted that only the first offence above (and none below) must be committed "wilfully". The others are offences if the act is done, even if done by mistake, or carelessly or unwillingly.

It is also an offence to do any of the following:

(5) Do any act for the purpose of preventing salmon or trout from passing through a fish pass.

(6) Take or attempt to take any salmon or trout in its passage through a fish pass.

(7) Place any obstruction, use any contrivance or do any act whereby salmon or trout may be scared, deterred, or in any way prevented from freely entering and passing up and down a free gap at all periods of the year.

An attempt to take a salmon or trout passing through a fish pass is an offence, therefore, but not where it is passing through a free gap if it is not scared, deterred or prevented from using the free gap.

Temporary bridge across free gap. It is not an offence to place a temporary bridge or board over a free gap to cross over it, provided it is taken away immediately after the person using it has crossed.[2]

Presumed guilt of owner or occupier. The owner or occupier of a dam shall be deemed to have altered it, if the dam is damaged or destroyed, or is allowed to fall into a state of disrepair, and if he fails to repair or reconstruct the dam within a reasonable time of receiving notice from the river authority or the Minister, so as to render the fish pass as efficient as before the damage.[3] The owner or occupier may therefore be guilty of an offence under s. 22 if he fails to comply with a notice to repair a dam, even if he had not done any of the things listed in (1) to (7) above.

---

[1] 1923 Act, s. 22(1), and see s. 73(1) for recovery under what is now the Magistrates' Courts Act, 1952.
[2] *Ibid.*, s. 22(4).
[3] *Ibid.*, s. 22(5).

Restrictions on Fishing Near Dams and Mills

Section 17 of the 1923 Act makes it an offence for any person to take or kill, or attempt to take or kill, except with rod and line, or scare or disturb any salmon or trout, in any of the following places:

(1) Within fifty yards above or one hundred yards below[1] any dam or any obstruction, whether artificial or natural, which hinders or retards the passage of salmon or trout.

(2) In any waters under or adjacent to any mill, or in the head race or tail race of any mill, or in any waste race or pool communicating with a mill.

(3) In any artificial channel connected with any dam or obstruction, artificial or natural, which hinders or retards the passage of salmon or trout.

The section is only out to protect salmon and trout and so other fish may be fished for in these places.

In *Onions* v. *Clarke*[2] a byelaw which deprived a riparian owner of the whole of his fishing rights without compensation was held not to be unreasonable.

The important point to note is that angling with rod and line is permissible in these places. "Rod and line" means a *single* rod and line.[3]

Exception for fishing mill dams and apparatus on dams. Legal fishing mill dams are excepted from these rules provided they have no crib, box or cruive, so no offence is committed if salmon or trout are taken above, below or in mill races etc. of such a fishing mill dam, and a similar exemption is given regarding "any fishing box, coop, apparatus, net or mode of fishing in connexion with and forming part of such dam or obstruction for purposes of fishing."[4]

No proceedings until compensation paid. Although it is an offence to fish for salmon and trout in the prohibited places near dams under s. 17 of the Act as described above, the Act states by s. 17(4):

"Where a fish pass approved by the Minister is for the time being attached to a dam or obstruction this section shall not be enforced in respect of the dam or obstruction until compensation has been made by the [river authority][5] to the persons entitled to fish in the waters for that right of fishery, such compensation to be settled in case of dispute by a single arbitrator appointed by the Minister."[6]

---

[1] These distances may be varied by byelaw – *Ibid.*, s. 17(1). They are to be measured in a straight line on a horizontal plane (Interpretation Act, 1889, s. 34).

[2] (1917) 116 L.T. 335.

[3] Salmon and Freshwater Fisheries Act, 1923, s. 92(1).

[4] *Ibid.*, s. 17(3).

[5] Formerly "fishery board" – see below.

[6] Salmon and Freshwater Fisheries Act, 1923, s. 17(4).

This is hardly a satisfactory way of providing for compensation to be paid to the owner of fishing rights, whose rights are curtailed or extinguished by s. 17 of the Act, but presumably it is supposed to mean that compensation can be claimed and arbitrated if necessary, and it is thought that the claim for compensation does not have to be made within two years of the completion of the dam, as s. 25 of the Act (see p.55 below), which lays down the two-years' rule, can hardly have application here. Proceedings for compensation for loss due to the river authority installing a fish pass must however be commenced within two years.

Application to river authority areas only. Section 17, as enacted in 1923, prohibited fishing near dams as described above "in any fishery district". Today fishery districts have been swallowed up in river authority areas. The effect of this is that the rules will apply in a river authority area, but not to the River Thames and the River Lee and its tributaries which, by a typically English quirk, are not included in any river authority area. This may seem of small importance, as it is today, but today live fish can actually be detected swimming, apparently not unhappily, in the murky waters of the Thames in Greater London. If the cleaning up of the Thames continues to advance the day may be seen again when salmon run up this river. In any case, trout are found in the upper Thames and the Lee. These are not migratory trout, but then s. 17 applies to all trout. So even today there is some significance in the rules not applying to these rivers.

Boxes and Cribs in Weirs and Dams

Where any weir or fishing mill dam is used for taking salmon or migratory trout, any box or crib used must conform to rules about their description and positioning laid down in s. 15 of the 1923 Act, otherwise an offence is committed.

Compulsory Purchase of Obstructions With or Without Fisheries

River authorities are given extensive powers to acquire artificial obstructions by purchase, lease or hiring, either by agreement[1] with the owner or, if the Minister's authority is forthcoming, by compulsion, and the same applies to "any fishery attached to or worked in connection with any such obstruction". The river authority may use the obstruction in any lawful way for fishing, and may exercise fishing rights in any fishery acquired. Or it may lease the obstruction or fishery to others who may enjoy the rights. Alternatively, the river authority may remove the obstruction it acquires, or it may alter it. If the obstruction or fishery is taken on lease, the river authority must adhere to the terms of the lease. The lease might, for example, prohibit the river authority from sub-letting the obstruction or fishery. In

---

[1] The appropriate parts of the Land Clauses Act, 1845, apply to sales by agreement, and also Local Government Act, 1933, s. 173, regarding property of the Duchy of Lancaster — see Salmon and Freshwater Fisheries Act, 1923, s. 16(2).

salmonless and troutless waters river authorities could not exercise these powers under the 1923 Act but could have recourse to their wider powers under the Water Resources Act, 1963.[1]

It should be noted that a river authority has no power under the 1923 Act to acquire compulsorily a fishery which is not attached to or connected with a dam it is acquiring. It can however purchase or lease a fishery or fishing rights separately by agreement.[2]

Compulsory purchase procedure. The procedure on a compulsory acquisition follows the standard pattern so that any interested party has an opportunity to object and be heard before the Minister can confirm the compulsory order.[3]

Confirmation by Minister is Conclusive

But the Act provides:

" . . . the confirmation by the Minister shall be conclusive evidence that the requirements of this Act have been complied with, and that the order has been duly made and is within the powers of this Act."[4]

This is hardly fair play, and might work harshly if the proper procedure has not been gone through.

Purchase Price and Compensation

If there is a compulsory purchase, the river authority must pay for what is acquired a purchase price assessed in accordance with certain statutory purchase rules. These are set out in the Land Compensation Act, 1961, s. 5, and broadly speaking require the acquiring authority (the river authority in this instance) to pay the fair open market value. If the purchase price cannot be agreed, either side can refer the question to the Lands Tribunal to decide what should be paid. The seller may be entitled to compensation in addition to the purchase price. This will be so if the compulsory purchase lowers the value of any remaining land of the seller. For example, in the case of a dam joining two parts of an estate and forming a means of access between them, were the river authority to compulsorily purchase the dam and destroy it, the two parts of the estate would be severed. The owner of the estate could then claim compensation for the consequent loss in value of his estate, in addition to the purchase price of the dam. This too would be assessed by the Lands Tribunal if the parties could not agree.

---

[1] E.g. Water Resources Act, 1963, s. 65, and see Chapter 22.
[2] Salmon and Freshwater Fisheries Act, 1923, s. 54(1)(*d*).
[3] *Ibid.*, s. 16 and Sch. 1.
[4] *Ibid.*, s. 16(5).

Compulsory Hiring of Obstructions and Fisheries

A hiring of a dam or other obstruction[1] by a river authority can only be for a period of not less than fourteen years and not more than thirty-five years.[2]

The Minister's order authorising the compulsory hiring must lay down the terms and conditions of the hiring other than the rent, and it must provide for covenants by the river authority to maintain the obstruction or fishery in good condition.[3] If the parties cannot reach agreement about what rent, or other payment, should be paid the Lands Tribunal decides, assessing it in accordance with the purchase rules in the Land Compensation Act, 1961, and Sch. 1 to the 1923 Act.[4]

Tenanted land. If the obstruction and fishery (if any) hired is part of land already let to a tenant, the Lands Tribunal is also given the task of assessing what rent the tenant should pay to his landlord for the residue of the premises in his lease if landlord and tenant cannot agree[5], and rules are laid down for assessing this.[6]

Dilapidations. At the end of the hiring, any amount payable by the river authority as outgoing tenant for dilapidations or breaches of covenant are not, in default of agreement, settled by the Lands Tribunal, but by an arbitrator appointed by the Minister.[7]

Gratings to Keep Migratory Fish from Artificial Channels

Approved gratings must be placed and maintained across all conduits or artificial channels (and their outfalls) into which water is diverted from waters frequented by salmon or migratory trout, if the diverted water is to be used for the purposes of a canal or water undertaking.[8] The purpose of the gratings is, of course, to prevent salmon or migratory trout descending the diversion channel or conduit.[8] The same applies if the water is to be used for the purposes of a mill but only if the conduit or channel has been constructed since 1923.[9] Where water is diverted for irrigation purposes, therefore, there is no obligation to instal gratings, but, as will be seen, the river authority may do so under s. 24 of the Act (see p.54). The obligation to instal and maintain the gratings falls upon the owner of the canal or water undertaking, or, in the case of a mill, upon the occupier of the mill. They must do it at their own

---

[1] See above p.51 for what may be hired.

[2] Salmon and Freshwater Fisheries Act, 1923, s. 16(4).

[3] *Ibid.*, 1st Sched., Part II. Where the object of the compulsory hiring is subject to a mortgage, the Law of Property Act, 1925, ss. 99 and 100, applies — see Salmon and Freshwater Fisheries Act, 1923, s. 16(6) as amended by that Act.

[4] 1st Sched., Part II, para. 4 as amended by Finance Act, 1963; Lands Tribunal Act, 1949, s. 1.

[5] Salmon and Freshwater Fisheries Act, 1923, 1st Sched., Part II, para. (3)(*c*).

[6] *Ibid.*, 1st Sched., Part II, para. (5).

[7] *Ibid.*, 1st Sched., Part II, para. (6).

[8] *Ibid.*, s. 23(1).

[9] *Ibid.*, s. 23(1) and (6).

expense, and they are entitled to no compensation for any cost or loss caused to them. The river authority, or the Minister, may however exempt anybody from the obligation to instal or maintain gratings.

The offence. Failure to place and maintain a grating in accordance with these rules is an offence if the omission is "without lawful excuse".[1] The 1923 Act does not usually recognise any excuses when creating its numerous offences, but the "lawful excuse" Parliament probably had in mind here was an exemption granted by the Minister or fishery board (now the Minister or river authority).

No interference with canal navigation. Section 23(5) lays down:

> "No such grating shall be so placed as to interfere with the passage of boats on any navigable canal."

Presumably this is getting at the Minister, because the person responsible for placing the grating must do so in a position approved by the Minister.

Byelaw exemption. The obligation to instal and maintain gratings may be lifted for a period in each year, by byelaws made under the 1923 Act by the river authority.[2]

Installation of Gratings by River Authority

Without relieving owners of canal or water undertakings, and occupiers of mills, from their duty to provide gratings as described above, river authorities may themselves instal and maintain them at their own expense. This may be done:

> "in any watercourse, mill race, cut, leat, conduit, or other channel for conveying water for any purpose from any waters frequented by salmon or migratory trout at or near the points of divergence and return, or either of them, or in any other suitable place".[3]

Written consent must first be obtained from the Minister, who must approve the device, and it must not obstruct any conduit or channel used for navigation or in any way interfere with the effective working of a mill.[3]

Works to maintain flow. Where the river authority instals gratings they may, again only with the written consent of the Minister, and at their own expense, widen or deepen the watercourse, or "take some other means to prevent the flow of water being prejudicially dminished or otherwise injured".[4] The river authority does not have to take steps to ensure the flow of water is kept up, but if it does not it may have to meet a claim for compensation (see below).

---

[1] *Ibid.*, s. 23(4).
[2] *Ibid.*, s. 23(6); and s. 59(1)(*l*).
[3] *Ibid.*, s. 24(1).
[4] *Ibid.*, s. 24(3).

Keeping salmon and trout out of danger. If the powers given above are insufficient to prevent salmon or trout getting into waters where they are likely to come to no good, the river authority may rely on the more general powers given by s. 24(4) of the 1923 Act to:

" . . . adopt such means as the Minister may approve for preventing the ingress of salmon or trout into waters in which they or their spawning beds or ova are, from the nature of the channel or other causes, liable to be destroyed, but so that no water rights used or enjoyed for the purposes of manufacturing or milling, or for drainage or navigation, be prejudicially interfered with thereby."

Offences Against Gratings and Other Devices

It is an offence to do any of the following things:

(1) Injure any grating or other device placed or maintained by the river authority under the powers described above; or

(2) Remove any such grating or other device, or any part of one, except during any period of the year during which under a byelaw gratings need not be maintained; or

(3) Open any such grating or other device improperly; or

(4) Permit any of the offences in (1), (2) and (3) above; or

(5) Obstruct any person, who has legal authority, whilst he is carrying out any of the river authority's powers regarding the placing or maintenance of any such gratings or other devices.[1]

Compensation for Injury by River Authority.

Anybody sustaining loss by reason of the river authority exercising any of its powers described above for installing and maintaining gratings or other devices, is entitled to compensation from the river authority. If agreement cannot be reached regarding the proper amount of compensation, it is to be settled by an arbitrator appointed by the Minister.[2] Compensation would be payable, for example, to the owner of fishing rights if gratings installed by the river authority deprived a fishery of fish. Proceedings to recover compensation must be instituted within two years from the completion of the work in respect of which the compensation is claimed.[3]

Control by Land Drainage Authorities

Under the Land Drainage Act, 1961, it is necessary to obtain the consent of the river authority before erecting any structure in, over or under any part of a *main river*, or before altering or repairing any structure in a way likely to affect the flow of water in a river or impede any drainage

[1] Salmon and Freshwater Fisheries Act, 1923, s. 24(5).
[2] *Ibid.*, s. 24(6).
[3] *Ibid.*, s. 25.

work.[1] "Main river" means any part of any river or stream which is marked on the map of the river authority as main river by the Minister.[2] Both river authorities and internal drainage boards are given power, where the flow of water in a watercourse under their jurisdiction is obstructed, to require the trouble to be remedied by the person who caused it, or the owner or occupier of adjoining land, or anyone having control of the watercourse.[3]

---

[1] Land Drainage Act, 1961, s. 31.
[2] Water Resources Act, 1963, s. 11.
[3] Land Drainage Act, 1961, s. 28.

CHAPTER 9

RIGHTS AND WRONGS ON LAND OF OTHERS

The pastime of angling entails so much use of other people's land, that it is of special importance to the angler that he does not endanger his relationship with the owners and occupiers of land by thoughtlessness and ignorance. "Heaving" rubbish over the hedge, or into the ditches — making fires — digging for bait — cutting branches from trees — are all unlawful, unless done with permission, and the kind of behaviour which brings out the "No fishing" notices.

The simple rule for the angler is to go only where he has permission or legal authority to go, and to do only what he has permission or legal authority to do. For example, the right to fish a river usually confines the angler to the river, the river bank and public rights of way.

This chapter deals first of all with the misdeeds which might be committed by the angler[1], or anyone else who uses the land of others. Some are civil wrongs (known as torts), some are crimes, and many are both. A civil wrong gives the injured party a personal remedy against the wrongdoer, who may usually be sued in a civil court (such as the County Court) where he may be ordered to pay damages to compensate the other party. Examples of torts are trespass, negligence and nuisance. A crime is an offence against the State, for which the offender may be prosecuted before a criminal court (such as a Bench of Magistrates) and punished. A crime is frequently a tort also, and it is worth noting too that by escaping the criminal law the wrongdoer does not necessarily escape the civil law.

Trespass to Land. This ancient (and, alas, also modern) wrongdoing means an entry upon the land of another without permission or lawful authority, and includes any unauthorised interference with it. The most obvious form of trespass is taking a "short cut" or stroll across private land without permission, but a person may trespass without himself going onto the land. A trespass may be committed by projecting something onto, over, into, or under another's land. Throwing a cigarette package over the hedge, or casting a bait into a swim can be trespasses, even if the trespasser himself never enters the private land. As far as the law is concerned, "land" includes not only the surface but everything fixed to it, everything beneath it, and the air space above it. For example, buildings, all things growing, fences, walls and waters are all included, and an interference with them may be a trespass.

---

[1] Though not you, I am sure, gentle reader.

Angling club cards or day tickets may state, for example, that digging for bait or cutting wood for rod rests is prohibited, but whether stated or not, such behaviour would be a trespass.

A lawful entry may be turned into a trespass, when a person with authority to enter land exceeds or abuses the authority by going beyond what he has the right to do.

Trespass, of itself, is not a crime, but a civil wrong.

Remedies for Trespass. The occupier may sue a trespasser even if *no* damage has been done. Normally there is little point in taking a trespasser to Court if no significant damage has been done, but if a trespasser is a persistent offender or threatens to do further acts of trespass, the Court may be asked to make an injunction against him. The injunction will be a court order, restraining him from trespassing. Anything then done in defiance of the order would be a contempt of court, and might be visited with condign punishment — such as imprisonment.

The occupier, however, does not have to resort to law to rid himself of a trespasser, but may exercise the age-old remedy of self-help. If a trespasser will not leave the land, the occupier does not break the law if he seizes him by the scruff of his neck and seat of the pants and gently deposits him onto the highway. This is because any person in possession of the land is allowed to eject a trespasser forcibly, but he may not use more force than is reasonably necessary for the purpose. Needless to say, this is a remedy to be used with discretion!

As trespass is a wrong against the person in possession of the land, the tenant in occupation of let land is usually the person who can exercise the legal remedies. The landowner who is not in possession may however take proceedings if the trespass is one that injures his interest — e.g. if long-term damage is done, such as cutting timber.

Interference with Goods. An unauthorised removal of, or interference with, goods is also a trespass.[1] We have seen above (p.57) what the law means by land, and for the sake of simplicity we can use the expression "goods" to mean everything else except persons.

This will include, therefore, livestock, preserved game[2], preserved fish[3], harvested crops or fruit. As with trespass to land, the possessor of goods may claim damages and an injunction against anyone wrongfully interfering with his goods, whether damage is done or not, and may use reasonable force to protect his property.

Interference with goods, may, of course, also be a crime — for example, stealing or malicious damage.

The possessor has no remedy, however, against a person with a justifiable excuse for the trespass in defence of himself, his property or a legal

---

[1] It may also be the tort of detinue or conversion.
[2] *Read* v. *Edwards* (1864) 17 C.B.N.S. 245.
[3] See p.60 below.

right. For example, a person lawfully on land may injure, or even kill, an attacking animal, if it is necessary to save himself from injury.

Criminal Damage

Since the first edition of this book the monumental Malicious Damage Act, 1861, has been repealed, almost in its entirety, and with it many other anti-wrecking laws. The short, but pungent, Criminal Damage Act, 1971, takes their place, replacing many detailed offences with a few sweeping ones. The first few words of section 1 says plenty:

> "A person who without lawful excuse destroys or damages any property belonging to another intending to destroy or damage any such property or being reckless as to whether any such property would be destroyed or damaged shall be guilty of an offence."

If the destruction or damage is by fire (arson) the maximum penalty is life imprisonment. Any other offence under the Act carries a maximum penalty of ten years imprisonment (s. 4).

A threat to damage or destroy property is also an offence if it is intended there will be fear that the threat will be carried out (s. 2).

"Property". This means "property of a tangible nature" and includes wild creatures, or their carcasses, which have been tamed or are ordinarily kept in captivity, or which have been "reduced into possession". This is explained below with regard to stealing fish, where it will be seen that in some circumstances fish, alive or dead, would come into this definition of property. Among things that do not count as property in this connection is the foliage of trees, but the unlawful damage or destruction of a tree, other than its foliage, flowers or fruit, would be the offence (s. 10).

"Without lawful excuse". Lawful excuses include the honest belief that you have consent to do the damage. Also it is excusable if the damage is done to protect other property (or rights in property, such as fishing rights) in immediate need of protection, provided the action is reasonable (s. 5).

Warrant to search and seize. If there is reasonable cause to believe someone has something which has been used, or is intended to be used, for committing criminal damage, a magistrate can issue a warrant authorising any constable to search for it and seize it (s. 6). An official water bailiff, being deemed a constable[1], can apply for such a warrant.

Dams, floodgates, sluices. The Criminal Damage Act, 1971, s. 11(5), retains the specific offence in section 9 of the 1923 Act of destroying or damaging, without lawful excuse, any dam, floodgate or sluice with intent to take or destroy fish.

Buoys. One of the few old offences still retained is unlawfully removing, casting adrift, sinking, damaging or concealing any buoy or other

---

[1] Salmon and Freshwater Fisheries Act, 1923, s. 67 (3).

guiding mark for navigation.[1]

Stealing Fish

In the law reforms since the first edition of this book, the dreaded Larceny Acts have been repealed and the crime of larceny abolished. This is no consolation to the criminal fraternity, however, because larceny has been replaced by a new crime to be known as "theft". It is much the same thing, but it is supposed to be easier to prove. The old Larceny Acts have been condensed into the Theft Act, 1968, which states in section 1:

"A person is guilty of theft if he dishonestly appropriates property belonging to another with the intention of permanently depriving the other of it."

Can fish be stolen? The rule of law is that "things which do not belong to any determinate possessor cannot be the subject of larceny"[2] — or, more simply, ownerless things cannot be stolen. The gruesome example beloved of jurists is a human corpse. Birds, beasts and fishes raise a problem. The Theft Act, 1968, summarises the position by stating "wild creatures, tamed or untamed, shall be regarded as property, but a person cannot steal a wild creature not tamed nor ordinarily kept in captivity, or the carcase of any such creature, unless . . . it has been reduced in to possession by or on behalf of another person . . . " — and one or two legal wrinkles are added.[3]

Broadly speaking, if there is a measure of control over birds, beasts and fishes by an owner, they can be stolen.

Domestic and farm animals and poultry are therefore capable of being stolen, but not wild animals at large. Wild creatures may, however, be brought under control sufficiently to change them in law from ownerless to owned — for example, on their being killed, captured or tamed — and then they normally become the property of the owner of the land on which they were taken. They have been "reduced into possession". Thus an angler who takes earthworms out of another's land does not steal them, but he does steal them if he takes them after they have been collected in a pot.[4]

Applying these rules to fish, it is clear that dead fish are capable of being stolen, and likewise fish in a tank. Also fish confined in a lake or pond can be stolen[5] but not fish at large in a running watercourse. In the old case of *R.* v. *Steer and Others*[6] the accused were charged with stealing carp from a private pond. Although there was a technical defect in the charge entitling them to acquittal, it is interesting to note that the judge refused to quash the charge because "the offence of fishing in other men's ponds, and taking away

---

[1] Malicious Damage Act, 1861, s. 48.
[2] Kenny *Outlines of Criminal Law* (15th edition, p. 219).
[3] s. 4(4).
[4] Christian "Game Laws" p. 79. In both cases of course he commits a trespass.
[5] *Gray's Case* (1594) Owen 20.
[6] *R.* v. *Steer* (1704) 6 Mod. Rep. 183

their fish, is too great to receive so much countenance". Hale relates that two men who took fish out of a *net* in a river were convicted of stealing them before Mr Justice Harvey at Cambridge in 1627.[1] Those fish could be stolen, because they were not at large but had been captured. The same would apply to lobsters caught in a pot.

The decision in *R.* v. *Howlett*[2] is intriguing, but also instructive, because the court held that mussels were wild animals. They could not therefore be stolen unless the owner of the land (in this case private foreshore) "reduced them into possession". Raking over the mussel beds from time to time was not sufficient to reduce them into possession, and the convictions of two men charged with stealing them were quashed.

Fish taken at sea become the property of the owner of the fishing boat as soon as they are put in the hold and they then become capable of being stolen.[3]

Fish Poaching Offences

Theft. Stealing fish (those capable of being stolen) is the offence of theft, as we have seen above. The maximum penalty is 10 years imprisonment.[4]

Illegal fishing in private waters. The Theft Act, 1968, provides for the poacher by specifying offences for which it is unnecessary to decide whether the fish are legally capable of being stolen or whether they have been "reduced into possession" — or whether any fish are actually taken.

(*a*) It is an offence unlawfully to take or destroy (or to attempt to) any fish in water which is private property or in which there is any private right of fishery, at night (i.e. one hour after sunset to one hour before sunrise). This offence is also committed if it is done (or attempted) in the daytime by any means *other than by angling*. The maximum penalty is a £50 fine on a first conviction, and three months imprisonment, and/or a £100 fine on a subsequent conviction.

(*b*) If it is done (or attempted) *by angling* in the daytime a different offence is committed for which a lighter maximum penalty is laid down — a fine of £20.[5]

The activity must be done "unlawfully" for it to be one of these offences, so that if the angler has a *bona fide* claim of right to fish the water he cannot be convicted, but he must show reasonable ground for the claim of right.[6] A genuine, but false, belief in the right to fish is no defence to the

---

[1] Hale P.C. 511.
[2] *The Times*, 7 February 1968.
[3] *R.* v. *Mallinson* (1902) 66 J.P. 503.
[4] Theft Act, 1968, s. 7.
[5] *Ibid.*, s. 32(1) and Sched. 1, para. 2.
[6] *Wells* v. *Hardy* (1964) 2 Q.B. 447 and see p.23 above (non-tidal waters).

charge, even if the public have fished the water unchallenged for a great many years.[1] Thus a claim by the accused of a public right to fish in non-tidal waters is no defence, because no such public right can be obtained.[2] The offence can be committed by fishing in tidal waters if it is a private fishery[3], but it is a good defence to plead a genuine belief that public fishing was allowed, and evidence of public fishing in tidal waters for many years is sufficient defence.[4] In *Hales* v. *Alder*[5], the accused was acquitted because he genuinely believed he had the permission of the tenant of the land.

Catching fish with rod and line, or by any other method, is "taking", whether the fish are carried away, kept temporarily in a keep net, or returned immediately to the water.[6]

The offence extends to the taking or destruction of any kind of fish, whether or not they can be caught by angling, including crayfish[7] and winkles.[8]

In *Barnard* v. *Roberts* in 1907[9] the Court decided that the two accused found using a line carrying baited hooks sunk in the River Llugwy by a stone and pegged to the bank, were not "angling".

Seizure of tackle. The Theft Act, 1968, has done away with the right of the landowner, or his bailiff etc., to confiscate the fishing tackle of anyone found fishing illegally, instead of prosecuting him. This was a useful deterrent, and usually suited all parties better than going to court. Now if somebody is committing an offence of illegal fishing in private waters (i.e. either offence (*a*) or (*b*) above) "any person" may seize for production in court anything the offender has with him at the time of the offence "for use for taking or destroying fish". On conviction the court can order forfeiture of such things (whether seized or not). The seizure may be done if there is reasonable cause to suspect the offence is being committed.[10]

Apprehension of offenders. "Any person" may arrest without a warrant anyone who is, or whom he, with reasonable cause, suspects to be committing the offence of poaching in private waters described in para. (*a*) on p.61 above, but not the offence in para (*b*)[11]. This means there is no general right of arrest of persons caught illegally fishing *by angling* in daytime, but there is of night offenders, and of offenders using non-angling means in the daytime. See Chapter 22 for the powers of water bailiffs to arrest.

Litter and The Litter Act, 1958. Leaving litter behind is the besetting

[1] *Booth* v. *Brough* (1869) 33 J.P. 694.
[2] *Paley* v. *Birch* (1867) 8 B. & S. 356.
[3] *Hudson* v. *MacRae* (1863) 4 B. & S. 585 and see Chapter 5.
[4] *R.* v. *Stimson*(1863) 4 B. & S. 307.
[5] (1874) 38 J.P. 407.
[6] *Wells* v. *Hardy* (1964) 2 Q.B. 447 and see p.23 above (non-tidal waters).
[7] *Caygil* v. *Thwaite* (1885) 49 J.P. 614.
[8] *Leavett* v. *Clark* (1915) 3 K.B. 9.
[9] (1907) 71 J.P. 277.
[10] Theft Act, 1968, Sched. 1, para. 2(3) and (4).
[11] *Ibid.*, Sched. 1, para. 2(4).

sin of the public, and a bad habit from which the angler is not, alas, immune. As well as being an unsightly nuisance it is not always realised that litter is frequently a source of danger, especially to livestock, many of which have suffered agonising deaths through swallowing polythene bags or have had to be killed after treading on sharp pieces of picnickers' jetsam. The angler should know that abandoned lengths of nylon fishing line are especially dangerous. An angling club was banned by the Severn River Authority from holding contests on any of its waters because of litter being left behind by anglers.[1]

Depositing anything on land without authority is a trespass, even if there is the right to go on the land for other purposes, so that the "litter bug" may be sued for damages. It may also be a crime.

The Litter Act, 1958, makes it an offence to throw down, drop or in any way deposit litter "in, into or from any place in the open air to which the public are entitled or permitted to have access without payment" and leave it there. It is therefore an offence not only to leave litter in an open air public place, or on a public highway or right of way, but also to throw it onto private land from a public place. Even if an angler pays for his *fishing* he would still be guilty if he left litter in any place in the open air to which the public had free access.

The offence consists of both *depositing and leaving*, so that the angler who tidies up properly before he leaves his swim, commits no offence even if he has been sitting for some time among his sandwich wrappings, empty ground bait bags, and escaped chrysalises. Leaving any abandoned thing may be the offence. The Act does not use the word "litter" but the words "anything whatsoever".

The offence can be committed even though there may be a roof over the "litter bug's" head. The Act lays down " . . . any covered place open to the air on at least one side and available for public uses shall be treated as a place in the open air".

The maximum penalty has been increased from a fine of £10 to £100 by the Dangerous Litter Act, 1971, which requires the court in sentencing to take account of the nature of the litter and the risk it causes to persons or animals, or damage to property.[2]

The Litter Act, 1958, has been little protection for the owner of private land because it only deals with public places — the "Keep Britain Tidy" campaign has probably been more effective — but if damage is caused by litter the offender might be punishable under the Criminal Damage Act, 1971, (see p.59). The Civic Amenities Act, 1967, goes further by making it an offence to abandon a vehicle or anything else on any land (public or private) in the open air, if it is taken to the land to dump it.[3]

---

[1] *Angling Times*, November 26, 1965.
[2] S. 1.
[3] S. 19.

Duty of Occupiers of Land Towards Anglers

Negligence. The landowner, or occupier, has a legal duty not to injure by his negligence anglers who enter upon his land. He may also have other duties laid down in the lease, if the anglers have a fishing lease from him.

Occupiers Liability Act, 1957. This Act, which set out to simplify the law on this subject, lays down that the occupier of premises owes a "common duty of care" to all his visitors, except insofar as he can and does alter his legal duty towards particular visitors, for example, by an agreement.[1] This duty of care is described in the Act as follows:[2]

"(2) The common duty of care is a duty to take such care as in all the circumstances of the case is reasonable to see that the visitor shall be reasonably safe in using the premises for the purposes for which he is invited or permitted by the occupier to be there."

"Premises" here has a wider meaning than in colloquial use, and has more the meaning of the property of the occupier. The use of this word in law is discussed in Chapter 13 in connection with the letting of fishing.

The duty of care owed by the occupier to anglers on his property is not therefore one of elaborate protection. If there are dangers on the property which anglers have access to, steps must be taken either to guard them or to give sufficient warning of the dangers. The occupier is allowed to rely on visitors to take an ordinary degree of care to look after themselves, and to guard against any special risks ordinarily met with in the exercise of their calling. If children are allowed to enter the land to fish, he must expect them by nature to be less careful and more adventurous than adults and take sufficient steps to safeguard them from dangers on the premises accordingly.[3]

Where anglers have acquired rights of fishing under an agreement (such as a fishing lease) with the occupier of the land, the occupier owes them the common duty of care, but he may qualify his duty in the agreement. The agreement could exonerate the occupier from all liability as regards the safety of anglers. If, however, such a thing is stipulated on "day tickets" given out to casual visitors as a receipt for payment for a day's fishing, the stipulation may well be of no effect. This is explained more fully with regard to pier tickets in Chapter 6.

Trespassers. The occupier does not owe the common duty of care to trespassers.

An appeal decision in the House of Lords has modified the old rule that the duty owed was no more than to avoid leaving a deliberate trap for the trespassers. The test is whether a humane person with the knowledge, ability and resources of the occupier could and would take steps to protect trespassers from any danger on the land.[4]

---

[1] Occupiers Liability Act, 1957, s. 2(1).
[2] *Ibid.*, s. 2(2).
[3] *Ibid.*
[4] *British Railways Board* v. *Herrington, The Times*, February 17, 1972.

A poacher, therefore, trespasses at his own risk, and has no redress against the occupier of the land if, for example, an unsound bridge collapses under his weight and he suffers an injury — or a wetting.

Bulls. May a farmer run a bull in a field where anglers have permission to fish? The answer is not straightforward. The owner of a domestic animal is not liable for any injury done by the animal, unless the injury could reasonably be expected. The courts have always had the strange notion that the bull at heart is kindly disposed towards man, and have classified it as one which its owner could not reasonably expect to attack a human being.[1] But if the owner knows a particular animal has shown a vicious tendency, he must take care to see that it does no injury by reason of the tendency, and will be liable for damage if it does. This rule is now spelled out in the Animals Act, 1971.[2]

In some areas the running of bulls in fields crossed by public footpaths is made an offence by byelaws. The practice would also be unlawful if it were contrary to an express prohibition in a fishing lease, and in any event might well be held to be contrary to the usual covenant for "quiet enjoyment" if the point were ever taken to court.

---

[1] *Lathall* v. *Joyce & Sons* [1939] 3 All E.R. 854.
[2] S. 2(2).

CHAPTER 10

THE ANGLING CLUB

An angling club or association is not recognised by English law as having any legal existence separate from its individual members, unless it is an incorporated body (a company). Most angling clubs are unincorporated and so they cannot undertake business transactions in their own name.

Incorporated Clubs

An angling club may be incorporated under the Companies Act, 1948, and if large enough in its activities this may have advantages. The club when incorporated becomes a "limited" corporate body (though the Board of Trade may excuse the appendage "limited" or "Company" after the name[1]) and becomes a legal "person" separate from its members. Its liability may be limited by shares or guarantee, and it has the convenience of being able to conduct business in the name of the club. The club itself can purchase or take leases of fishing rights or premises, instead of having to form a trust, and it may sue or be sued and borrow money in its own name (provided its articles allow borrowing, which they should).

Liability of Members. Usually an incorporated sports club is limited by guarantee, and the guarantee, which will be that of its members, will be for a modest sum. The club being a company, the individual members will not be liable for any debts and obligations undertaken by the club unless and until the company is wound up, and then the liability of a member will be limited to the amount of his guarantee (which may be, say, £1) or, if the company is limited by shares, to the amount unpaid on his shares.[2]

Club Rules. The internal affairs of the club as between members are governed by the club's rules, the incorporation affecting mainly relations with the "outside world". The club's Aims and Objects will be set out in the Memorandum of Association, and it is important for these to be wide enough to cover anything (however remote) the club is ever likely to want to do. The Club Rules are often appended to the Memorandum of Association. See below for a further note on club rules, and Appendix A for a model set of rules.

Formalities. Incorporation is not usually worth while for the small club, because when incorporated the club must adhere to the rules laid down in the

---

[1] Companies Act, 1948, s. 19.
[2] Companies Act, 1948, s. 212.

Companies Acts — for example an annual return must be made in a specified manner.

Unincorporated Clubs

An unincorporated club is one which is not registered as a company under the Companies Acts.

In an unincorporated club, the members of the club are jointly entitled to its assets, because the club as such (being non-existent at law) can own nothing. No member can realise his share of the club assets, except when the club comes to an end.[1] Until that unhappy day, each member can enjoy the privileges of the club according to the club rules.

Acquisition of fishing. As an unincorporated club cannot obtain the legal title to fishing, or anything else, in its own name, it is necessary to appoint a trustee (or trustees) to take rights or property on behalf of the club, and hold it in trust for the members. For example, one of the members may take a lease of fishing rights in a river and hold it in trust for the club members. Although the trustee then has the legal ownership of the lease, as a trustee he is not free to deal with the lease as he pleases, but must treat it as if it belonged to the members. On the other hand, he will be responsible under the lease to see that the rent is paid, and all the terms are observed.

The club rules should provide for the appointment of trustees, and also for indemnifying them against any liabilities they properly undertake on behalf of the club. Unless the rules provide for it, the trustees cannot claim to be indemnified by the club members.[2]

Clubs belonging to the Anglers' Co-operative Association (the Association formed to fight pollution) can appoint, if they want, the A.C.A. Trustee Company Ltd to hold the ownership or leases of fishing as trustees on behalf of the club. This will have the advantage of the club retaining control of the fishing in the usual way, but if it should be necessary to take action against polluters, the A.C.A. could act directly on behalf of the club.

A model form of fishing lease is given in Appendix B.

The Committee. The day to day business and management of the club will, of course, be delegated to the club committee. The election of committee members and their powers will depend upon the club rules. The committee members will be personally responsible for anything done by them beyond the authority given by the rules or given by the membership in accordance with the rules. If the rules do not provide that the committee can pledge the credit of the members, the committee may not claim from the members if they over-commit the club funds. Should the committee act without authority the members in general meeting can ratify their action, but otherwise the committee members are personally liable.

The Rules. The Rules form part of a legal contract between the members of the club, and so are legally binding upon the members. The rules

---

[1] *Abbatt* v. *Treasury Solicitor* [1969] 3 All E.R. 1175.
[2] *Wise* v. *Perpetual Trustee Co.* (1903) A.C. 139.

can only be altered or amended in accordance with the rules themselves. It is therefore important for the rules to provide for this, otherwise members are not bound by a change of rule even if carried by a vote, unless every single member consents.[1] When this situation arose in *Abbatt* v. *Treasury Solicitor*[2] and a club in general meeting voted by a majority to adopt new rules, the Court of Appeal held that, although express consent was not given by each member, the new rules became binding because no dissenting voter objected, but, on the contrary, the membership as a whole acquiesced by their conduct. Giving the committee or a meeting powers to carry out the general business or purposes of the club, does not enable them to change the rules.[1]

Rules of an Angling Club should provide for the admission and election of members, and their resignation and expulsion. Expulsion of members, however, should be handled carefully. A member may only be expelled if the rules allow it, and then only in accordance with the rules, and in good faith in the interests of the club.[3] The rules of natural justice apply, which means that a member should be given the opportunity to be heard before he is expelled.[4] The rules should also regulate the angling of the members, and require members to conform to the terms of fishing leases held on behalf of the club, and any byelaws. A model set of Angling Club rules is given in Appendix A.

Law Suits

An unincorporated club cannot sue or be sued in its own name, nor can the Secretary, or other officer, sue or be sued in the name of the club, even if the rules say they can.[5] As it is not practical for all the club members to be parties to an action the Court can make an order for one or more of them to represent them all — or so many as have the same interest in the proceedings.

The trustees may take proceedings or be sued regarding fishing rights held by them on behalf of the club and regarding any contracts entered into by them on behalf of the club.

An incorporated club can sue and be sued in its own name.

Supporting litigation. The case of *Martell* v. *Consett Iron Co. Ltd*[6] cleared up the question of whether it was legal for an association of anglers and riparian owners which was not a party to an action to give financial support and encouragement to a litigant in the interests of angling. The Court decided it was, thereby allowing the Anglers' Co-operative Association to carry on its work of cleaning up polluted waters and deterring new pollutions by underwriting the legal costs of members who face proceedings against polluters.

---

[1] *Harrington* v. *Sendall* [1903] 1 Ch. 921.
[2] [1969] 3 All E.R. 1175.
[3] *Tontussi* v. *Molli* (1886) 2 T.L.R. 731.
[4] *Lawlor* v. *Union of Post Office Workers* [1965] Ch. 712.
[5] *Gray* v. *Pearson* (1870) L.R. 5 C.P. 568.
[6] [1955] 1 All E.R. 481.

Protecting its Angling Interests

Angling clubs have opportunities to promote or defend angling interests in addition to organising angling for their members, as appears here and there in this book.[1] A summary of some of these may be helpful:

Pollution. By acquiring the ownership of riparian land abutting on waters in which it has fishing rights, an angling club places itself in the strongest position to prevent pollution of its waters. (See Chapter 20.) One club owning a short stretch of river bank can save miles of river from being fouled, by its right to injunctions to restrain pollution. The ownership of only a few yards of waterside land is sufficient.

If leases of fishing are obtained from riparian owners, clubs are advised to obtain a covenant from the landowner, if possible, to join in any proceedings the club may take against polluters. This can be coupled with an indemnity against the landowner's costs.

Water abstraction. Under the Water Resources Act, 1963, an angling club whose fishing might be attacked may object to the draft statement of "minimum acceptable flows" proposed by river authorities, and, if it does object, has a right to be heard either at a public inquiry into the proposals, or at a private hearing held on behalf of the Minister.[2] The same applies to any proposal by a river authority to amend a statement of minimum acceptable flows.[3] There is no obligation upon river authorities to give angling clubs notice of their proposals for minimum acceptable flows, but they must give notice to every person who has requested them to do so.[4] Clubs are advised to make this request.

Where an application is made for a licence to abstract water it must be advertised. If an angling club's fishing might be affected by the abstraction, it is advisable at least to examine the application and take advantage of the procedure outlined in Chapter 21.

Owners of fishing rights who sustain loss or damage because of water abstraction can apply to the Minister to revoke or vary abstraction licences, provided no minimum acceptable flow has been fixed for the waters.[5]

Regulation of fisheries. A club or association which in the opinion of the Minister sufficiently represents the fishing interests in an area can apply to the Minister to make an order regulating the fisheries in the area.[6] A club also has the right to object to any draft order made by the Minister to regulate fisheries[7], and to object to any byelaw which may affect its fishing.[8]

---

[1] Fuller advice for clubs, and notes on tax problems, may be found in *All For Fishing*, by Gregory and Seymour, (London, Charles Knight, 1970).
[2] Water Resources Act, 1963, s. 19 and Sched. 7 and see Chapter 21.
[3] *Ibid.*, s. 20 and Sched. 7.
[4] *Ibid.*, Sched. 7, para. 4(g).
[5] *Ibid.*, s. 47 and see Chapter 21.
[6] Salmon and Freshwater Fisheries Act, 1923, s. 39(1), and see Chapter 22.
[7] *Ibid.*, s. 40.
[8] Water Resources Act, 1963, s. 119 and Sched. 12.

General fishing licences. As appears in Chapter 4 a general licence to fish for salmon or trout can be obtained from the river authority by an association entitled to an *exclusive* right of fishing in a fishery where a river authority licence (i.e. a rod licence) is needed. If an angling club obtains a general licence to fish, any member of the club may fish in the waters covered by the licence without any other licence, but the Secretary must give him written authority.[1]

Diseases of fish. An angling club which suspects that any of its waters may be infected with a disease of fish, can require the Minister to have the waters examined by an inspector, and is entitled to a free copy of the inspector's report.[2]

Grants for Angling

These are available to clubs — see p.166.

---

[1] Salmon and Freshwater Fisheries Act, 1972, s. 6(8).
[2] Diseases of Fish Act, 1937, s. 5 and see Chapter 18.

CHAPTER 11

FISHERIES

Fishing Rights

The right to fish in a certain place is often called a fishery, or, more learnedly, a piscary. Fishing rights may be owned together with the land on which the water is situated (that is, "the soil"), or separate from the ownership of the land.[1] They might be held by the owner-occupier, the landlord owner, the tenant of the land, a tenant of the fishing only (for example, an Angling Club), an owner of other land which may or may not be neighbouring the fishing, by an owner of the fishing alone (that is, not connected with the ownership of any land), or they may be shared between the landowner and another or others. Other permutations may be possible but enough has been said to indicate that a search for the fishing rights in any water may lead the enquirer anywhere.

A profit à prendre. When a fishery is separated from the ownership of the land, it is called a profit à prendre. (The more legalistic angler might give it its full multi-lingual description of a *profit à prendre in alieno solo* — or he might simply call it a profit, for short.) A profit à prendre is the right to take something out of another's land (in this case, fish). If the land is not owned by the owner of the profit, it is called an *incorporeal fishery*. Where the fishery goes with the ownership of the soil, it is a *corporeal fishery*.

Kinds of Fishery

Fisheries may be private or public, and a private fishery may be a "several fishery" or a "common of fishery".

No further divisions or subdivisions are necessary, but a short glossary of the various terms used in describing fisheries should be useful.

Common Fishery — the right of public fishing in tidal waters.

Common of Fishery — where two or more persons share the same right of fishing.

Corporeal Fishery — where the same person owns the soil and the fishing rights. It may be either a several fishery or a common of fishery.

Exclusive Fishery — another term for several fishery.

---

[1] *Hanbury* v. *Jenkins* (1901) 2 Ch. 401.

Fishery — used in two different senses at law — viz. (1) the right to fish in a given place; and (2) the place where the right of fishing is exercised.

Fishery in Gross — a right of fishing not attached to the ownership of any land.

Franchise Fishery — a right granted to a subject to take royal fish.[1]

Free Fishery — a term best avoided. It has sometimes been used to describe a several fishery and sometimes a common of fishery.

Incorporeal Fishery — where the fishing rights and the soil are owned by different persons. The fishing rights are then a "profit à prendre".

Piscary — a fancy name for fishery.

Royal Fishery — the right of the Crown to royal fish in territorial waters.[1]

Several Fishery — a sole and exclusive right of a person to the fishing, whether or not he owns the soil.

Soil — when used in connection with fishing rights, it is the land over which the water stands, flows or ebbs and flows.

Sole Fishery — another term for several fishery.

Territorial Fishery — another term for corporeal fishery.

Private Fisheries

Several Fishery. This sole and exclusive right of a person to fish in a given area may exist in either tidal or non-tidal waters. As the Crown has not been able since Magna Carta to deprive the public of their right to fish in tidal waters, all several fisheries now existing in tidal waters originated before 1192. The only way in which a private fishery could now be created in public waters would be by Act of Parliament[2], Parliament having the power to enact anything, even such a heinous measure as this.

The law presumes[3], if there is no evidence to the contrary, that the owner of a several fishery owns the soil[4], and that the owner of the soil owns the fishing rights in waters on his land.[5] In tidal waters the soil is presumed to belong to the Crown for the benefit of all subjects of the realm. Several fisheries may be freehold or leasehold.[6] A several fishery, however, may be owned apart from the ownership of the land. For example, on selling part of his estate a landowner might retain for himself fishing rights in the land he sells. In this way the fishing rights in a river or lake may be found to belong to the land "next door". Or an individual, syndicate or Angling Club might purchase fishing rights without purchasing any land. In such a case the fishing

---

[1] For royal fish, see Chapter 2.
[2] *Malcolmson* v. *O'Dea* (1863) 10 H.L.Cas. 593.
[3] For presumptions, see pp.95–98 below.
[4] *Hanbury* v. *Jenkins* (1901) 2 Ch. 401.
[5] *Carlisle Corp.* v. *Graham* (1869) L.R. 4 Exch. 361 at p.368.
[6] E.g. *Grove* v. *Portal* (1902) 1 Ch. 727.

rights might belong to a person or body who owned no land at all. Where a landowner on selling land reserves the fishing rights to himself, he retains the *exclusive* right to fish.[1]

The exclusive right of the owner of a several fishery need not be an exclusive right to take all kinds of fish. It may, for example, as was found to be the case in *Seymour* v. *Courtenay*[2] (1771) be divided up so that one person has the right to take oysters and another the right to take all floating fish. In such a case there are two several fisheries (and not a single common of fishery) as long as the owners of the fishing rights have each the sole right to certain kinds of fish.

Common of Fishery. A common of fishery arises where one or more persons share the same right of fishing either with the owner of the soil, or with others none of whom own the soil. It must not be confused with a "common fishery" which is quite different, being the right of the public to fish in public waters.

The private right to fish in common with others may go with the occupation of land, or with a house situated apart from the land where the fishing is enjoyed. (This is known as a "common appurtenant" to land.) It might be neighbouring land, or land elsewhere. Where the right to fish in another's water is attached to a particular piece of land or a house, the law assumes that it was granted, as Blackstone said "for the sustenance of the tenant's family"[3] and it is limited to the needs of the occupier and his household. He may not therefore sell the fish he catches. The common of fishery appurtenant to land passes to each owner of the land for the time being.

A common of fishery may also be held "in gross" — i.e. not connected with the ownership of any land. For example, the members of an angling club might be granted the right to fish a water together with the owner of the land.

When a landowner grants a "fishery" or "a free fishery" to another, he does not relinquish his own right to fish unless the grant clearly says so.[4]

"Free Fishery". The reader has been advised to avoid this term, but the author cannot take his own advice because unfortunately the term has been used freely and requires some explanation. Mr Justice Willes commented in the case of *Malcolmson* v. *O'Dea* in 1863[5] that there had been confusion in the use of the term over the centuries from a Year Book of Henry VII to the Court of Queen's Bench in *Holford* v. *Bailey* reported in 1849.[6]

---

[1]*Paget* v.*Milles* (1789) 3 Doug. 43.
[2](1771) 5 Burr. 2814.
[3]Blackstone II, p. 35. *Lord Chesterfield* v. *Harris* (1908) 2 Ch. 397, affirmed *sub nom. Harris* v. *Chesterfield* [1911] A.C. 623.
[4]See *Bloomfield* v. *Johnston* (1868) I.R. 8 C.L. 68.
[5](1863) 10 H.L.Cas. 593.
[6](1849) 13 Q.B. 426.

The great jurist Blackstone says[1] that the term free fishery is properly used to describe a several fishery in tidal waters, but the Irish Judge Baron Fitzgerald, in *Bloomfield* v. *Johnston*[2], referring to Blackstone, said "free fishery, when used, as all admit it may be used, in the sense of fishing not exclusive, is, if *in alieno solo*, not distinguishable from common of fishery", which, to say the least, is a pity.

It would seem more logical to suppose that "free" has been used to contrast the right with a right in common, as it has been used for instance in "free warren", and that Blackstone knew a thing or two.

Incorporeal Fishery. The term incorporeal fishery describes all rights of fishing held in the land of another. A several fishery or a common of fishery is incorporeal when owned by a person who does not own the soil. The grant of an incorporeal right of fishing does not therefore give a right to occupy or interfere with the soil, unless such a right is expressly granted together with the fishing rights.

No devices for fishing may be fixed to the soil by the holder of incorporeal rights. Lord Herschell in *Attorney-General* v. *Emerson*[3] confirming this also thought that stakes could be *temporarily* driven into the soil to hold nets, as being ancillary to the right to fish.

A *corporeal fishery* is one held by the owner of the soil. Normally the owner of corporeal rights will own land adjacent to the water, but if the soil beneath the water only is owned, it will be a corporeal right of fishing.[4] In *Hesketh* v. *Willis Cruisers*[5], the Court of Appeal emphasised that a corporeal fishery was *land* and not a right appurtenant to land. On a transfer of land other than the soil of the fishery together with "rights appurtenant to the land", they held that a corporeal fishery previously owned with the land was not transferred.

A corporeal fishery and an incorporeal fishery may exist in the same water, if, for example (again, as in *Seymour* v. *Courtenay*[6]), the owner of the soil has the right to take oysters, while another has the right to take floating fish.

Public Fisheries

Common Fishery. The right of the public to fish in tidal waters is called a common fishery, and where it may be enjoyed has been examined in Chapter 5 above. It must not, of course, be confused with a common of fishery (see p.73 above). The public right of fishing stems from the Crown's ownership of the soil of tidal waters.

---

[1] II Com. 39.
[2] (1868) I.R. 8 C.L. 68.
[3] (1891) A.C. 649, 656.
[4] *Marshall* v. *Ullswater Steam Navigation Co.* (1863) 3 B. & S. 732.
[5] (1968) 19 P. & C.R. 573, following *Micklethwait* v. *Newlay Bridge Co.* (1886) 33 Ch. D. 133.
[6] (1771) 5 Burr. 2814 (see p.73 above).

The rule that the Crown has been unable since Magna Carta to grant away or restrict public fishing rights[1] is qualified by the Crown's power to re-grant fishing rights in tidal waters where there has once been a private fishery. Lord Blackburn in *Neil* v. *Duke of Devonshire* in 1882[2] quoted with approval in the House of Lords the words of the Master of the Rolls in Ireland in the court below:

> "It is not law, and this can never be too often repeated, that the Crown cannot grant a several fishery in tidal waters since Magna Carta. Such a statement is illusory and contrary to law. It can grant a several fishery in such waters since Magna Carta, *if that fishing existed before Magna Carta.* If a tidal water in which there was *prima facie* a right in the public to fish was appropriated by an individual or by the Crown before Magna Carta, that individual or the Crown, if the Crown has got it back, can grant it after Magna Carta."

No individual member of the public may place "fixed engines" (e.g. salmon baskets) in public waters[3], but the public may use any lawful means of fishing which does not involve an appropriation of the soil. They may therefore draw nets or lay lines[4], provided they comply with the 1923 Act (see Chapters 7 and 8).

The public may take any kind of fish, except royal fish. Shell fish may be taken from public waters, even if they were laid down by someone else[5] (but not, of course, from a private fishery).

---

[1] See p.22 above.
[2] (1882) 2 App. Cas. 135.
[3] *Att.-Gen. for British Columbia* v. *Att.-Gen. for Canada* (1914) A.C. 153, 171.
[4] *Bevins* v. *Bird* (1865) 12 L.T. 306, 307.
[5] *Truro Corporation* v. *Rowe* (1902) 2 K.B. 709.

CHAPTER 12

PROTECTION OF FISHING RIGHTS

Nature of Fishing Rights

Ultimately the rights of the owner of fishing depend upon the wording of the grant, and the rights in any case will be affected by Acts of Parliament and byelaws. But the owner of fishing rights at common law has the right to fish for and catch every fish in his fishery, and take away the fish caught. A person who enjoys fishing rights over another's property obtains the legal right to take away the catch only if the fishing rights were granted by deed. This is because a profit à prendre (see p.71 above) can only be legally granted by a formal grant under seal. This is clearly established in cases to do with shooting rights, such as *Mason* v. *Clarke.*[1] Here the landlord of a farm, who had reserved in the farm tenancy agreement the right to take rabbits, granted the rabbiting for one year to the local garage proprietor — an expert rabbit catcher. This case shews that a person granted a profit à prendre (such as the right to take rabbits, or fish) has a remedy against anyone interfering with his right even though it is not granted by deed, provided he has taken steps to exercise his right. This is because of the legal doctrine of "part performance", which enables a person having an informal agreement to demand a formal grant in certain circumstances. The niceties of this need not be examined here because normally there is no objection raised to anglers taking away fish provided the rules of the water are adhered to. If legal issues should arise on this score, *Mason* v. *Clarke*, being the latest pronouncement on the subject, and from the highest appeal court in the land (the House of Lords) may be referred to. It is enough to relate here, that in this case the unfortunate rabbiter immediately ran into trouble with the farm tenant who apparently had a grievance against the landlord. In the words of the rabbiter, who was accepted by the Court as a truthful witness, the tenant "behaved like a lunatic", "flew at" him and his assistants, ordering them off the land, and ripping up snares which they had set. The House of Lords held that the expert rabbiter was clearly entitled to an action for trespass against the farmer, and awarded damges and an injunction (that is a court order restraining the farmer from interfering with the rabbiting under threat of imprisonment for disobedience).

The owner of fishing rights who does not own the soil (i.e. who has an incorporeal right), may not interfere with or fix anything in the soil (see

---

[1] [1955] A.C. 778.

p.74), but where the soil is owned fishing rights carry the right to place "fixed engines" in the bed, subject, of course, to the restrictions upon obstructing the passage of fish laid down in the Salmon and Freshwater Fisheries Act, 1923 — see Chapter 8.

Who may fish. In the past the right to fish was not considered, as it is nowadays, a right to enjoy a pastime, but was thought of more as a means of providing dishes for the household. Usually, therefore, the owner of fishing rights is free to exercise them either personally, or by his servants. This was challenged unsuccessfully in the case of the disporting gamekeepers, *Wickham* v. *Hawker.*[1] On the conveyance of land there was reserved to the seller and excepted from the grant "free liberty, with servants or otherwise . . . to hawk, hunt, fish and fowl". When the gamekeepers of the owner of these rights entered the land after game, the landowner took an action against them for trespass, but the judge, Baron Parke, would not allow the claim. "If there be a personal licence of pleasure", he said in his rather quaint Chancery language, "it extends only to the individual, and it cannot be exercised with or by servants; but if there is a licence of profit, and not for pleasure, it may." He added, "It appears to us, that the liberties to hawk, hunt, fish and fowl, granted to one, his heirs and assigns, are interests, or profits à prendre, and may be exercised by servants in the absence of masters".

Right of Action. Fishing rights are a legal property. This simple point of law is of immense importance for the protection of anglers, and indeed for the preservation of the pastime against polluters and others who would harm the interests of anglers. It means that the owner of fishing rights, or any person in possession of them, such as a fishing tenant, can take proceedings against anyone unjustifiably interfering with the fishery, or its use or enjoyment. An action in court may be taken for trespass or nuisance, and this right is available whether or not the fishery owner owns the land, and whether or not he is entitled to take away the fish he catches.

The old case of *Child* v. *Greenhill*[2] (1638) showed that the owner of an incorporeal fishery (i.e. where no land is owned in connection with the fishery) has a right of action for trespass against anyone taking fish out of his waters — in that case one hundred eels. Lord Justice Lindley, however, disposed of any argument about it once and for all in *Fitzgerald* v. *Firbank*[3] when he said:

"You cannot draw any distinction with reference to the right of taking away the fish between one kind of right of fishing and another. If a person chooses to pay for the amusement of catching fish and leaving them in the water, of course he can do so,"

and Lord Justice Rigby agreed, saying:

---

[1] (1840) 7 M. & W. 63.
[2] (1638) 4 Cro. Car. 553.
[3] [1897] 2 Ch. 96.

"I hold that the grantees of the incorporeal hereditament [that is, the fishing] have a right of action against any person who disturbs them either by trespass or nuisance, or in any other substantial manner."

As we have seen, *Mason* v. *Clarke* (above p.76) confirms that this is so even where the grant is not by a formal deed.

The importance of this for angling societies combating pollution is brought out in Chapter 20.

The Ely Beet Sugar Factory Cases. The pollution of the Cambridgeshire Ouse by a sugar beet factory gave rise to litigation in the 1930s which cleared up some further points about the fishery owner's right of action. The owner of two fisheries some way downstream from Ely claimed that effluent from the factory killed fish in his fisheries. In the first action he was awarded £200 damages[1], but was refused an injunction (that is, a court order) to restrain the factory from further pollution, because measures had already been taken at considerable expense to purify the factory's discharge for the future. Mr Justice Farwell held that the owner of the fisheries had a right of action even though the effluent was not discharged directly into the fisheries but was carried into them by the stream. "This is not strictly speaking a trespass", he said. "It is nuisance."

The defendants argued that the Ouse had at one time been tidal at Ely, and so the plaintiff could not take an action against them unless he proved a grant of the fisheries. If they could not prove such a grant was made before Magna Carta, the law would presume the fisheries belonged to the Crown. The judge answered this by saying firstly that the defendants could not defend themselves by setting up a *jus tertii* against the occupiers of the fisheries. In other words, it was no use saying they belonged to someone else, i.e. the Crown. Secondly, he held that there was sufficient proof of title to the fisheries by the claimant.

In a second action[2] the same owner of the same fisheries again alleged effluent from the same factory was killing his fish. This time he was unsuccessful because he was unable to satisfy the trial judge that the injury to his fisheries was caused by the factory. The defendants raised some further ingenious defences on this occasion. They said that even if the factory had polluted the fisheries, the owner could not claim because he could not prove any pecuniary loss. The Court of Appeal rejected this contention, holding that the disturbance of a fishery was an invasion of a legal right. It was not necessary to show pecuniary loss because the injury to the legal right carried with it a right to damages.

The defendants then argued that pollution was an offence under s. 8 of the Salmon and Freshwater Fisheries Act, 1923, which enacted (s. 8(3)):

"Proceedings under this section shall not be instituted except by the

---

[1] *Nicholls* v. *Ely Beet Sugar Factory Ltd* [1931] 2 Ch. 84.
[2] *Nicholls* v. *Ely Beet Sugar Factory Ltd* [1936] Ch. 343.

fishery board or by a person who has first obtained a certificate from the Minister that he has a material interest in the waters alleged to be affected."

and so the owner of the fisheries was out of order in bringing a private action. The Master of the Rolls gave this argument short shrift, saying:

"It struck me at once as a very hard proposition to say that an Act like this which imposes penalties on grounds of public policy in order to prevent certain things being done and which is for the benefit and protection of owners of fisheries, should have the singular effect of depriving them of their common law remedies."

The Judges in the Court of Appeal made testy remarks about the amount of time, money and ingenuity that had been wasted in the action over what they thought was not very much. Even so the two cases of *Nicholls* v. *Ely Beet Sugar Factory Ltd* settled some important law for anglers, which can be summarised thus:

An action by the occupiers of a fishery:
(1) May be taken in nuisance, if not trespass, against upstream occupiers of lands or premises who disturb or injure the fishery;
(2) Cannot be combated by setting up a *jus tertii* (i.e. title belongs to someone else), whether the action is in trespass or nuisance;
(3) May be taken and damages and/or an injunction obtained without proving pecuniary loss; and
(4) May be taken even though the conduct complained of is an offence punishable under the criminal law.

The old case of *Courtney* v. *Collet*[1] shews that downstream anglers could have their troubles before pollution had ever menaced angling. In that case the upstream occupier removed a dam — or as the contemporary report has it, "threw down a certain wear" — and flooded another's fishery. The report says:

"It seemed to the Court that this was a plain trespass, for the causing of a superfluity of water to drown or overflow the land or fishery of the plaintiff, is a plain trespass."

Modern support for this view is found in the judgment of Lord Justice Kennedy in *Fraser* v. *Fear*[2] where he indicated that if a new hatch were brought into operation in a mill, which when opened caused such a rush of water as to drive fish into a quieter cut and prevented them entering an

---

[1] (1697) 1 Ld. Raym. 272.
[2] (1912) 107 L.T. 423.

angler's pool, the owner of the fishing in the pool could claim damages and an injunction. In this case, however, the angler failed to prove his case.

In the recent case of *Rawson* v. *Peters*[1], where the Bradford Waltonians A.C. sued canoeists on the River Wharfe, the Court of Appeal decided an action could be taken against canoeists who interfered with fishing rights even if no one was fishing at the time and no damage was done. Nominal damages of 50p with costs were awarded with liberty to apply to the County Court for an injunction.

Compensation for Statutory Works

An interference with a fishery may be authorised by statute, giving an authority (or possibly, even, a commercial company) powers to execute works. Normally, where a statute authorises works which may interfere with private land, no common law claim for nuisance may be made, but provision is made to compensate owners and occupiers who suffer loss or damage – this includes the owners and occupiers of fisheries. In any event statutory authorities are liable for damages if fishing is injured by their negligence.

Land drainage works. The Land Drainage Acts, 1930 and 1961, specify powers and duties of drainage authorities. The "general powers" are to maintain drainage works, to improve existing works (e.g. deepening or widening watercourses) and to construct new works. "Works" include watercourses.[2] If the exercise of these powers causes injury to "any person" the drainage authority "shall be liable to make full compensation".[3] "Injury" has its usual legal meaning of loss or damage.

The Lands Tribunal in the recent case of *Burgess* v. *Gwyned River Authority*[4] awarded £7,000 damages to an owner of fishing rights in the River Dovey as compensation for injury to the fishing by drainage works carried out to prevent flooding. In an earlier case the High Court had decided that no compensation was payable unless there was an "actionable wrong"[5] but the President of the Tribunal giving judgment in this case said:

> "a river authority has a duty to the owners of fishing rights to carry out any necessary protective works in such a way as to do no unnecessary damage to those rights, and if they do not, their action is unreasonable and is an actionable wrong and an 'injury' within the meaning of the Act[3] for which they must pay full compensation."

Another recent decision throws light on the compensation liability of drainage authorities when they widen watercourses and dispose of spoil. The Act states they may "appropriate and dispose of any matter removed" in

---

[1] *The Times*, November 2, 1972.
[2] Land Drainage Act, 1930, s. 34(1).
[3] *Ibid.*, s. 34(3).
[4] (1972) 24 P. & C.R. 150.
[5] *Marriage* v. *East Norfolk Rivers Catchment Board* [1949] 2 All E.R. 1021.

widening, deepening or dredging a watercourse without making payment for the "matter". If the "matter" is deposited on the banks (as it may be within strict limits) the authority *may* pay compensation "if they think fit" − but they *must* pay full compensation if the injury caused could have been avoided by reasonable care.[1] In *Pattinson* v. *Finningley Internal Drainage Board*[2] the Lands Tribunal, awarding damages with interest, to two farmers, held that trees removed in widening a drain were not "matter" and so the Board was not exempt from paying for them. The land taken was "matter removed", but although no payment was to be made for it compensation was payable for loss of the use of the land.

Pipeline Crossings. Pipelines laid every year now involve numerous river crossings. Under the Acts empowering pipeline construction − e.g. the Gas Act, 1972, (gas mains), the Public Health Act, 1936 (sewers and water pipes), the Water Act, 1945 (water mains) and the Pipelines Act, 1962 (commercial pipelines) − compensation is payable for damage to fishing rights. River authorities will be consulted, but in some cases it will be important for the owners of fishing to make representations for the protection of their interests − such as to ensure the timing of a river crossing is planned to avoid interference with the migration of fish.[3]

Registration of Commons and Common Rights

The Commons Registration Act, 1965, gave three years for claimants to register (1) land in England and Wales said to be common land or town or village greens; (2) rights of common claimed over such land; and (3) ownership of such land. A further two years was given to lodge objections to registrations. It is now too late either to register or to object to claims. Registration under the Act, or under the Land Registration Acts, 1925 and 1936, is conclusive. For anglers this means that any *common of piscary* (common fishing rights) not now registered has lapsed. Likewise, no land can be recognised as a town or village green unless it was registered before 31st March 1970 − i.e. land allotted under any Act for the recreation or exercise of inhabitants of any locality, or on which they have a customary right to indulge in sports and pastimes, or on which they have so indulged as of right for at least 20 years.

The stage has been reached for the determination of disputed claims by Commons Commissioners. In one of the first cases to be heard the Chief Commons Commissioner decided that a "pastime" in the definition of a town or village green could be sea fishing, but it must be a right confined to inhabitants of a defined locality. The claimant failed to prove that a piece of Devon seaboard known as Top Jetty qualified as a town or village green and so the registration as such was not confirmed.[4]

---

[1] Land Drainage Act, 1930, s. 38 as amended by Land Drainage Act, 1961, s. 29.
[2] (1971) 22 P. & C.R. 929.
[3] The British Standard Code of Practice for the Installation of Pipelines in Land (CP 2010) expressly requires the protection of fishing rights.
[4] *In the Matter of Top Jetty, Woody Bay, Martinhoe, Devon*, Ref. No. 9/D/9, decided May 22, 1972.

CHAPTER 13

ACQUISITION OF FISHING RIGHTS

All land was originally owned by the Crown throughout the Kingdom. Theoretically it still is, all land ownership being on tenure from the Crown. The fishing rights in all waters were therefore originally owned by the Crown. The Crown's sovereignty extended over the coastal foreshore, and today reaches out over territorial waters. The public's right to fish in tidal waters is through the ownership of the soil by the Crown.

Time was when only the landowners (usually the Crown) had the fishing rights, so that today all ownership of fishing rights is derived from ownership of the soil. The Crown, however, took to disposing of fisheries as a separate grant, severing them from the ownership of the land. Magna Carta stopped the Crown once and for all from granting away fisheries in tidal waters, as we have seen (p.22). The Crown would also at times keep back fisheries when granting land. The *Royal Fishery of Banne Case*[1] (1610) is an example. The Crown granted away the land through which the River Banne ran, but retained the soil of the river and the fishing.

Disposal of fishing. Fishing rights have therefore become a separate commodity in the property market, and may be disposed of and acquired in the same way as other interests in land — bought and sold, given away or leased.

Basically, the fishing still goes with the land when it changes hands, unless expressly separated from it, as will be seen from the following notes on modes of acquisition.

Modes of Acquisition

Grant. The law presumes that the landowner owns the fishing, unless there is evidence to the contrary.[2] As the ownership of the soil and the fishing go together, a grant of fishing will pass the soil to the acquiring party unless a different intention is shown in the grant.[3]

It has been held, however, that if the landowner grants "the soil" (just using those words) to another, this only passes the soil and not the fishing.[4]

---

[1] (1610) Dav. Ir. 55.
[2] See p.89 below for prescription.
[3] *Duke of Somerset* v. *Fogwell* (1826) 5 B. & C. 875; *Att.-Gen.* v. *Emerson* (1891) A.C. 64.
[4] *Scratton* v. *Brown* (1825) 4 B. & C. 485.

Where the fishing is granted without the land (an incorporeal fishery) it must be by deed — a formal legal document signed, sealed and delivered.[1]

Lease of Land. A lease of land, whether or not it is agricultural land, gives the tenant a tenancy of the sporting rights, unless the landlord expressly reserves them in the lease. If, therefore, a river runs through the let land, and there is no reservation of fishing rights, the tenant has the right of fishing to the exclusion of his landlord. However, in cases where this is not the intention of the parties, and evidence can be brought forward to show it, the Court will infer a reservation of the fishing to the landlord.[2] A reservation or exception of the fishing by the landlord in a lease of land has the effect in law of a grant back to the landlord by the tenant[3], but no formal conveyance or re-grant is needed.[4]

In *Jones* v. *Davis* (1902)[5] where there was a reservation to the landlord in the tenancy of game rights, but nothing was said about fishing rights, it was decided that the landlord could not prosecute a person for unlawfully fishing on the land, if the fishing was with the permission of the farm tenant.

A lease of riparian land (land on the bank of a river) raises a presumption that the tenant may fish to the centre line of the river (see Chapter 14 for presumptions).

Fishing Leases. Fishing may be leased by itself. If it is leased without the land, it must be done by a formal deed, though if it is let without the formality of a deed the owner may still claim the rent for the use and occupation of the fishing.[6] If no rent is fixed for the fishing, the landlord is entitled to a reasonable rent.

A lease of fishing can be made subject to restrictions on the tenant's right — for example, limiting him to certain methods of fishing, or certain kinds of fish. The landlord may also retain the right for himself to fish as well as the tenant. This would give him a personal right to fish, ending on his death. In *Re Vickers Lease* (1947)[7] the landlord reserved "one rod for his own use", and this was held to give him only a personal contractual right to fish, and not a legal property which could be passed on to someone else.

A lease which prohibits assignment or subletting the premises does not disallow the tenant from permitting another person to fish, unless the covenant prohibits subletting part of the premises. In *Grove* v. *Portal*[8] a licence for two rods granted by the tenant was held not to be a breach of such a covenant.

A model fishing lease is given in Appendix B.

---

[1] *Neil* v. *Duke of Devonshire* (1882) 8 App. Cas. 135.
[2] *Browne* v. *Marquis of Sligo* (1859) 10 I Ch.R. 1.
[3] *Doe d. Douglas* v. *Lock* (1835) 2 Ad. & El. 705.
[4] Law of Property Act, 1925, s. 65.
[5] (1902) 86 L.T. 447.
[6] *Holford* v. *Pritchard* (1849) 3 Ex. 793.
[7] *Re Vickers Lease, Pocock* v. *Vickers* (1947) Ch. 420.
[8] (1902) 1 Ch. 727.

Security of Tenure under Fishing Leases

"Business Premises". An interesting and important question that has not as yet been clearly answered by the courts, is whether a syndicate or club which has been let fishing rights can claim as of right a new lease under the Landlord and Tenant Act, 1954, when the old lease comes to an end. Part II of the Act gives a right to tenants to claim new leases of what are broadly termed "business premises" and if claimed the landlord can only resist a new lease on proving one of the special grounds laid down by the Act. At first glance it seems quite absurd to suggest that a letting of fishing to a group of sportsmen solely for their recreation could possibly be a letting of business premises. "Business premises" however, although an adequate description of the generality of what falls under the wing of Part II of the 1954 Act, is by no means a good term to describe what many a lawyer thinks can be brought in by a side wind.

Section 23(1) of the 1954 Act introduces Part II of the Act by providing:

" ... this Part of the Act applies to any tenancy where the property comprised in the tenancy is or includes premises which are occupied by the tenant and are so occupied for the purposes of a business carried on by him or for those and other purposes."

So far it could not possibly apply to a fishing lease. But then s. 23(2) provides:

"In this part of the Act the expression 'business' includes a trade, profession or employment, and includes any activity carried on by a body of persons, whether corporate or incorporate."

A syndicate of anglers fishing a fishery, and possibly maintaining it, under a lease, is an "activity carried on by a body of persons", on the literal meaning of the words. It seems too that the courts will not put a restricted meaning on the word "activity". In *Addiscombe Garden Estates* v. *Crabbe*[1] the Court of Appeal rejected the suggestion that the word "activity" in the section must mean a business kind of activity. The case decided that a member's lawn tennis club was entitled to a new lease of tennis courts and a club house because the club was a body of persons carrying on an activity. On the other hand in *Abernethie* v. *Kleiman Ltd*[2], where a man ran a voluntary Sunday-school with assistants, Lord Justice Widgery said, "What a man does in his spare time in his home is most unlikely to qualify for the description 'business' unless it has some direct commercial involvement in it, whether it be a hobby or recreation or the performance of a social duty."

---

[1] [1958] 1 Q.B. 513.
[2] [1969] 2 All E.R. 790.

The obvious answer to the contention that a fishing lease falls within the ambit of Part II of the 1954 Act, would be that s. 23(1) only applies where the leased property "includes premises". The letting of a fishery does not normally include "premises" as the word would be understood by an honest fisherman. This, however, does not dispose of the argument, because a question mark hangs over the meaning of the word "premises" in the section. If "premises" has the legal meaning of the forepart of a deed or conveyance which describes the subject matter of the transaction (the part known as the *habendum*), then a fishing lease, and indeed every lease, will include "premises". Learned articles in legal journals[1] have argued that this is the meaning to be given to the word for the purposes of s. 23. This, however, is not the only meaning given to the word "premises", even by lawyers. The Oxford Dictionary also gives the more popular meaning:

"A house or building with its grounds or other appurtenances."

The point is not an easy one, and in cases not concerned with the 1954 Act, the court has insisted on the word "premises" being given the meaning of the aforementioned subject matter of a document.[2] In *Gardiner* v. *Sevenoaks R.D.C.*[3] Lord Chief Justice Goddard said, " 'premises' is no doubt a word which is capable of many meanings," and held that one of them, at least, covered a cave with a door (for the purposes of s. 1 of the Celluloid and Cinematograph Film Act, 1922). More recently the courts have decided the word means a "building" in the Licensing Act, 1964, s. 20[4], but "must be given its normal wide meaning" in the Rent Act, 1965.[5]

What is more important, is that the House of Lords included fishing rights under the Landlord and Tenant Act, 1927, s. 5 (now repealed). The then *Whitley* v. *Stumbles*[6] where a new lease was granted of a hotel and fishing rights under the Landlord and Tenant Act, 1927, 5 (now repealed). The then Lord Hailsham, delivering the judgment of the Court, agreed that the Act sometimes used the word "premises" in the colloquial sense "contemplating rather the buildings in which the trade is carried on than the whole of the subject matter of the lease", but added, "yet it does not intend to exclude other things which are properly described as premises in the strict legal sense *when it is appropriate that they should be included*".[7] This case, however, did not decide that fishing rights by themselves could be business premises for which a new lease could be claimed under the Act. Indeed Lord Hailsham left the point wide open, saying:

---

[1] See, for example, (1962) 106 Sol. Jo. p.543.
[2] See Roland Burrows, *Words and Phrases*, (1944), and *Bracey* v. *Read* [1962] 3 All E.R. 472 (gallops) under the 1954 Act.
[3] [1950] 2 All E.R. 84.
[4] *R.* v. *Hastings Licensing Justices, ex p. Lovibond Ltd* [1968] 2 All E.R. 270.
[5] *Thurrock U.D.C.* v. *Shinah* (1972) 23 P. & C.R. 205.
[6] [1930] A.C. 544.
[7] Author's italics.

"I do not wish to be understood as accepting the view that if the profit à prendre [the fishing rights] here included had not formed part of the premises . . . the county court judge would have had power to compel the appellant to grant a new lease of those rights."

Although because of its special features it did not clear up the point, the recent case of *Jones* v. *Christy* in 1963[1] gives some guidance. A lodge and grounds were let together with fishing rights in a stretch of a Welsh river, and with an option to take fishing rights in *another stretch* of water (described as "the blue fishing rights"). The lease contained a covenant by the tenant to use the premises for no other purpose than a private residence or for the profession of a veterinary surgeon. The tenant took up the option and for some years carried on the activity of letting out the "blue fishing rights" at profitable rates, making a room in the lodge available to the anglers as a drying room. When the lessors served a notice to quit, the tenant claimed a new lease on the ground that he had a lease of business premises which came under Part II of the 1954 Act.

From the report of the case (which could be a little clearer) it seems that the County Court Judge, Judge Pennant, decided that it was not a letting of business premises, and there had been substantial breaches of covenant by the tenant. The report of the Court of Appeal's decision states that the Master of the Rolls, Lord Denning, said that "the letting of the fishing rights had been done on such a scale that in his view it amounted to carrying on a business". Though his Lordship doubted whether the mere letting of an incorporeal hereditament could be occupation such as to be the subject of a new tenancy within the 1954 Act, this business was also carried on at a room in the lodge, and to that extent his Lordship differed from the County Court Judge. But once the tenant had put his case under the Act on the footing that the business was carried on by him in that way, he exposed himself as being in breach of the covenant in the lease not to use the premises or any part thereof for any other purpose than as a private residence or for the profession of veterinary surgeon. In view of the breach of covenant the Master of the Rolls decided the tenant ought not to be granted a new tenancy.

It appears therefore that the Court of Appeal decided that the lease was subject to the 1954 Act because the business activities were "carried on at a room in the lodge" − in other words in *premises*, in the more popular meaning of the word. The Master of the Rolls, it will be noted, echoing Lord Hailsham in *Whitley* v. *Stumbles* (above), also doubted whether mere letting of fishing as an incorporeal hereditament (that is without land or buildings) would fall within the ambit of the 1954 Act.

The Act was clearly intended to deal with business-like activities in premises, as the word is colloquially understood, even if its wording could be interpreted otherwise. It is suggested, therefore, that a mere letting of fishing rights alone should not give the fishing tenant the right to claim a new lease

---

[1] (1963) 107 Sol. Jo. 374.

under the Act, even if the tenant is a syndicate or association of anglers.

When fishing rights are let together with business premises – as, for example, was the case in *Jones* v. *Christy*, above – a new lease ordered by the Court to be granted under the 1954 Act will include "rights enjoyed by the tenant in connection with the holding" (e.g. fishing rights) unless the parties agree to the contrary, or the Court in its discretion excludes them.[1]

Fishing Let with Cottages. In certain areas such as Wales it is a common practice to let fishing together with a cottage. The question of security of tenure then arises under the Rent Acts.

Frequently the letting is for a short period, such as weekly, and the cottage is let furnished. Anglers being honourable folk, and in these cases usually on holiday for a fixed period, it is believed to be rare for a landlord to encounter any difficulty through tenants staying on beyond the period of the letting. It is a general principle of the Rent Act, 1965, however, that occupiers of dwellings may not be evicted otherwise than by an order of the court. By s. 32:

"It shall not be lawful for the owner to enforce against the occupier, otherwise than by proceedings in the court, his right to recover possession of the premises",

and by s. 30(1):

"If any person unlawfully deprives the residential occupier of any premises of his occupation of the premises or any part thereof or attempts to do so he shall be guilty of an offence".

He could be fined up to £100 or imprisoned for six months, or both, on a first offence, or £500 and/or six months' imprisonment on a subsequent offence (s. 30(3)).

The effect of ss. 30 and 32 together is that if the landlord removes an occupier of a dwellinghouse otherwise than by a court order, he commits a criminal offence, even if the occupier has ceased to have any right to occupy. Harassment of the "individual occupier of any premises" is also a criminal offence, punishable with the same penalties (s. 30(2)).

These laws can be an encouragement to tenants of dwellings who "know their Rent Act" to stay on after their right to remain has ended until ordered by the court.

An occupier who rents a furnished dwelling does not obtain the automatic security of tenure and rent control given by the Rent Act, 1968, in the case of unfurnished lettings. But Part VI of the Act gives a measure of protection where the right to occupy a dwelling "as a residence" is granted "in consideration of a rent which includes payment for the use of furniture or

---

[1] Landlord and Tenant Act, 1954, s. 32(3) as amended by Law of Property Act, 1969 s. 8.

for services" (s. 70) (provided it is not in a specially excepted area (s. 68) and is within certain rateable value limits (s. 71)).

The Act then gives the "furnished tenant" a right to apply to a Rent Tribunal to review the rent and get security of tenure for a time. No security of tenure can be given, however, where the letting is for a fixed period, such as for three months, or a fishing season, though the Rent Tribunal in these cases has jurisdiction to review the rent.

The Rent Act, 1968, s. 70(5), further makes it clear that a house let furnished for a holiday is not to be treated as occupied "as a residence", and so a holiday letting does not give the tenant a right to go to the Rent Tribunal. It has been reported that a furnished houseboat was held not to be within the ambit of the Rent Acts.[1] Caravans have been held to be subject to the Acts, but it depends on the circumstances of the case. If the caravan is fixed in one place, it will fall under the jurisdiction of the Rent Tribunal, but if it is free to be moved it will not (but the occupier is protected against harassment).[2]

Premises let as unfurnished dwellings are almost bound to be caught by the Rent Acts, giving the tenant virtually permanent security of tenure. These are exceptions and qualifications which it would be inappropriate to discuss here because the owner or manager of a fishing cottage would be well advised not to let it unfurnished — at least until he has gone into the implications of the Rent Acts with his lawyers.

The moral for the owners of fishing cottages therefore is to protect their interests by: (1) letting them furnished and not unfurnished, and either (2) letting them for holidays only, or (3) letting them for fixed periods only, and not, for example, from year to year.

Licence. The word licence here has nothing to do with official licences issued by river authorities and dealt with in Chapter 4. It means the owner of the fishery giving "leave and licence" to another to fish. Unlike a lease a licence gives the angler no legal interest in the land, but only a permission to fish. Unless the permission is given by a formal deed (signed, sealed and delivered), the licence to fish does not give a right to take away fish, and the licence can be revoked at any time by reasonable notice.[3] What is reasonable notice will depend on the circumstances. In the case of an annual licence to shoot, the court held that three weeks' notice, given outside the shooting season, was reasonable.[4]

It is sometimes difficult to know whether an arrangement allowing somebody to fish is a lease or a licence. All the circumstances must be looked at to decide this, because it depends upon the *nature* of the arrangement, and what the parties intended.[5] What the parties call it is not conclusive, because

---

[1] (1949) 113 J.P. News 376 R.T.
[2] Caravan Sites Act, 1968; *R.* v. *Guildford Area Rent Tribunal, ex p. Grubey,* (1951) E.G. 469 — earlier at (1951) E.G.D. 286. But see the rating case — *Field Place Caravan Parks Ltd* v. *Harding (V.O.)* (1966) 64 L.G.R. 399.
[3] *Mellor* v. *Watkins* (1874) L.R. 9 Q.B. 400.
[4] *Lowe* v. *Adams* (1901) 2 Ch. 598.
[5] *Isaac* v. *Hotel de Paris* [1960] 1 All E.R. 348

an arrangement in the nature of a lease is no less a lease for being called "a licence". It used to be thought that the criterion was whether exclusive possession was given. If it was, it was a lease. But this, though an important factor, is not the deciding factor.[1] The points to look for are whether a payment is made in the nature of a rent; whether exclusive possession was intended; whether the occupier has tenant-like rights and obligations; and whether the owner has landlord-like rights and obligations — all these factors, if present, indicate a lease rather than a licence.[2]

Prescription — Long Use

If a right is exercised over someone else's property for a long period, the courts will tend to presume that the right is lawful, if it could have had a legal origin. This is known as prescription, and a right to fish, just as a right of way, may arise by prescription. In other words, the law will generally assume that the right to fish was lawfully granted at some time, if it has been enjoyed by a person long enough without dispute.

Prescription at Common Law. The question — how long? — raises some legal complications which the reader of this book will be spared as far as possible. It is enough to know that the common law basis of prescription is that if a right has been enjoyed from "time immemorial" it is an absolute right. Time immemorial is fixed at 1189, the first year of Richard I. Before the Prescription Act, 1832, made things easier, proof of the exercise of a right for twenty years raised a presumption that it had been used since time immemorial, but the claim could be defeated by the landowner showing that there was a time after 1189 when the right claimed did not exist. The claim could also be defeated by other means — e.g. by proving that the right had been granted for a fixed period only and it had expired.

The Prescription Act, 1832. The Prescription Act, 1832, has saved lawyers much raking about in the abysses of history, by laying down that if a right can be shown to have been enjoyed for a relatively short period, it cannot be defeated by someone proving there was a time after 1189 when the right did not exist. Unhappily the Act laid down differing periods for different kinds of rights.

The position regarding *fishing rights* is:

(a)   When the right has been enjoyed continuously for thirty years, the claim to the right cannot be defeated by the landowner proving that there was a time since 1189 when the right did not exist. The claim might, however, be defeated by any other means, such as by proving that the right to fish was allowed under a temporary arrangement only.

---

[1] *Addiscombe Garden Estates Ltd* v. *Crabbe* [1958] 1 Q.B. 513.
[2] See *Thurrock U.D.C.* v. *Shinah* (1972) 23 P. & C.R. 205.

(b)   When the right has been enjoyed for sixty years the claim to fish
may be defeated in one way only — by production of a *written grant*
which shows that the right has come to an end, or that it can be
revoked.[1]

For the acquisition of a *watercourse* (the use of water without taking
fish), the respective periods are twenty years and forty years.[2]

For the acquisition of an *easement*, such as a right of way, the
respective periods are also twenty years and forty years.[2]

Where there is no prescription. Prescription assumes that the person
enjoying the right has been given an absolute grant of the right at some time
but the grant has been lost. This is a legal fiction, but it is a convenient one
and serves to show that prescription operates only where the claimant could
have a permanent right. A tenant who under his tenancy occupies the land for
sixty years and enjoys the fishing, could not thereby claim a right for ever —
nor, of course, could a tenant under a fishing lease.

The courts have also held that "a fluctuating and uncertain body", such
as the general public, or the inhabitants of a parish, cannot obtain fishing
rights by long use, "and indeed cannot be the grantee either of a several
fishery or any other kind of real property".[3] This rule was analysed by Mr
Justice North in the Thames fishing case of *Smith* v. *Andrews*:

> "Any requisition of rights must be founded upon either custom,
> prescription, or lost grant. It is well settled that the public cannot have any
> right to fish founded upon custom, however long the practice has
> continued ... Can any such right be acquired by prescription? It is clear
> settled law that it cannot",

and finally:

> "There can be no presumption of a lost grant with respect to a
> matter which cannot be the subject of prescription."[4]

As will be seen, however, at p.99, the Court found a way round this
rule in *Goodman* v. *Saltash Corporation*[3], by holding that the inhabitants of
the town, who had enjoyed the right to fish for oysters in the tidal Tamar
since time immemorial, had the fishing rights.

Nor can a claim to fishing under the Prescription Act, 1832, be made
through anglers enjoying the right "in gross" — i.e. not attached to the
occupation by them of any land — because an incorporeal right cannot be
acquired by prescription.[5]

---

[1] Prescription Act, 1832, s. 1.
[2] Prescription Act, 1832, s. 2.
[3] *Goodman* v. *Saltash Corporation* (1882) 7 App. Cas. 633.
[4] (1891) 2 Ch. 678, 699-700.
[5] *Shuttleworth* v. *Le Fleming* (1865) 19 C.B.N.S. 687.

Fishing Rights in Ponds and Large Lakes. The ownership of an estate in land includes land covered by water, so that the landowner owns the fishing rights in ponds and lakes on his land unless the fishing has been granted away.[1] The landowner owns standing water on his land, and all that is in it — but not flowing water (see Chapter 21).

Planning permission is not needed to construct a fish pond in rural land or in a garden, but it would be needed if it was to be accompanied by substantial structures such as shelters and lavatories which were not in the "curtilage" of a dwellinghouse.

Although at common law the landowner has the right to construct fish ponds on his land, he may not do so if it interferes with the rights of commoners.[2]

Where land abuts on a lake, the riparian owner is presumed to have the fishing rights up to the middle of the lake in the same way as with non-tidal rivers (see Chapter 14, p.96 below), even if the lake is a large one.[3] If land in several different ownerships abuts on a lake, the presumption, presumably, is that each riparian owner is entitled to the fishing opposite his own land up to the middle point halfway between his bank and the bank of the landowner opposite.[4] On some large lakes the fishing rights have been separated from the ownership of the land, as with Coniston Water where in *Shuttleworth* v. *Le Fleming*[5] there was proved to be a fishery attached to no land (i.e. a fishery in gross). On Whittlesea Mere there is a common fishery.[6] But as with non-tidal rivers the public cannot acquire fishing rights in ponds and lakes, even if the public have customarily fished there and their enjoyment of the fishing can be traced back over a long period[7], and even if public rights of navigation are enjoyed on the water.[8]

Canals and Reservoirs. These two can be taken together because they are usually artificially constructed under powers given by Act of Parliament — often a Private Act. The general rule applies here, as elsewhere, namely that the owner of the soil is entitled to the fishing rights unless the fishing is expressly separated from the ownership of the land. The owner of the soil, having the fishing rights, may dispose of them as he pleases. He may therefore keep them in hand, let them out or sell them. Usually the authority responsible for the canal or reservoir obtains the ownership of the soil, and will have powers of compulsory acquisition given by the Act of Parliament under which it operates. The enabling Act of Parliament may, however, make special provision regarding the fishing.

---

[1] *Clarke* v. *Mercer* (1859) 1 F. & F. 492.
[2] *Reeve* v. *Digby* (1638) Cro. Cas. 495.
[3] See *Bristow* v. *Cormican* (1878) 3 App. Cas. 641, 666 and *Toome Eel Fishery (N.Ireland) Ltd* v. *Cardwell* [1966] N.I. 1.
[4] *Marshall* v. *Ullswater Steam Navigation Co.* (1863) 3 B. & S. 732.
[5] (1865) 19 C.B.N.S. 687.
[6] 2 Hundred Rolls 646 and see Chapter 11 for meaning.
[7] *Johnston* v. *O'Neill* [1911] A.C. 552.
[8] *R.* v. *Burrows* (1869) 34 J.P. 53.

If a river in which there are already fishing rights is canalised, the owners are not deprived of their rights, unless the Act of Parliament empowering the works provides to the contrary.[1]

The public cannot obtain fishing rights in canals and reservoirs by grant, custom or prescription.[2] However, although it has never been done, were the enabling Act for the construction of a canal or reservoir expressly to provide that the public would have the right of fishery, the provision would have legal effect.

---

[1] *Hargreaves* v. *Diddams* (1875) L.R. 10 Q.B. 582.
[2] See p.89 for the meaning.

CHAPTER 14

EVIDENCE AND PROOF OF FISHING RIGHTS

The origin of fishing rights is so often lost in the mists of history, that the courts have at times had to undertake fascinating detective work examining evidence traced back over centuries, to discover whence fishing rights came and to whom they went. In the course of such exercises, rules and presumptions have evolved to guide in this business of proof.

Documentary Evidence. When the fishing is separated from the ownership of the land, the title to the fishing rights is normally found in a deed of grant, or lease. Where the title cannot be so clearly shown, the courts have admitted in evidence all kinds of documents which indicated something about the fishing in times past.

For example, the courts have looked at old charters[1], old court rolls[2], former court proceedings about the fisheries, such as actions against trespassing fishermen[3], and convictions[4], accounts of rent collectors or stewards[5], surveys[6], tithe maps, awards or assessments[7], rate books[8], land tax assessments[9], old settlements[10] and also leases and counterparts.[4]

Proof of the authentic execution of an ancient document (i.e. one twenty-five years old or more[11]) is not needed if the document is produced from "proper custody".

A modern illustration of the eivdence sometimes needed to prove the existence of fishing rights is the case of *Stephens* v. *Snell*[1] in which a "sole and several fishery" was claimed to exist in Axmouth Harbour, Devon. An action was taken for an injunction (i.e. a court order) to restrain a local fisherman, Henry Snell, from trespassing on the fishery with his boats and nets. The claimant asserted a right of fishing granted before Magna Carta. He relied on a charter made in 1331, the fourth year of Edward III's reign. This

---

[1] *Stephens* v. *Snell* [1939] 3 All E.R. 622.
[2] *Att.-Gen.* v. *Emerson* (1891) A.C. 649; *Rogers* v. *Allen* (1808) 1 Camp. 309.
[3] *Stephens* v. *Snell* (above); *Neil* v. *Duke of Devonshire* (1882) 8 A.C. 135.
[4] *Malcolmson* v. *O'Dea* (1863) 10 H.L.C. 593.
[5] *Percival* v. *Nanson* (1851) 7 Exch. 1; *Att.-Gen.* v. *Emerson* (above)
[6] *Edgar* v. *English Fisheries Special Commns.* (1870) 23 L.T. 732.
[7] *Palmer* v. *Andrews* (1902) Stuart Moore "History of the Law of Fisheries", 147.
[8] *Smith* v. *Andrews* (1891) 2 Ch. 678.
[9] *Doe d. Strode* v. *Seaton* (1843) A. & E. 171.
[10] *Johnston* v. *O'Neill* (1911) A.C. 552.
[11] Evidence Act, 1938, s. 4.

ancient charter recorded the contents of two earlier charters granted by "Lord Henry of famous memory, formerly King of England" and "Lord Henry of good memory, formerly King of England", making sundry grants to the Abbot and monks of the Abbey of St. Mary of Monteburg, including " . . . another manor which is named Auxemund in Devon, with the church of the same manor, and a fishery, and two draughts which are there, to drag with nets." The charter also recorded a confirmation and re-grant of these by Edward III. "Auxemund" was established as Axmouth, but it was important to decide whether "famous" and "good" Henry was Henry I or II, both of whom reigned before Magna Carta, or Henry III, who reigned after. The judge decided it was not Henry III. A grant by Edward VI in 1552 was also proved, passing to one Walter Earle the lordship of the manor of Axmouth together with "fisheries, fishings and woods", and a later action for trespass on the fishery against Sir William Templer De La Pole which was won by the lord of the manor.

This together with modern evidence satisfied Mr Justice Bennett of the origin and continuance of the fishing rights in favour of the claimant.

How Far Back Proof is Needed. To establish title to fishing rights (i.e. a several fishery[1]) in tidal waters, evidence of a grant before Magna Carta is needed, either by proving the grant or other facts from which it will be assumed that the fishery existed before that date.[2] The judgments of the House of Lords in *Malcolmson* v. *O'Dea*[3] are a guide to the evidence that is necessary. It is important to show that the fishing was exercised as a separate right, and not simply enjoyed by the claimant as a member of the public. Evidence of exercise of the fishing rights in modern times, coupled with ancient documents, will be sufficient if there is nothing to indicate the original grant was *post* Magna Carta.[4] Proof of use for one hundred and ten years was sufficient in *Duke of Northumberland* v. *Houghton*[5] without ancient documents, and in other cases fifty years[6], and even twenty years[7] sufficed.

In non-tidal waters, proof of title to fishing rights need be proved no further back than for any other property rights.

Proof may be by prescription, where this is possible and continuous long use can be shown without being defeated in one of the permissible ways (see Chapter 13).

Evidence of Exercise of Fishing Rights. Evidence of possession of the fishing rights is an important part of establishing a claim. Documentary evidence alone is not sufficient to establish title to a fishery in tidal waters.

---

[1] See p.72 for meaning.
[2] *Att.-Gen. for British Columbia* v. *Att.-Gen. for Canada* (1914) A.C. 153.
[3] (1863) 10 H.L.C. 593.
[4] *Neil* v. *Duke of Devonshire* (1882) 8 A.C. 135; *Ashworth* v. *Browne* (1860) 10.I.Ch.R. 421.
[5] (1870) 22 L.T. 491.
[6] *R.* v. *Downing* (1870) 23 L.T. 98.
[7] *Hales* v. *Alder* (1874) 38 J.P. 407.

To exclude the public it is also necessary to show private enjoyment of the fishing rights.[1] What is sufficient evidence of possession will depend on the circumstances — this was discussed in the House of Lords in *Lord Advocate* v. *Lord Lovat*[2]. Where the title to fishing is in dispute, the court will look for evidence of the kind of conduct which could be expected of the fishing owner taking into account the nature of the fishery. For example, acts of ownership such as stocking with fish, or weed cutting, possession of fishing rights, and payment of rent[3] are clear evidence.

Receipt of rent under a fishing lease[4], or granting a fishing lease[5] are acts indicating ownership of fishing rights. Other acts which have been given in evidence as showing ownership of the fishing (or else of the soil and thereby the fishing) are: using "fixed engines" to catch fish[6], using nets[7] extracting sand and gravel from the bed, fencing off cattle drinks, doing revetment works to prevent bank erosion, and building piers.[8]

The presence of weirs in a navigable river is strong evidence of an ancient fishery, because of the statutes which forbade the introduction of new weirs between 1350 and 1861.[9]

Limitation of Actions. In order to prevent litigants bringing stale claims to court, the Limitation Acts bar claims if they are not brought within a certain lapse of time. For this reason a person occupying land unchallenged, and without leave or licence, for twelve years, obtains a title to the land which cannot be defeated. This is commonly called "squatters rights". It should be noted, however, that possession of incorporeal fishing rights (for meaning, see p.72) for however long will not give "squatters rights" to the fishing.[10]

Legal Presumptions and Burden of Proof. The task of settling issues is made easier than it might be by certain presumptions, which are part of the law of evidence. Presumptions are inferences which the law requires to be drawn once certain facts are established. Legal presumptions are usually rebuttable — that is, they hold good only if the contrary is not proved. (There are conclusive presumptions known to the law, but none concerns fishing rights.) Presumptions also serve the purpose of deciding who has the burden of proving what.

Fortunately some of these presumptions help solve questions about title to fishing rights, and the following presumptions prevail until the contrary is proved.

---

[1] *Neil* v. *Duke of Devonshire* (above).
[2] (1880) 5 App. Cas. 273, 288.
[3] *Bristow* v. *Cormican* (1878) 3 App. Cas. 641.
[4] *Greenback* v. *Sanderson* (1884) 49 J.P. 40.
[5] *R.* v. *Inhabitants of Alresford* (1786) 1 Term. Rep. 358.
[6] *Lord Fitzhardinge* v. *Purcell* (1908) 2 Ch. 139.
[7] *Lord Advocate* v. *Lord Lovat* (above).
[8] *Att.-Gen.* v. *Emerson* (1891) A.C. 649.
[9] See *Williams* v. *Wilcox* (1838) 3 Nev. & P.K.B. 606 and 17 Hals. 314 (Third edn.).
[10] The definition of land in the Limitation Act, 1939, s. 31(1), does not include incorporeal rights, so s. 4 does not apply.

Presumptions – Non-Tidal Waters

(1) *Ownership of riparian land to middle of river*

Where land is bounded by a non-tidal river, there is a presumption that the riparian owner (i.e. the owner of land abutting the river) owns the soil to the middle line of the river. The law has the Latin tag *"usque ad medium filum aquae"* (up to the middle thread of the water). There is also a presumption that the owner of the soil also owns the fishing. If, therefore, the opposite banks of the river are in different ownerships, each riparian owner may fish from his bank to the middle of the river.[1]

If both banks are in the same ownership, there is a presumption that the landowner owns the fishing across the entire river.[2]

What is the "middle thread" of a stream which in winter may be swollen by freshets, and in summer drought may trickle lamely in a shrunken channel? Although the courts apparently have not had to decide this point yet as regards non-tidal rivers, the answer seems clear from the decision in *Hindson* v. *Ashby* in 1896[3], in which Lord Justice Smith held that the bed of a river is so much of the soil as contains the water at its average and mean flow throughout the year, ignoring abnormal floods and droughts. Presumably the dividing line for riparian fishing rights is the middle line of the bed.

Although the presumption does not apply to tidal waters, the courts have had to consider what is the "middle thread" of a tidal river, and seem to have concluded that the line would be halfway between the high water mark of ordinary tides on each side of the river.[4] Stuart Moore, however, holds, more realistically, that the line should be the centre of the channel at ordinary low water.[5]

Where there is an island in the river, the presumption is that the riparian owners own the soil and fishing to the middle line between the island and the bank.[6]

This presumption of riparian ownership was well illustrated in *Lamb* v. *Newbiggin*[7] where the court held that the owners of the land abutting on a river within a manor were presumed to have the fishing, unless the lord of the manor could prove by evidence manorial fishing rights.

The Courts have recognised that in practice the "middle line" must be treated as elastic. As Mr Justice Sargent put it in *Long* v. *Gowlett*[8], "when the opposite banks of an ordinary non-navigable stream are in separate ownership and occupation, the ordinary every-day relationships between the two riparian owners admit of the user of the stream by either of them for

---

[1] *Lord Chesterfield* v. *Harris* (1908) 2 Ch. 397.
[2] *Tracey Elliott* v. *Earl Morley* (1907) 51 S.J. 625.
[3] (1896) 2 Ch. 1.
[4] *Thames Conservators* v. *Smeed, Dean and Co.* (1897) 2 Q.B. 334.
[5] *History and Law of Fisheries*, p.118, et seq.
[6] *Great Torrington Commons Conservators* v. *Moore Stevens* (1904) 1 Ch. 347.
[7] (1844) 1 Car. & Kir. 549.
[8] [1923] 2 Ch. 177, 196.

such purposes as boating or fishing, without any meticulous examination of the question whether the boat or the blades of the oars, or the lure for the fish, may be on the one side or the other of the medium filum of the bed". Crossing the line was not evidence of long use sufficient to prove that rights had been extended.

The length of the fishery owned by the riparian owner is determined by the length of his land abutting on the river.

(2) *Ownership of soil*

We have seen that the owner of the soil is presumed to own the fishing. Similarly it is a presumption that the owner of the fishing owns the soil. Where someone owning the soil grants away the fishing, the ownership of the soil passes as well as the fishing unless a contrary intention is expressed in the grant.[1] This presumption prevails over the presumption in favour of the riparian owner.[2] The ownership of the soil and the fishing may be separated, and if it is proved the presumption is, of course, rebutted.[3]

Where weirs are permitted a right of fishing is given, also ownership of the soil where the weirs are constructed, or where there is a right to construct weirs for fishing.[1]

Presumptions — Tidal Waters

(1) *Ownership of foreshore and soil of tidal rivers*

There is a presumption that the Crown owns the foreshore between the mean high and low water marks of ordinary tides, and also the soil of tidal rivers as far as the tide ebbs and flows (see Chapter 5 for further discussion of this). By reason of this presumption in favour of the Crown, there arises the presumption that the public have the right to fish in tidal waters. That presumption can only be rebutted by proof of a several fishery (for meaning see Chapter 11) granted by the King before Magna Carta.[4]

Ownership of riparian land does not raise a presumption of ownership to the middle of a tidal river or estuary on which the land abuts. The presumption is that the Crown in granting land adjacent to tidal waters did *not* grant any part of the foreshore.

(2) *Several fishery*

Proof of the existence of a several fishery in tidal waters raises a presumption that the owner of the fishing also owns the soil. This is so whether the fishery is on the foreshore[5], or in a tidal river.[6]

---

[1] *Hanbury* v. *Jenkins* (1901) 2 Ch. 401.
[2] *Hindson* v. *Ashby* (1876) 2 Ch. 1, 9.
[3] *Marshall* v. *Ullswater Steam Navigation Co.* (1863) 3 B. & S. 732.
[4] *Malcolmson* v. *O'Dea* (1863) 10 H.L. Cas. 593.
[5] *Att.-Gen.* v. *Emerson* (1891) A.C. 649.
[6] *Duke of Somerset* v. *Fogwell* (1826) 5 B. & C. 875.

There is *no* presumption, however, that the owner of the soil in tidal waters is the owner of the fishing. This presumption does not arise, because Magna Carta restrained the King from granting private fishing rights in tidal waters — a grant of the soil in tidal waters therefore does not give the fishing rights.[1]

Even so, if the sea suddenly encroaches on private land, or is artificially diverted onto private land, the public right of fishing does not follow it. The landowner then has the right of fishing over his own land[2], unless according to Hale he himself deliberately diverts a tidal river over his land for his own advantage.[3]

Burden of Proof. Once the facts are established which raise a legal presumption, the burden of proof is thrown upon any person who asserts the contrary. Arising from the presumptions therefore the burden of proof falls upon any person claiming fishing rights over another's land, and upon any person claiming a private (i.e. a several) fishery in tidal water.[4]

Evidence of Extent of Fishing Rights

Although the existence of fishing rights may be proved without calling for historical evidence from far back, it may sometimes be necessary to delve into the past in order to settle the boundaries of the fishery.

Riparian land. Where the fishing rights arise from the ownership or occupation of land adjacent to a river, the length of the fishery will be according to the length of land abutting on the river, unless documents of title show a different boundary.

A manor. As regards a manorial fishery, Mr Justice Bennet in *Stephens* v. *Snell*[5] confirmed the statement in Halsbury[6] that in the absence of evidence to the contrary the length of the fishery is determined by the bounds of the manor.

We have seen above (p.94) the importance of evidence of possession of a fishery, but where possession can be shown it is not always necessary to prove acts of ownership over every part of the fishery claimed. It depends on the character of the water in question. In some cases it would be reasonable to assume that the whole of a certain water, or section of a river, would be in one ownership, in which case evidence of, say, fishing or stocking in one part, would indicate possession of the whole.[7]

When there are separate titles to different parts of a water evidence of acts of ownership in one part would not, of course, be evidence of ownership

---

[1] *Att.-Gen.* v. *Emerson* (1891) A.C. 649.
[2] *Carlisle Corp.* v. *Graham* (1869) L.R. 4 Exch. 361.
[3] *De Jure Maris.*
[4] *Lord Fitzwalter's Case* (1674) 1 Mod. Rep. 105.
[5] [1939] 3 All E.R. 622 (see p.93 above).
[6] "Laws of England" (3rd edn., vol.15, p.54).
[7] *Jones* v. *Williams* (1837) 2 M. & W. 326, 331.

of another part[1], and ownership claimed by prescription must be proved as extensively as it is claimed.[2]

Proving a Common of Fishery. A common of fishery (the right of one or more persons to share the fishing with the owner) may be established by proving a grant, custom or prescription. Such joint fishing rights may exist in tidal waters just as a several fishery may, thereby excluding the public right of fishing.[3]

Legal difficulties have arisen where it has been claimed that the local inhabitants have customarily enjoyed the right of fishing in certain waters. The court in *Bland* v. *Lipscombe*[4] held that inhabitants of a parish being a fluctuating body could not claim a profit à prendre[5] and therefore could not claim fishing rights for themselves. The House of Lords in *Goodman* v. *Saltash Corporation*[6] got round this difficulty neatly. The Mayor and Corporation took an action for trespass against a number of inhabitants for taking oysters from the tidal Tamar. The Corporation could prove that it had a several fishery which it had enjoyed from time immemorial. The defendants could also prove that from time immemorial "the free inhabitants of ancient tenements within the borough" had exercised a right to dredge the oysters from February 2 to Easter eve in every year. The Corporation could by law claim its right by prescription, but the inhabitants, not being an incorporated body, could not. Lord Selborne in his judgment said that a lawful authority for the inhabitants' use of the fishery should be presumed if possible, and a majority of the court decided that the presumption should be drawn that the original ancient grant to the Corporation was subject to a trust or condition that the free inhabitants should be allowed to dredge oysters annually between Candlemas and Easter. This presumption could be drawn because it was not inconsistent with any of the facts or documents produced in evidence.

In the recent sea-coal case of *Alfred F. Beckett Ltd* v. *Lyons*[7] the Court declined to follow the example of *Goodman* v. *Saltash Corporation* in respect of the inhabitants of the County Palatine of Durham.

Apparently commoners of a manor are not such a fluctuating body that they cannot obtain fishing rights by proof of continued long use.[8]

---

[1] *Neil* v. *Duke of Devonshire* (1882) 8 A.C. 135, 151.
[2] *Rogers* v. *Allen* (1808) 1 Camp. 309.
[3] *Carter* v. *Murcot* (1768) 4 Burr. 2162, 2164.
[4] (1854) 4E. & B.713n.; and see *Bluett* v. *Tregonning* (1835) 3 Ad. & El. 554.
[5] For meaning see Chapter 11.
[6] (1882) 7 A.C. 633.
[7] [1967] 1 All E.R. 833, and see Chapter 5 above.
[8] *Allgood* v. *Gibbon* (1876) 34 L.T. 833; *Lord Rivers* v. *Adam* (1878) 3 Ex. D. 361.

CHAPTER 15

WATERSIDE RIGHTS AND FISHING

Riparian Rights. Land on the banks of a river, or other water, is known as riparian land, and its owner a riparian owner. Rivers very commonly form boundaries between properties in different ownerships, and because of the legal presumptions in favour of riparian owners (see p.96) fishing rights are most usually owned through the proprietorship of land adjacent to the river. In addition to fishing rights, the riparian owner has certain other rights which derive entirely from his ownership of riparian land, for example rights of access to, and use of, the water, and most important for our purposes, the right to receive water unpolluted.

These other rights are important for the riparian owners' enjoyment of their fishing, when they own the fishing, and when they do not the owners of fishing and riparian owners must exercise their rights with reasonable consideration for each other. The angler must not interfere with the exercise of riparian rights, nor must the riparian owner spoil the angler's fishing.[1]

The riparian rights are presumed at law to go with the riparian land whether or not the landowner also owns the soil of the neighbouring water, or the fishing.[2]

As appears in Chapter 21 on water abstraction the basic right of the riparian owner is to receive the water flowing through his land undiminished in quantity or quality, and to take and use it for any purpose not inconsistent with the similar rights of other riparian owners.[3] The Water Resources Act, 1963, however, has cut so deep into the riparian owner's common law right to take water flowing through or past his land, that the position is now governed by this statute rather than the common law.

If an Act of Parliament authorises any interference with riparian rights, this may be done only to the extent that is necessary for a reasonable exercise of the statutory powers.[4]

Severance of Land from Riverside. Subject to what is said below about tidal waters, the land must abut directly onto the water if riparian rights are to be enjoyed. An artificial connection with the water is not sufficient. Furthermore, if land enjoys riparian rights, they are lost if the land becomes

[1] *Bridges* v. *Highton* (1865) 11 L.T. 653.
[2] *Lyon* v. *Fishmongers' Co.* (1876) 1 A.C. 662.
[3] *Mason* v. *Hill* (1833) 5 B. & A. 1, at p.17. But in *Rugby Joint Water Board* v. *Walters* [1966] 3 All E.R. 497 spray irrigation was held not to be an ordinary riparian purpose.
[4] *Edinburgh Water Trustees* v. *Sommerville & Son* (1906) 15 L.T. 217, at p.218.

cut off from the river. For example, if the riparian owner sells part of the land, but none of the part sold abuts on the river, then the riparian rights do not pass with the land to the purchaser even if he has a right of way to the river across the remaining part of the riparian owner's land. This point arose in the case of the Merseyside waterworks (*Stockport Waterworks Co.* v. *Potter*[1]) in 1864. The Stockport Waterworks were on land which at one time had been part of land abutting on the Mersey, but had become severed from the river. Water was fed to the waterworks from the river by "conduits and tunnels". The Court held that the waterworks company could not take an action against manufacturers whose refuse fouled the river water — though one of the appeal judges, Baron Bramwell, dissented. Chief Baron Pollock said that if the waterworks were to have riparian rights by reason of their being connected to the river by conduits, so would every house in Stockport to which the water flowed in pipes.

Land Abutting on Tidal Rivers. The owner of land abutting on a tidal river has the same riparian rights as the owner on the banks of a non-tidal river. His land need not be in contact with the water at all times, but to enjoy riparian rights it must be in contact with the flow of the water at least at ordinary high tides, even if at low tide there is an expanse of uncovered foreshore between the riparian land and the stream. In *Lyon* v. *Fishmongers' Company*, Lord Selborne said:

> "It is, of course, necessary for the existence of a riparian right that the land should be in contact with the flow of the stream; but lateral contact is as good, *jure naturae*, as vertical . . . It is true that the bank of a tidal river, of which the foreshore is left bare at low water, is not always in contact with the flow of the stream, but it is in such contact for a great part of every day in the ordinary and regular course of nature, which is an amply sufficient foundation for a natural riparian right."[2]

The riparian owner of land abutting on a navigable river must exercise his riparian rights not only consistently with the rights of other riparian owners, but also so as not to inferfere with the public right of navigation[3] (see Chapter 19).

Riparian Right of Access to the Water

The riparian owner is entitled to access to the water that flows through or past his land in order to enjoy his riparian rights, whether or not he owns the soil.

Public navigation. If the water is a public navigable river he may go onto the river at any point on his land. This is because a public navigable river

[1] *Stockport Waterworks Co.* v. *Potter* (1864) 10 L.T. 748.
[2] (1876) 1 A.C. 662 at p.683.
[3] *North Shore Ry.* v. *Pion* (1889) 14 A.C. 612 at p.620.

is a public highway, and as a member of the public he is entitled to navigate it. In *Lyon* v. *Fishmongers' Company* (above) Lord Selborne said that:

> "The only practical advantage to the owner of a river frontage might consist in the access there afforded him to the water for the purpose of using, when upon the water, the right of navigation common to him with the rest of the public."

The sea, and, in general, tidal rivers are waters navigable by all subjects of the realm. Non-tidal waters are open to public navigation if the public has acquired the right (e.g. by dedication, long use or statute) but not otherwise. It should be noted that the existence of public fishing rights does not necessarily mean that there is also the right to public navigation. The character of the channel might rule out navigation rights — even if it is wide and deep enough to allow the passage of a boat.[1] Conversely, the existence of public navigation rights does not necessarily mean that there are public fishing rights, because although the public can obtain the right to navigate non-tidal waters, they cannot obtain the right to fish in them.[2] The riparian owner therefore has no right to fish from a boat on a public navigable river unless he has the fishing rights or the river is tidal and the public have fishing rights.

Should there be a sea wall[3] or a highway[4], constructed between the riparian owner's land and the river, his right of access is not extinguished. Nor can it lapse through not being exercised.[3] A riparian owner has the right to go ashore and cross all intervening land at low tide to get to his land, even though he has no ownership of the soil of the foreshore[5], and even if it is privately owned.[6]

When an acquiring authority in the exercise of compulsory powers deprives a riparian owner of his access to the water, or injuriously affects it, compensation is payable under compulsory purchase law.[7]

Use of Riparian Bank and River Bed

Riparian Right to Moor. The angler exercising his public right to fish or navigate in tidal or navigable water does not have the right to moor on private land or to lay or maintain private moorings.[8] The riparian owner is permitted to moor along his own bank whether or not he owns the soil of the river, provided he does not thereby obstruct navigation in a navigable river. He may

---

[1] *Cf. Sim E Bak* v. *Ang Yon Huat* [1923] A.C. 429.
[2] *Smith* v. *Andrews* [1891] 2 Ch., 678 and see Chapter 5.
[3] *Port of London Authority* v. *Canvey Island Commissioners* [1932] 1 Ch. 446.
[4] *Tetreault* v. *Montreal Harbour Comms.* [1926] A.C. 299.
[5] *Macey* v. *Met. Board of Works* (1864) 10 L.T. 66.
[6] *Att.-Gen. for Straits Settlement* v. *Wemyss* (1888) 13 A.C. 192.
[7] *Metropolitan Board of Works* v. *McCarthy* (1874) L.R. 7 H.L. 243.
[8] *Fowley Marine (Emsworth) Ltd* v. *Gafford* [1968] 1 All E.R. 979.

float a boathouse or wharf moored to his land under the same condition.[1]

Although this is certainly so at reasonable times, and for ordinary business purposes such as for loading and unloading[2], it is not clear whether it would be so for the purposes of private angling. Where the riparian owner, however, has fishing rights in the river it is submitted that it would be a reasonable use of his riparian land to moor boats, landing stages or pontoons as ancillary to the exercise of fishing rights, provided they did not impede navigation.

In any event a riparian owner must not obstruct the right of access of other riparian owners to their land, and must move a moored vessel without delay if necessary to afford access.[3]

In the "man of Bosham" case in 1960, *Iveagh (Earl)* v. *Martin*[4], Mr Justice Paull declared that a "man of Bosham" could, because of age-old rights given to "tenants in the ancient demesne" of the Manor of Bosham, moor permanently on the foreshore free of charge if the boat was used primarily for fishing, and could use the quay owned by the lord of the manor for reasonably short periods for embarking, disembarking, unloading fish from the boat, or loading fishing tackle on to it.

"River Bank" and "River Bed". The meaning of "river bank" and "river bed" need definition because often they are in different ownerships and sometimes special rights may be exercised over one or the other. For example, a fishing lease might require anglers to keep banks in good repair, and drainage authorities are empowered to deposit spoil on the banks of watercourses.[5]

"Bank". In *Jones* v. *Mersey River Board*[6], the Court of Appeal decided that banks of a river, at least in the context of land drainage, meant so much of the land adjoining or near to it as performed or contributed to the performance of the function of containing the river. This was also the sense of previous meanings given to the word in both English and American decisions.

"Bed". This was defined in the American case of *State of Alabama* v. *State of Georgia*[7] and repeated in the English case of *Hindson* v. *Ashby*.[8]

"The bed of a river is that portion of its soil which is alternatively covered and left bare as there may be an increase or diminution in the supply of water, and which is adequate to contain it at its average and mean stage during the entire year without reference to the extraordinary freshets of the winter or spring, or the extreme droughts of the summer or autumn."

---

[1] *Booth* v. *Ratté* (1889) 62 L.T. 198.
[2] *Original Hartlepool Colliers* v. *Gibb* (1877) 5 Ch. D. 713.
[3] *Land Securities Co.* v. *Commercial Gas Co.* (1902) 18 T.L.R. 405.
[4] [1960] 2 All E.R. 668 at p.684, and see below, Chapter 19.
[5] Land Drainage Act, 1930, s. 38; Land Drainage Act, 1961, s. 29.
[6] [1957] 3 All E.R. 275.
[7] (1859) 54 U.S. 427.
[8] [1896] 2 Ch. 1.

(i) *Generally*. The banks of rivers belong to the riparian owners, at least in the case of a non-tidal river.[1] This is an important factor in deciding who may do what, where the riparian land and the fishing is separately owned. In such cases the fisherman and the landowner must act with reasonable consideration for the rights of each other. Although the landowner must not interfere unjustifiably with the fishing interests, he is entitled to make a natural reasonable use of his land.[2] He may, for example, carry out revetment works to protect his banks from erosion, and fence off drinking places for his cattle.[3] On the other hand he must not fix structures in the soil which impede or damage the fishery, such as obstructions which prevent the passage of fish or deprive the fishery of water.[3]

Where the riparian owner is also owner of the river bed and fishing — which is the normal case — he is entitled at common law to make use of the river bed and banks in much the same way as he may the dry land he owns. He is entitled to erect structures on them, so long as he does not interfere with the riparian rights of other owners upstream or downstream from him.[4] Planning permission under the Town and Country Planning Act, 1971, will usually be needed before above-ground, or above-water, structures can lawfully be erected, such as a landing stage with ancillary works[5], but not for a houseboat. Furthermore, in the case of a navigable river he may not do anything which materially obstructs or endangers navigation.

The river authority is empowered by the 1923 Act to purchase so much of the bank adjoining a dam as may be necessary for making or maintaining a fish pass, and can exercise compulsory powers for this purpose.[6]

(ii) *Obstructions to Navigation*. The law about obstructing the passage of fish is dealt with in Chapter 8 and the respective rights of anglers and navigators where the two conflict in Chapter 19. The riparian owner who owns the soil of a navigable river must exercise his rights with a weather eye open for the navigation rights on the river. Obstructing a public navigable river is a "public nuisance" at common law for which the offender may be proceeded against by the Crown, or the Attorney-General, on behalf of the public.[7] It may also be a "private nuisance" for which he may be sued by any person who suffers special injury from it over and above that suffered by the public at large.[8] Such a person may also abate the nuisance but must use the least injurious means to get rid of it. A person who abates the nuisance cannot take court proceedings as well.

---

[1] *Hanbury* v. *Jenkins* [1901] 2 Ch. 401.
[2] *Cf. Peach* v. *Best* [1931] 1 K.B. 1, 14 as explained in *Mason* v. *Clark* [1955] A.C. 778, 796.
[3] *Bridges* v. *Highton* (1865) 11 L.T. 653.
[4] *Orr-Ewing* v. *Colquhoun* (1877) 2 A.C. 839.
[5] (1951) J.P.L. 665.
[6] Salmon and Freshwater Fisheries Act, 1923, s. 20(7) and see Chapter 8.
[7] *R.* v. *Russell* (1827) 6 B. & C. 566.
[8] *Colchester Corp.* v. *Brooke* (1845) 7 Q.B. 339.

Even though the owner of the bed of a public navigable river must not erect obstructions which hamper navigation, there is no obligation upon him to see that the river bed does not become obstructed, and no obligation upon him to dredge the river in order to keep it navigable.[1] On the other hand, if tolls are charged for maintaining the navigation, the owner is under a duty to take reasonable care to see that craft are not endangered by obstructions, such as unmarked sunken boats[2], or submerged piles[2], or of course disused, or for that matter used, "fixed engines" for catching fish. The owner of dilapidated structures on the river bank, or bed, or the seashore or sea-bed, which may be a danger to navigation must either remove the danger or give warning of it.[3]

(iii) *Working Minerals.* Where the soil and fishing are in separate ownerships, winning minerals from the bed of a river might seriously interfere with the fishing interests. In such a case, it is suggested that exploiting minerals is a natural and usual use of land, and indeed is in the national interest, so that the mineral owner would be entitled to win them, provided the work was carried out in a reasonable manner and with due consideration of the rights of others, and provided there was no express prohibition on the title to the land (such as a restrictive covenant). His right is, of course, subject to statutory restriction; planning permission would be required under the Town and Country Planning Act, 1971, before he could lawfully work the minerals. The powers of the river authority or internal drainage board to restrain operations which obstruct the flow of water, do not apply to mining operations or brine pumping.[4] Even so, mineral working is almost sure to fall foul of a byelaw or two if carried out in the bed of a river under the jurisdiction of a river authority or in the district of an internal drainage board. This need by no means prove fatal to the enterprise. Consultation with the authority concerned should normally lead to a working arrangement which has its indulgence, provided, in the case of a navigable river, the work can be carried out without undue interference with navigation.

Anglers' Rights to Use Banks. It must not be assumed that the grant of fishing rights automatically gives the right to go onto the river banks[5] or shore in order to fish. In the venerable case of *Inhabitants of Ipswich* v. *Browne*[6] in 1581 the Court said that fishing rights which can be exercised without recourse to the neighbouring land were rights over water only. The fishing can be carried out from boats, which do not need to land on private property adjoining the fishery.

The right to use adjoining land for fishing frequently goes with the fishing, however, as incidental to the grant. The right may also be acquired by

---

[1] *Simpson* v. *Att.-Gen.* [1904] A.C. 476.
[2] *Parnaby* v. *Lancaster Canal Co.* (1839) 11 A. & E. 223.
[3] *White* v. *Phillips* (1863) 9 L.T. 388.
[4] Land Drainage Act, 1961, s. 28. See further Chapter 8.
[5] *Ball* v. *Herbert* (1787) 3 T.R. 253.
[6] (1581) Sav. 11, 14. See also Woolrych *Law of Waters* (2nd ed.), p.167.

custom, or prescription. In *Lockwood* v. *West*[1] the local fishermen had spread out their nets to dry on private land from time immemorial, and it was held to be a customary right of the fishermen of the parish.

We have seen (p.89) that fishing rights may be acquired by prescription if the circumstances are right. So may the right of anglers to use river banks. In *Gray* v. *Bond*[2] in 1821 proof of fishermen using the shore for twenty years was said by the judge to be sufficient for the jury to presume a valid right. In *Hanbury* v. *Jenkins*[3] Mr Justice Buckley thought the right to use the river banks could be acquired by prescription as incidental to fishing where the fishing was an incorporeal right (i.e. not attached to any ownership of land) even though incorporeal rights cannot be acquired by prescription. He gave this rather unorthodox opinion on the ground that it was natural for the two rights to go together – or rather, not unnatural.

More recently Mr Justice Plowman held in *Rice* v. *Dodds*[4] that a fishing path along the bank is to be implied on the grant of fishing rights, if the rights cannot be exercised without it. He made a declaration to this effect – and also rectified a conveyance which inadvertently had omitted the reservation of the fishing rights on the sale of the land!

Use of Highways and Towpaths

Highways by waters. If a public right of way adjoins a river bank, may anglers fish from it? The answer is, no. All public rights of way are highways, and although every member of the public is entitled to use a highway, he may only use it for the purpose of passage – or, as the lawyer loves to put it, "for the purpose of passing and re-passing". The Highways Act, 1835, defined "highways" to be "all roads, bridges, footways, causeways, churchways and pavements" (s. 5). Angling is permissible from none of them.

The fact that a public right of way leads to a water does not give the public the right to fish if they have not the fishing rights in the water.

Interference by highway users. The public may only use a highway in a reasonable manner, and a member of the public may not take advantage of his right to use a public way in order to interfere with anglers who are lawfully fishing. In this respect it should be noted that although the public have the right to use a highway, the soil remains in the ownership of the landowner. The same presumption arises in respect of highways as it does regarding the ownership of the soil of rivers[5] – namely, that the owners of land adjoining each side of a highway own the soil to the centre line of it, and if a landowner owns the land on both sides of the highway, he owns the entire highway, subject to the public's right of passage. The soil of a highway,

---

[1](1844) 6 Q.B. 50 and see Chapter 5 for use of foreshore.
[2](1821) 2 Brod. & Bing 667.
[3][1901] 2 Ch. 401, 422.
[4](1970) 213 E.G. 759 cf. also *Re Webb's Lease* [1951] Ch. 808.
[5]See p.96.

though, does not necessarily belong to a private owner, because the Ministry of Transport or the highway authority may have purchased the land outright.

Where the highway is privately owned — which will usually be so in the case of footpaths and bridleways — an unreasonable use of it by a member of the public will be a trespass against the occupier of the land.

Equally the occupier of the land has redress if his fishing or other sporting rights are interfered with by members of the public making unreasonable use of the highway. As we have seen before, anglers do not seem to get into scrapes as shooting men do, and so here again the classic example which makes the point of law clear is about shooting rights.

In *Harrison* v. *Duke of Rutland*[1] the Duke was on a shooting expedition on his grouse moors with a party of friends. When the guns were in the butts and the birds were being driven towards them a man came along a highway and did his utmost to prevent the birds from crossing the highway and reaching the butts. The Duke's keepers asked him to desist but he refused, whereupon the keepers tackled him and lay on him until the drive was over. Everyone therefore had plenty of sport! The man then took proceedings for damages against the Duke and the assailants. The Court of Appeal decided that the man was a trespasser, even though he remained on the highway throughout his antics, because he was not using the highway for passage but to spoil the sport of the owner of the land. The assault on him was therefore permissible in the circumstances, and the occupier was entitled to damages and an injunction (i.e. a court order) to restrain the transgressor from further trespassing.

As far as fishing is concerned, it follows that members of the public using rights of way have no right to stop and spoil the sport of anglers lawfully practising their art. Small boys, for instance, will be entitled to cross bridges which are part of the highway, but they must not pause to hurl debris at anglers or fish, or both, below; and the loud-mouthed spectator with the flashing clothing, given to standing on the towpath immediately behind the angler, terrifying the fish from his swim, may be asked to "move along".

The foreshore. The public has no right of way on the foreshore unless a path has in a particular place been dedicated as a right of way, as we have seen in Chapter 5. The public frolicking on the beach or in the sea, therefore, having no entitlement to be there, may not interfere with anglers who have, and even less may they require the angler to give place.

Highways Crossing Waters

Bridges. Bridges which carry a public way across a river are part of the highway, and may be used by the public, as of right, for the purposes of passage but not for other purposes. The public are not therefore entitled to fish from a bridge, whether or not the public have fishing rights in the water below. That is to say, the public can have no right to use for angling the part

---

[1] [1893] 1 Q.B. 142.

of a bridge which is the continuation of the highway. Whether an angler may employ other parts of a bridge to angle in waters which he is entitled to fish, is another question — and one not likely to come before the Courts for decision. It is not entirely academic, however, because it is common to see small boys, in particular, angling from bridges obviously contrary to the laws of highways. They could be "moved along", or even charged with an offence. Equally, it is not unknown to see small boys astride buttresses or pursuing other "cliff hanging" modes of angling from bridges. One feels the courts, if asked to deal with such youthful enterprise, would say that the whole structure was part and parcel of the highway, and not to be used for adventures other than a reasonable mode of passage. This would seem to be borne out by other parts of the law relating to bridges which, being of a complex nature, will not be found here.

Frequently the bridge, although carrying the highway, will belong to the landowner, who will have the right to exclude anglers from fishing from it, unless they had been given the right so to use the bridge in the grant or lease of the fishing.

Other crossings. Where a highway goes across a waterway by way of a ferry, ford or stepping stones, the public have the right of passage across the water as with any other part of the highway. By analogy with the public right of navigation in navigable rivers, it must be assumed that the angler must give way and not impede anyone reasonably using a highway to cross the water. The Highways Act, 1959, lays down that the public by long use of a crossing may acquire a right of way over land covered with water in the same way as any other land. Where, therefore, the public have enjoyed a way across water:

> "As of right and without interruption for a full period of twenty years, the way shall be deemed to have been dedicated as a highway unless there is sufficient evidence that there was no intention during that period to dedicate it." [1]

Although it is thought the highway user has the right of way in such cases, he must exercise his right of passage in a reasonable manner, and with reasonable consideration for the rights of anglers. If (Heaven forbid!) a dispute should arise as to who has the right of way as between the user of a highway across public navigable waters, and the navigator, the law has laid down no priorities between them. No doubt the test would simply be, what is reasonable in the circumstances of the case? — the law's sensible answer to many a knotty point.

Towing Paths

There is no right at common law for the public to use a towpath along the bank of a public navigable river or canal. It can therefore only be used for

---

[1] Highways Act, 1959, s. 34(1) and see s. 34(11).

towing or passage if the right has been acquired in some way. A towpath may be a private path, or a public highway. The public may acquire rights by the landowner dedicating the towpath to the public use. In such a case the dedication may be restricted to certain forms of use — such as for passage on foot or horseback only and for towing vessels — but although the kind of use it may be put to can be stipulated by the dedicator, he cannot in dedicating a towpath, or other way, to the public, restrict it to particular sections of the public.[1] The use may, for example, be restricted entirely to towing barges by horses[2], but it must be open to all members of the public who want to take horse-drawn barges along the waterway.

The public right to use a towpath may also be acquired by custom[3] or by prescription[4], or else an Act of Parliament governing the watercourse may give the public rights to use the towpath, or enable the rights to be given (for example The Thames Conservancy Act, 1932, s. 77).

Towing paths by canals. In the case of man-made watercourses, such as canals, the right to use the towing path will depend upon the statute which enabled the watercourse to be constructed. The public can have no right to fish from the towing path in these cases, though there be a right of way, because a grant of fishing rights cannot be made to the public.[5] The rights of the owner of the fishing in a canal will also depend upon the terms of the enabling statute, or on the terms under which the landowner originally conveyed the soil to the company or authority who constructed the canal.[6] The rights of the owner of the fishing could be no greater than these terms allowed, though it would be possible to restrict them further on a disposal of the fishing by the original owner.

Landowner's right to use towpaths. As we have seen, where the landowner dedicates a way to the public as a highway he does not lose the ownership of the soil. The same applies if he grants a private right of way to a person or a body of persons. The soil of a towpath, therefore, frequently belongs to the riparian landowners, though in some cases it will have been transferred to the navigation authority by statute.[7] What then are the landowner's rights and duties where there is a towpath?

In the first place, where the management of the watercourse is governed by statute, it all depends on the statute, which may or may not entitle neighbouring landowners to fish from the towpath. Whether the soil of the towpath is owned by the landowner or the navigation authority, the landowner must not obstruct the towpath to prevent or hinder its use for navigation. If he does so the navigation authority — such as the conservators

---

[1] *Dawes* v. *Hawkins* (1860) 8 C.B. (N.S.) 848.
[2] *Winch* v. *Thames Conservators* (1874) L.R. 9 C.P. 378.
[3] *Wyatt* v. *Thompson* (1794) 1 Esp. 252.
[4] *Ball* v. *Herbert* (1789) 3 Term. Rep. 253 and see p.89 for prescription.
[5] See Chapter 5.
[6] *Staffordshire & Worcestershire Canal Navigation* v. *Bradley* [1912] 1 Ch. 91, 100.
[7] See *Bruce* v. *Willis* (1840) 11 A. & E. 463.

of the river — may obtain a court injunction to restrain him.[1] Subject to this qualification, the riparian owner who owns the soil of the towpath may use it for any of his own purposes so long as he does not create any dangers or obstructions for those entitled to use it for towing, or passage, and so long as he complies with any byelaws relating to the towpath.

The landowner accommodates the public by dedicating the way, and does not have to alter or improve it to suit the convenience of the public.[2] Anglers using a towpath, as members of the public, must take it as they find it, and cannot blame the landowner, if, for instance, tree roots impede the way.

The position is different, though, when the owner of the soil takes a toll. If the towpath is kept open by the navigation authority and they collect a toll from users of navigation, then they have a duty of care, to see that the towpath is kept free from dangers. In *Winch* v. *Thames Conservators*[3] where the conversators took a toll they were held to be liable to pay damages when horses, drawing a barge along the Thames, fell into the river owing to the dangerous condition of the towpath, and were drowned. The conservators might have escaped liability if they had taken more care to prevent such a danger, or had warned of the danger, or if the danger had been a hidden one which would not have been noticed with reasonable care on their part.

This case also decided that the towpath is not confined to the beaten track, but includes as much of the bank of the watercourse as is normally used in the course of towing vessels.

---

[1] *Lea Conservancy Board* v. *Britton* (1879) 45 L.T. 385.
[2] *Fisher* v. *Prouse* and *Cooper* v. *Walker* (1862) 31 L.J.Q.B. 212 (both case taken together).
[3] (1874) L.R. 9 C.P. 378.

CHAPTER 16

WHEN RIVERS ALTER COURSE
OR THE COASTLINE CHANGES

We have seen in Chapter 14 the law presumes (until the contrary is proved) that the ownership of fishing rights goes with the ownership of the soil, and that the owner of riparian land has the fishing rights up to the middle line of the river. These presumptions frequently determine conclusively who is the owner of the fishing in particular parts of the river. What happens to the fishing rights, then, if a river changes its course and flows in a different channel over different soil, or if a bank erodes away? Does somebody lose fishing, and another gain it? Rivers are fickle, and this is by no means an uncommon happening. The sea, even more so, is constantly taking land here and giving it back there.

The short answer is that where the change in a river's course is gradual and imperceptible the fisheries follow the changed channel of the river. When the change is sufficiently sudden to be perceptible the fisheries do not follow the new channel. A similar rule applies to erosions and accretions of coastal land. This is not the whole story, however, and the position becomes clearer when actual examples are taken, though one aspect of the law (to do with marking of boundaries) remains in doubt as we shall see.

Gradual and Imperceptible Changes. The effect of the general rule is most easily followed where the bed of a river is in one ownership right across from bank to bank. In this case, where there are imperceptible changes in the river's bounds, the owner of the bed owns it wherever it gets to. If the river gradually encroaches on the land of an opposite landowner who owns none of the river bed, then the owner of the bed gradually acquires the land as it becomes part of the river bed. This is not so if the change is sudden and perceptible. It is suggested also that it is not so where the original boundaries remain ascertainable even though the change may be imperceptibly gradual — but it is on this point that the law is in doubt. If the ownership of the soil follows the new boundaries of the river, so will the fishing rights which go with ownership of the soil, and vice versa.

The case of *Carlisle Corporation* v. *Graham*[1] in 1869 illustrates the rule neatly. The Carlisle Corporation by a grant from the Crown had the fishing rights (i.e. a several fishery) in a loop of the tidal river Eden. Late in the seventeenth century the water began to recede from this loop and pass along

---

[1] (1869) L.R. 4 Exch. 361.

a ditch which "cut off the corner", as it were. This ditch, known as "The Goat", along the whole of its length ran through land not owned by the Corporation, and formerly carried little water and was partly dry. Gradually the river Eden changed its course from the loop to "The Goat" until the loop dried up completely. The Corporation than claimed that its fishing rights were in "The Goat", but the landowner claimed that as owner of the soil he had the fishing rights in "The Goat".

The court held that the Corporation's fishery did not follow the river when it changed its course from the loop to "The Goat". Although the change in this instance took place slowly it happened in such a way that the whole of the channel was clearly in the ownership of the landowner on whose land it was. Chief Baron Kelly, following the Irish case of *Murphy* v. *Ryan*[1] pointed out that as:

> "the right of the Crown to grant a several fishery in a tidal river to a subject is derived from the ownership of the soil, which is in the Crown by the common law, a several fishery cannot be acquired even in a tidal river if the soil belong not to the Crown, but to the subject."

The facts were less unusual in *Foster* v. *Wright*[2] in 1878 where Mr Justice Lindley shed light on the whole problem in a case concerning a non-tidal river. The River Lune was the boundary of the plaintiff's land, and he owned the fishery right across the river from bank to bank. The river gradually began to encroach onto the land of the opposite owner who owned none of the river bed or fishing, but the encroachment was so gradual that it could not be perceived, though over a period of years it could be shown that a strip of the opposite land had become part of the river. So the opposite landowner started to fish in this strip, and the plaintiff claimed he was thereby trespassing on his fishery.

Mr Justice Lindley held that it was trespass, because the plaintiff owned the whole of the river bed, and as the change in the bed was gradual and imperceptible the right of fishing was not lost by the change. He said:

> "The question we have to determine is whether the plaintiff's exclusive right of fishing extends over so much of the water as flows over the land which can be identified as formerly part of the defendant's property.
>
> "I am of opinion that it does. The change of the bed of the river has been gradual; and although the river bed is not now where it was, the shifting of the bed has not been perceptible from hour to hour, from day to day, from week to week, nor in fact at all, except by comparing its position of late years with its position many years before. Under these circumstances, I am of opinion that, for all purposes material to the

[1](1868) Ir. R. 2 C.L. 68.
[2](1878) 4 C.P.D. 438.

present case, the river has never lost its identity, nor its bed its legal owner.

"Gradual accretions of land from water belong to the owner of the land gradually added to (*Rex* v. *Yarborough*)[1]; and conversely land gradually encroached upon by water ceases to belong to the former owner (*In re Hull & Selby Railway Co.*).[2] The law on this subject is based upon the impossibility of identifying from day to day small additions to or subtractions from land caused by the action of running water."

Later in his judgment Mr Justice Lindley added this for our guidance:

"But supposing the plaintiff's right of fishing not to have been the consequence of his ownership of the soil — supposing him to have had only a right to fish in the Lune — I am of opinion that he has the same right of fishing in the river in its present bed as he had of fishing in the river in its old bed."

He then showed how this case differed from *Carlisle Corporation* v. *Graham*[3], saying of that case:

"In that case the old and the new beds of the river existed as two distinct beds: the new bed was not, as here, formed by the old one gradually shifting its place; there, the water gradually left the old bed, and followed an entirely new course always distinguishable from the old; whilst here, there has been and is only one bed, and its change of place has only become perceptible after the lapse of years."

Where Former Bounds Remain Ascertainable. Mr Justice Lindley's decision in *Foster* v. *Wright* (above) is helpful in showing the basis of the general rule, but one essential element, or qualification, of the rule the decision leaves confused. The rule that boundaries move with the gradual and imperceptible changes in the bed of the river, where the bed determines boundaries, stems from early times, occurring in a Year Book of an Assize of Edward III[4], and being reiterated by Hale.[5] Both of these early authorities expressed the rule as being subject to the original boundaries not being lost. The Year Book qualified the rule by adding: "if certain bounds be not put and found before whereby one can perceive this increase". Hale added to his statement of the rule the qualification in these words: "but there be other known boundaries, as stakes on extent of land".

In *Ford* v. *Lacy*[6], although there was a gradual and imperceptible change in the bounds of the river it was held that the:

---

[1](1824) 3 B. & C. 91.
[2](1839) 5 M. & W. 327.
[3]See above p.111.
[4]Y.B. 22 Ed. III, fol. 106, pl. 93.
[5]*De Jure Maris*, cap.i., p.371 (1787).
[6](1861) 7 H. & N. 151.

"strip of land formerly part of the river bed but later left high and dry still belonged to the owner of the river bed because the strip was still identifiable as part of the former river bed, and the owner of the bed had always treated it as his."

The river concerned was the Lee in a stretch where it formed part of the boundary between Essex and Middlesex. The bed was wholly in Essex. The strip that became dry by the river gradually shifting its course was on the Middlesex side, but when the case came up for decision the jury decided that the strip was still in Essex, and the appeal court upheld the decision.

Mr Justice Lindley, in his judgment in *Foster* v. *Wright* (above), would not accept the principle that the rule of gradual accretion did not apply where the old boundaries were not lost, and said:

"In *Ford* v. *Lacy* the ownership of the land in dispute was determined rather by the evidence of continuous acts of ownership since the bed of the river had changed, than by reference to the doctrine of gradual accretion."

He said:

"The title so gradually and imperceptibly acquired cannot be defeated by proof that a portion of the bed now capable of identification was formerly land belonging to the defendant of his predecessors in title,"

and he called in aid the earlier decision, *In re Hull and Selby Railway Company.*[1]

The two Stuart Moores, authors of *The History and Law of Fisheries*[2] point out that *In re Hull and Selby Railway Co.*[1] was not authority for dismissing the qualification of the Year Book and Hale, and other cases which adopted the doctrine, because in that case, which was to do with an encroachment by the sea, there was no way of establishing the old boundary. They conclude that if the old boundary is marked or ascertainable physically, or even by reference to plans or maps, the gradual movement of the river bank does not extinguish the old boundary at law. This would seem to be the better view, at least so far as the old boundary can be ascertained by physical marks, and it should be noted that in later years Mr Justice Lindley, then a Lord Justice, expressed some doubt about the validity of his former judgment. In *Hindson* v. *Ashby*[3] he said of it:

"I may, perhaps, have gone too far. I am not, however, satisfied that I did, for in that case the river was the boundary."

---

[1] (1839) 5 M. & W. 327.
[2] (1903) p.129, *et seq.*
[3] [1896] 2 Ch. 1 at p.12.

But he left the point open, saying:

> "But it is unnecessary to dwell more on this question, and I leave it for reconsideration and decision when it shall arise."[1]

What then is the answer in practice? The owner of the soil of a river or of riparian land would be advised, when losing land gradually by shifting the river, to mark the bounds both on the ground and on a plan, if possible, because all the legal signposts, except for *Foster* v. *Wright* (above) seem to point to the conclusion that if the boundary is not lost, changes in the course of a river, whether gradual or not, do not alter the legal boundaries. This, after all, is basically the reason for the decision in *Carlisle Corporation* v. *Graham* (above). Another clue may be found in the remark of Chief Baron Pollock during the argument of counsel in the case of *Ford* v. *Lacy* (the Essex/Middlesex case (above)). He said, "If for fifty years the land has been treated as part of the County of Essex, we must presume that the water receded suddenly."

Sudden and Perceptible Changes. Where a river changes its course, or expands or contracts, suddenly and perceptibly, the fishing rights and the ownership of the bed do not follow the new channel. This is shown by the cases dealing with changes of the foreshore[2] by advances and retreats of the sea, and is accepted in the cases referred to above.

It is suggested, however, that it is not a question so much of whether changes are sudden, but whether they are perceptible, and that in spite of the "red herring" of *Foster* v. *Wright* (above) the main consideration is whether the old boundaries are lost when the changes take place. This appears to be the right conclusion when the meaning given to the law in this context to "perceptible" and "imperceptible" is considered.

What is "Imperceptible"? Lord Tenterden in *R.* v. *Yarborough*[3] said imperceptible meant "imperceptible in its progress, not imperceptible after a long lapse of time". Baron Alderson in the *Hull & Selby Railway* case (above) said "That which cannot be perceived in its progress is taken to be as if it never had existed at all". Going back to Hale[4] dealing with recessions of the sea, he says the test is was it "so insensible that it cannot be by any means found that the sea was there". If therefore the physical marks of the old boundary remain, changes, however gradual or sudden, would normally be perceptible as they happen.

Land and Fishing Rights Won and Lost from the Sea. The principles explained above derive as much from changes that have taken place regarding the foreshore as from non-tidal rivers changing their course. This is important

---

[1] At p.13.
[2] E.g. *Att.-Gen.* v. *Reeve* [1885] 1 T.L.R. 675 and *Lloyd* v. *Ingram* (1868) cited in *Hindson* v. *Ashby* (above).
[3] (1824) 3 B. & C. 91.
[4] *De Jure Maris.*

as regards fishing rights because the public are entitled to fish on the foreshore between high and low water marks unless the right was lost before Magna Carta (see Chapter 5). If the high water mark advances over coastal land the question arises whether the public right of fishing goes with it. The same rules apply for the sea as for rivers, so that if the high water mark advances imperceptibly, the public right of fishing goes with it. But this right stems from the Crown's ownership of the soil of the foreshore, so if there is a "sudden" and perceptible advance over coastal land the public right of fishing does not extend over the private land lost to the sea, because the ownership of the land is not then lost by the landowner.

The case of *Scratton* v. *Brown*[1] in 1824 laid down that the foreshore was in law a moveable freehold. As Lord Justice Lindley put it[2], the case was:

"A very important authority to show that water boundaries of land may fluctuate in law as well as in fact."

The Privy Council in *Government of the State of Penang* v. *Beng Hong Oong*[3] recently reviewed the law, and decided that where on a conveyance of land a boundary is described as the "sea beach" it means the high tide line which may be moveable, and the conveyance will include land added by gradual and imperceptible recession of the sea.

Effect of Imperceptible Changes on Fishing Rights. To sum up, the position where imperceptible changes take place is this:

(1)   Where the public have the right to fish on the foreshore, their fishing rights move with the foreshore;

(2)   Where the fishing rights in a river are in the same ownership right across from bank to bank, they move with changes in the river so that they remain in the whole width;

(3)   Where opposite landowners each have fishing rights to the middle line of a river, the limits of their respective rights will vary as the course of the river varies, and will be from each bank to the mid-line for the time being.

---

[1] (1825) 4 B. & C. 485.
[2] In *Hindson* v. *Ashby* [1896] 2 Ch. 1 at p.11.
[3] [1971] 3 All E.R. 1163, applying *Terrunanse* v. *Terrunanse* [1968] C.L.Y. 229 and *Musselburgh Magistrates* v. *Musselburgh Real Estate Co.* (1904) Sc.L.R. 247; distinguishing *Mellor* v. *Walmsley* [1905] 2 Ch. 164.

CHAPTER 17

RATING OF FISHING RIGHTS

Fishing Rights Severed from Land. Fishing rights are normally subject to rating. The General Rate Act, 1967, sections 16(*e*) and 29 make fishing and other sporting rights rateable where they are severed from the occupation of the land — in other words, where someone other than the occupier of the land has the fishing rights. Where sporting rights are let, they are only to be treated as severed from the land if the letting is by formal deed under seal. Giving a right to fish by a mere licence[1] does not therefore sever the fishing rights from the land.[2] But they are severed if the landowner lets the land and reserves the sporting rights to himself.[3] Where they are severed from the land the owner of the fishing rights is responsible for paying the rates, and not the occupier of the land.

"Land covered by water". Where sporting rights are not severed from the occupation of the land, they are not rateable. This does not avail the owner of fishing rights as much as the owner of other sporting rights because "land covered by water" is a separate rateable hereditament — that is, it is to be assessed for rating as a separate part of the land whether or not the occupier enjoys the fishing.

Exemption of Agricultural Land. "Land covered by water" will not be rateable if it counts as "agricultural land" for the purposes of the rating law. This is because agricultural land and buildings are exempted from rating.[4] Fishing rights which are not severed from the occupation of the land may therefore escape rating, if they are in waters which rank as agricultural land.

The definition of agricultural land is therefore important both for what it includes and for what it excludes. The relevant parts of the long statutory definition are:

> " 'Agricultural land' means any land used as arable meadow or pasture ground only, land used for a plantation or a wood or for the growth of saleable underwood . . . but does not include land occupied together with a house as a park, gardens . . . pleasure grounds, or land kept

---

[1]For meaning see Chapter 13.
[2]*Swayne* v. *Howells* [1927] 1 K.B. 385.
[3]*Lord Hastings* v. *Revenue Officer for Walsingham R.D.C.* [1930] 2 K.B. 278.
[4]General Rate Act, 1967, s. 26(1).

or preserved mainly or exclusively for purposes of sport or recreation . . . "[1]

Fortunately for the farmer the courts have decided that the word "only" in the definition does not mean only. Even if "land covered by water" is used for fishing as well as arable, meadow or pasture ground, it still ranks as agricultural land if the fishing is so subsidiary and ancillary as not to take away the general agricultural character of the land. This was decided in *Watkins* v. *Hereford Assessment Committee* (1935)[2] where a farmer was the owner-occupier of a farm through which two rivers ran. Cattle drank from the river and sheep were washed in them. The fishing in the rivers was let out for £14 a season, but there was no written agreement. The Divisional Court held that the river beds were "agricultural land" in spite of the fishing and in spite of the word "only" in the definition quoted above.

On the other hand, in *Clay and Clay* v. *Newbiggin (V.O.)* (1956)[3], it was decided that the fishing predominated over the use of the river for draining woodland and watering cattle. The owner employed a keeper and there was evidence that he acquired the agricultural land neighbouring the river so as not to be disturbed in his fishing.

The Lands Tribunal (Mr Erskine Simes, Q.C.) reached an interesting conclusion in *Govett (Exors.)* v. *Wand* (1959)[4] — the Bramsbury Common case. The land was bounded by the River Test on one side and the River Dever on another and the river banks were fenced off from the rest of the land which was pasture. Although the Tribunal decided the "land covered by water" (the river beds) was not agricultural land because the rivers were "kept and preserved mainly for purposes of sport" (see the definition of "agricultural land" above) it also decided that the rivers were land used as pasture even though the rivers were fenced off from the cattle — but in this case they were not pasture "only". The Tribunal was satisfied that works of improvement to the rivers and fencing them off "was designed to improve the grazing on Bramsbury Common and has been successful in that object". The work also improved the fishing which then became the main use of the rivers. The Court of Appeal[5] upheld the decision saying it was a finding of fact based on proper material, and that land used for pasture grounds could yet be kept and preserved mainly for sport.

Assessing the Rateable Value

Fishing rights. The net rateable value to be entered on the Valuation List for fishing rights is the estimated rent at which they might reasonably be

---

[1] *Ibid.*, s. 26(3)(*a*).
[2] (1935) 154 L.T. 262.
[3] (1956) 1 R.R.C. 13.
[4] (1959) 5 R.R.C. 232.
[5] *Garnett* v. *Wand (V.O.)* (1960) 7 R.R.C. 99 (same case, but different name on appeal).

expected to be let from year to year, if the tenant undertook to pay all usual rates and taxes, and to bear the cost of the repairs, insurance and other expenses (if any) necessary to maintain the fishing in a state to command that rent.[1]

Where the fishing is let, the actual rent paid is not necessarily its net annual value, and so the rateable value to be entered on the list might be different. In *Olding* v. *Denman* (1951)[2] the Lands Tribunal made allowance for the fact that a high rent for sporting rights had been agreed without realising that it might be the basis for the rating assessment.

The Valuation Officer, therefore, must judge what the open market rental value of the fishing rights are in each particular case, and will take into consideration: the quality of the fishing and the kinds of fish caught; the extent of the fishing rights; any special advantages and disadvantages of the water from an angling point of view; what demand there is for fishing in the area and whether the waters are reasonably accessible to prospective tenants; the extent of interference from navigation; whether the public have access to the banks, and, if so, the likely extent of interference; the estimated cost of maintenance including the cost of a water bailiff, weed-cutting, stocking, feeding, clearing unwanted fish, and care of the banks, where any of these items of expense would arise. The Valuation Officer calls on his knowledge of rents paid for any comparable fishing in the district and his experience of rating fishing rights. It was decided in *Colne Fishery Co.* v. *Essex C.V.C.* (1931)[3] that a public right of naviation in the river did not prevent the owners of oyster beds from having exclusive occupation of them, and so they were properly rateable.

No Gross Value is to be shown on the Valuation List for fishing rights.

Assessing "land covered by water". Where the fishing rights are not severed from the land, and "land covered by water" comes up for valuation, the fishing as such is not what is being valued. The fishing, however, may enhance the value of the land that is being assessed. Where the "land covered by water" is not agricultural land and the fishing is minimal, it may be appropriate to enter a nominal value only on the list. Where it is agricultural land, of course, no value is to be entered at all.

Rating relief for clubs. By section 40 of the General Rate Act, 1967, the rating authority has a discretion to reduce or remit the payment of rates where a "hereditament . . . is occupied for the purposes of a club, society or other organisation not established or conducted for profit and is wholly or mainly used for recreational purposes". This can and should avail a club, on application to the rating authority, in respect of rates on their fishing and club premises. If a club makes a financial gain or surplus, it does not follow

---

[1] General Rate Act, 1967, s. 19(3).
[2] 167 E.G. 633.
[3] (1931) 15 R. & I.T. 148.

that it is established or conducted for profit.[1] Relief under section 40 can be obtained in other cases which will apply to certain associations — e.g. charities and associations formed for educational purposes.

Drainage Rates. Occupiers of fishing are liable for drainage rates. Both the occupiers and owners rate will be levied on the occupier, but a tenant is entitled to recoup the owners rate by deducting it from the rent.[2]

---

[1] *Newton-le-Willows Cricket etc. Club* v. *Newton-le-Willows U.D.C.* (1966) 12 R.R.C. 32.
[2] Land Drainage Act, 1930, s. 24.

CHAPTER 18

DISEASES OF FISH

Diseases of Fish Act, 1937. The Diseases of Fish Act, 1937, enables the Minister and river authorities to take measures to check the spread of disease among fish, rather after the fashion that foot and mouth and other notifiable diseases of cattle are checked.

In this Chapter the Diseases of Fish Act, 1937, is called "the 1937 Act" for short.

Restriction on Importations of Live Fish and Eggs

Live Salmon and Trout. The 1937 Act prohibits absolutely the importation into Great Britain of "any live fish of the salmon family"[1] which is defined to include "all fish of whatever genus or species belonging to the family Salmonidae".[2] Trout are therefore included.

Import Licences. Live freshwater fish, or live eggs of fish of the salmon family, or of freshwater fish, may not be imported into Great Britain except under a licence issued by the Minister to the person they are consigned to.[3]

Freshwater fish are also defined in the 1937 Act, and include any fish living in fresh water, except fish of the salmon family or any kinds of fish which migrate to and from tidal waters.[4] Live eels may therefore be imported without a licence.

The licence from the Minister may lay down conditions regarding the quantities or kinds of live fish or eggs which may be imported under the licence, and also regarding the disposal, transport, inspection, cleansing and disinfection of the fish or eggs and of anything they may be transported or kept in, and any other precautions for avoiding the spread of disease among fish. A licence may be granted for any period up to twelve months, but may be suspended or revoked.[5]

Contravention of any of the 1937 Act's rules regarding the importation of live fish or eggs of fish, or of any condition in a licence is an offence punishable by a fine under the 1937 Act. Any police officer, or officer of Customs and Excise, or Ministry inspector who has reason to suspect an

---

[1] Diseases of Fish Act, 1937, s. 1(1).
[2] *Ibid.*, s. 10(1).
[3] *Ibid.*, s. 1(2).
[4] *Ibid.*, s. 10(1).
[5] *Ibid.*, s. 1(3).

offence has been committed may seize and detain any fish or eggs involved, and detain them until proceedings have been taken and disposed of, or until the Minister decides that no proceedings are likely to be taken.[1]

Re-exportation. The Commissioners of Customs and Excise may lift the rules set out above, in cases where fish or eggs are brought to Great Britain "solely with a view to the re-exportation thereof after transit through Great Britain only by way of transhipment".[2]

Infected Areas. If at any time the Minister is satisfied that waters in any area are infected with furunculosis, columnaris, or any disease of fish, which the 1937 Act may be extended to by Order in Council[3], he may make an order declaring the area to be "an infected area". This enables him to use special powers to prevent the spreading of the disease. In river authority areas, the control of the disease may be carried out by the river authority, except that fish farms are to be dealt with by the Minister (through his inspectors).

Orders regulating transport. Where an area is declared "an infected area" the Minister may by orders prohibit or regulate the transport of live fish, or eggs of fish, or of foodstuff for fish, from the area. Failure to carry out the orders is an offence.[4]

"Foodstuff for fish" means any substance used, or intended or likely to be used, as food for fish, including natural food.[5]

The occupiers of waters in an infected area are entitled to a free copy of the report upon which the Minister decided to declare the area infected.[6]

Directions to remove infected fish. The Minister may serve a notice upon the occupiers of waters in an infected area, directing them to remove dead or dying fish, and telling them how they are to be disposed of.[7] This applies to fish farms, and waters outside river authority areas, because in river authority areas, the Minister has no power to serve a notice except on fish farms — the duty there falling on the river authority (see p.123 below). The directions state the time by which the infected fish are to be disposed of, and if the occupier fails to do it within the stated time the Minister may authorise an inspector to do it, and the reasonable expenses incurred by the inspector may be recovered from the occupier as a civil debt.

If anybody does anything prohibited by the Minister's notice, he commits an offence unless he did not know about the prohibition.[8]

If the Minister thinks it necessary to protect the stock of fish in an infected area he can give written authority to the occupier of any waters to

---

[1] Diseases of Fish Act, 1937, s. 1(4).
[2] *Ibid.,* s. 1(5).
[3] *Ibid.,* s. 13. The Act was extended to apply to columnaris by the Diseases of Fish Order, 1966, S.I. 1966 No. 944.
[4] *Ibid.,* s. 2(1).
[5] *Ibid.,* s. 10(1).
[6] *Ibid.,* s. 2(3).
[7] *Ibid.,* s. 2(4).
[8] *Ibid.,* s. 2(5).

remove any fish, even in breach of an agreement to the contrary, and by otherwise illegal methods and by any agent.[1] The occupier must then dispose of the fish in any way he is directed to by the Minister, and failure to comply is an offence.[2]

Within seven days (or such longer time as the Minister may allow) from removing dead or dying fish, or removing fish under the Minister's written authority as described above, the occupier must notify the number of the fish removed. In a river authority area the river authority must be notified (except for fish farms), otherwise the notification must go to the Minister.[3]

Who is the "occupier"? Section 10(1) and (2) gives the answer to this as:

" 'Occupier' means in relation to any waters a person entitled, without permission of any other person, to take fish from the waters."

In short, the person having the fishing rights, whether as owner or tenant, is the occupier. A person who obtains the fishing rights for a year or less is not counted as the occupier, but in that case the occupier is the person from whom the right was acquired. Members of an angling club or association are not to be taken as individual occupiers of the waters, but in that case the occupier is the person having the management of the waters on behalf of the club or the association.[4]

No directions, therefore, to remove fish can be given to club members (except the manager) but where a notice has been served in an affected area, the club members must not do anything prohibited by the notice, provided they know of the prohibition.

Powers and Duties of River Authority

Reporting and removing infected fish. A river authority having grounds to suspect that any waters (except fish farms) are infected with furunculosis or columnaris "or in which the causative organisms of either of those diseases are present"[5] (or any disease of fish to which the 1937 Act is applied by Order in Council) must report it to the Minister, and may take any practical steps for getting dead or dying fish removed from the infected waters.[6] On receiving a report from the river authority the Minister must have an investigation made to check whether the waters are infected.

In an area declared "an infected area", the Minister may authorise the river authority to remove any fish (whether dying or not) from any waters in

---

[1] Diseases of Fish Act, 1937, s. 2(6).
[2] *Ibid.,* s. 2(7).
[3] *Ibid.,* s. 2(8).
[4] *Ibid.* ,s. 10(2).
[5] *Ibid.,* see s. 10(1), definition of "infected waters" as amended by Diseases of Fish Order, 1966.
[6] *Ibid.,* s. 3(1).

the infected area (except fish farms) and by any agents and any methods (including methods otherwise illegal).[1]

When a river authority removes fish under any of these powers, it must "properly dispose" of them, and when directed by the Minister must send him a return both of the number of fish removed by them, and of the number notified to them as having been removed by the occupiers of infected waters.[2]

Infected Fish Farms. Fish farm is defined by the 1937 Act:[3]

> " 'Fish farm' means any pond, stew, fish hatchery or other place used for keeping, with a view to their sale or to their transfer to other waters (including any other fish farm), live fish of the salmon family, live freshwater fish, live eggs of fish, or foodstuff for fish, and includes any buildings used in connection therewith, and the banks and margins of any water therein."

Restriction of transport. A Ministry inspector having reasonable grounds for suspecting the waters of a fish farm are infected with furunculosis or columnaris (or other disease of fish to which the 1937 Act is applied by Order in Council) must straight away serve a notice upon the occupier and report the facts to the Minister. No live fish, eggs of fish or foodstuff for fish must, without the Minister's permission, be transported from the fish farm during the following 16 days — unless within that time the Minister gives a written intimation that permission is no longer required.[4] Any person transporting anything prohibited from the fish farm, commits an offence unless he can prove he did not know it was forbidden.[5] This is a case where the burden of proof is thrown on the accused.

Removal of infected fish. This is dealt with by the Minister's directions as described above (p.122), an inspector carrying out the directions if the occupier defaults.[6]

Duty to Report Infection. Anybody entitled to take fish from any waters, or employed to have care of any waters, who has reasonable grounds for suspecting the waters are infected with furunculosis or columnaris (or other disease of fish to which the 1937 Act is applied by Order in Council) must forthwith report the facts by letter or telegram to the Minister if the waters are a fish farm, or outside a river authority area. In a river authority area, the river authority must be notified. Failure to report it without reasonable excuse is an offence. This duty falls upon any person entitled to fish, and would include individual members of an angling club.[7]

---

[1] Diseases of Fish Act, 1937, s. 3(2).
[2] *Ibid.*, s. 3(3).
[3] *Ibid.*, s. 10(1).
[4] *Ibid.*, s. 4(1).
[5] *Ibid.*, s. 4(2).
[6] *Ibid.*, s. 2(4) and (5).
[7] *Ibid.*, s. 4(3).

Minister's Duty to Inspect. The river authority or the occupiers of any waters can require the Minister to have an examination made by an inspector with a view to discovering whether waters are infected. A report of the result must then be provided free of charge to the river authority or occupier. If the waters are found to be infected, the Minister can be required to make another examination at any time, but the Minister can always decline to make an examination if he thinks it too soon after the last one.[1]

"Waters." The word "waters" here and throughout the 1937 Act, means waters frequented by, or used for keeping, live salmon or freshwater fish[2], eggs or food of fish, and includes the banks and margins of the waters, and any buildings used in connection with them.[3]

Powers of Entry, Seizure and Inspection. Any Justice of the Peace may issue a warrant, valid for up to one week, authorising anybody, where there is good reason to suspect an offence under the 1937 Act, to enter on any land[4] and seize any offending or suspected fish, fish eggs or foodstuff of fish, or article.[5]

A Minister's inspector has power: (*a*) to inspect any waters in which fish, or eggs or foodstuff of fish are likely to be found, and to take samples of them or any water, mud, vegetation or other matter; and (*b*) for the purpose of exercising his powers or carrying out his duties, to enter any land upon producing his authority.[6]

It is an offence to refuse to admit or to obstruct an inspector in the pursuance of his powers.[6]

An inspector who takes a sample of fish and finds that none in the water is infected, must pay the market value of any fish sampled.[7]

The river authority may also authorise persons to enter on land, on producing their authority, to carry out river authority duties, and it is an offence to refuse to admit, or to obstruct such a person in carrying out his duties.[8]

Penalties. Anybody committing an offence under the 1937 Act can be fined £20 on conviction, or £100 if it is a second or subsequent offence, and the court may order the forfeiture of any fish, eggs or food of fish, or any article concerned in the offence.[9]

---

[1] Diseases of Fish Act, 1937, s. 5.
[2] For meaning see p.121.
[3] *Ibid.*, s. 10(1).
[4] Land includes waters, s. 10(1).
[5] *Ibid.*, s. 6(1).
[6] *Ibid.*, s. 6(2).
[7] *Ibid.*, s. 6(3).
[8] *Ibid.*, s. 6(4).
[9] *Ibid.*, s. 8(1).

CHAPTER 19

FISHING VERSUS NAVIGATION AND
OTHER WATER USERS

Public Navigation Prevails. Where the public right of navigation conflicts with fishing rights, navigation is paramount. This is always the case where the public have the right to navigate in tidal waters, and will be so in non-tidal waters unless the grant of navigation rights was made subject to the right of fishing. Where there is no right of navigation, the recent canoe case, *Rawson* v. *Peters*[1], shews that the navigator will be liable for interference with fishing rights, even if nobody is fishing at the time and no damage is done.

Usually there is a public right of navigation in tidal waters, though not everywhere. Andrew Phelan, who gives a useful account of the right to navigate in his book *The Law for Small Boats*[2], says (at p.46):

> "Though the flowing of the tide is strong presumptive evidence of the existence of a public navigable waterway, whether particular water is navigable seems to depend, in the light of modern authority, on evidence of the situation and character of the channel . . . not every ditch or cutting forms part of the navigable river, even though it is large enough to admit the passage of a boat."

Unlike public fishing rights, the right of public navigation may be, and often has been, acquired in non-tidal rivers, by dedication by the owners of the soil[3], or by immemorial usage by the public[4] or by statute.[5] This is because the right to navigate is a right of way akin to a right of way on dry land.[6]

Scope of Public Navigation. The public right of navigation includes not only the right of passage but also the right to moor, to anchor[7], and even to ground a vessel, if it becomes necessary, in both tidal[8] and non-tidal[6] waters.

---

[1] *The Times*, November 2, 1972.
[2] London, Charles Knight, 2nd edition, 1970.
[3] *Simpson* v. *Att.-Gen.* (1904) A. C. 476.
[4] *Bower* v. *Hill* (1835) 2 Scott 535.
[5] E.g., Thames Conservancy Act, 1932, s. 79.
[6] *Orr-Ewing* v. *Colquhoun* (1877) 2 App. Cas. 839.
[7] *Gann* v. *Free Fisheries of Whitstable* (1865) 11 H.L. Cas. 192, but not to lay or maintain permanent moorings (*Fowley Marine (Emsworth) Ltd* v. *Gafford* [1968] 1 All E.R. 979).
[8] *The Swift* [1901] p.168.

Although writers have expressed doubts about the right to anchor in non-tidal waters, where there is a right of public navigation there must be the right to anchor at least in the case of necessity, and no doubt where the right has been acquired by custom. This view is supported by the Scottish Case of *Campbell Trustee v. Sweeney.*[1]

The right of navigation is not suspended when the tide is too low to float the vessel, so that a vessel does not have to keep out of a tidal river until it can come in on the tide.[2]

The right of public navigation extends over the whole width of a tidal river[3], but as the right in non-tidal rivers depends on a grant (express, or implied by law) the right may be restricted to certain parts or channels. Furthermore the right is not the same for all vessels, because the suitability of the river for navigation must be taken into account. A large ship may therefore have no right, on account of the narrowness of the channel, to penetrate where a small boat may legally go.[4]

It may also be noted here that when a tidal river changes its course the public right of navigation always follows it to its new channel, even if the fishing rights do not.[5]

Navigation to be Exercised Reasonably. Although the public right to navigation prevail over fishing, this rule is subject to the important qualification that it must be exercised reasonably with due regard to the rights of anglers and others.

In real life the law has been mainly concerned with conflicts between vessels and oyster beds, rather than with the rod and line angler, and also with trouble arising from fishing weirs impeding navigation, but the principles that have evolved from these cases apply generally to mariners and fishermen of all kinds. The qualifications that have evolved to the general rule that navigation prevails, are as follows:

(1) *Navigators must not wantonly disregard anglers.* As one might expect, the law requires the sailor and the angler to pay due regard to each other's rights. This was well brought out by Baron Wood in a nameless case at Durham Assizes in 1808 which, in spite of its lasting significance, is reported only as a footnote in Campbell's Reports.[6] A ship moored against a rock fitted with mooring rings in the River Tweed, and thereby hindered the owner of the fishing rights who took less fish, we are told, than he would have otherwise, and claimed damages. The judge directed the jury in these words which sum up the law even one hundred and sixty years later:

"A navigable river is a public highway, and all persons have a right to come there in ships, and to unload, moor and stay there as long as they

---

[1] [1911] S.C. 1319.
[2] *Colchester Corp. v. Brooke* (1846) 7 Q.B. 339.
[3] *Williams v. Wilcox* (1838) 8 A. & E. 314.
[4] *The Octavia Stella* (1887) 57 L.T. 632.
[5] *Carlisle Corp. v. Graham* (1869) L.R. 4 Ex. 361; Hale *De Jure Maris* p.1, c.6, p.34, and see Chapter 16.
[6] *Anon.* (1808) 1 Camp. 516n.

please. Nevertheless, if they abuse that right so as to work a private injury, they are liable to an action. The question will therefore be whether the defendant has abused his right. The privilege of the plaintiff[1] must be subservient to the right of the public. It would be of very mischievous consequence if the owner of a fishery could prescribe to the public how and where they are to moor in a navigable river. The only case I remember like this was where a man obstinately refused to move his ship from opposite a wharf although it would have been just the same if he moved one way or the other; and he therefore abused his right and the plaintiff recovered.[2]

"The defendant had a right to moor and remain where his ship lay, as long as convenience required. Yet if he acted wantonly and maliciously for the purpose of injuring the fishery, the plaintiff is entitled to a verdict, but not otherwise."

(2) *Navigators must not negligently harm fishing.* This is brought out by the leading case on oyster beds, *Colchester Corp.* v. *Brooke* in 1846.[3] A vessel in the Colne making for Colchester missed the tide and grounded on an oyster bed belonging to the Corporation. Instead of mooring carefully to avoid further damage, the master anchored her in such a way that the vessel swung round and made not only "divers large holes" in the oyster bed "but also crushed and destroyed divers large quantities of oysters". The judge, Lord Denman, did not hold the master responsible for the damage done to the oysters by the original grounding, but he was held liable for negligently allowing the vessel to swing and cause additional damage which could have been avoided.

The liability for negligence is not over-strict for vessels. In *The Octavia Stella*[4] a compulsory pilot, who should have known better, took the vessel, an Italian barque, and anchored her on an oyster bed in the River Helford in Cornwall, damaging the oysters. When the master was notified that he was on an oyster bed, he took all reasonable measures to move his ship as speedily as possible. The judge, Sir James Hannen, assisted by Trinity Masters, held that the pilot was negligent and liable for damages, but the master of the ship had not been negligent. Although damage was done to the oyster bed while the ship was in the master's control (and after the pilot had handed over) he had navigated in a reasonable manner and was not liable.

On the other hand, refusing to move when told that the vessel is on an oyster bed makes the master liable for damage caused by his remaining on the oysters.[5] He is also liable for damages if he takes no heed of a warning to keep off an oyster bed, and then grounds on it.[6]

---

[1] That is, to fish.
[2] The judge was referring to the recovery of *damages* not health or temper.
[3] (1846) 7 Q.B. 339.
[4] (1887) 57 L.T. 632.
[5] *Addison* v. *Hussey* (1896) unreported, but referred to in Stuart Moore, *History and Law of Fisheries*, (1903) p.90.
[6] *The Swift* [1901] P. 168.

In *The Bien*[1] the harbour authority were guilty of negligence when they failed to move a wreck which was damaging an oyster fishery.

(3) *The right to navigate carries no right to fish.* In *Micklethwaite* v. *Vincent*[2] it appeared that the defendant and others had been in the habit of fishing and shooting on part of the Norfolk Broads without permission from the owners. Mr Justice Romer held that the water was not tidal and so there was no public right to fish, although there was a public right of navigation. The shooting and fishing were illegal.

If it is borne in mind that the public's rights on a watery highway are akin to those on dry land, it can be seen what they are limited to: Mr Justice Paull put it graphically in the "Man of Bosham" Case:[3]

> "It must always be remembered that there are rights attached to navigation and that the rights of navigation are analogous to the rights of the public on a highway on land; that is to say, the right of coming and going and doing those things incidental thereto. On the highway I may stand still for a reasonably short time, but I must not put my bed on the highway and permanently occupy a portion of it. I may stoop to tie up my shoe lace, but I may not occupy a pitch and invite people to come on it and have their hair cut. I may let my van stand still long enough to deliver and load goods, but I must not turn my van into a permanent stall. In the same way, so far as navigation is concerned, I may have to wait for a favourable wind; I may have to load or discharge cargo, and I may have to do repairs necessary or desirable before again setting out to sea, but I may not *permanently* occupy a part of the water over a foreshore."

The importance of this for anglers is that although public navigation prevails over public or private angling, it only does so insofar as the vessel and crew are carrying out activities which are part of the right of navigation. The mariner may, of course, have the right to fish for other reasons — for example, because he owns the fishing rights or because he is afloat on public fishing waters — but fishing rights never derive from the right to navigate. The fishing is a right of property: the navigation is a right of way.[4]

(4) *The Rules of the Road at Sea must be observed.* These are laid down in the International Regulations for Preventing Collisions at Sea. Revised collision regulations came into force on 1st September, 1965.[5]

It is not the place of this book to go into shipping law and regulations, except to note that they do provide for sea traffic avoiding a fishing boat while fishing is taking place.

---

[1] [1911] P. 40.
[2] (1892) 67 L.T. 225.
[3] *Iveagh* v. *Martin* [1960] 2 All E.R. 668 at p.683.
[4] *Orr-Ewing* v. *Colquhoun* (1877) 2 App. Cas. 839.
[5] See The Collision Regulations (Ships and Seaplanes on the Water) and Signals of Distress (Ships) Order, 1965.

(5) *Byelaws must be observed*, in particular byelaws made under the Prevention of Pollution Acts prohibiting or regulating the use of sanitary appliances on vessels from which polluting matter might pass into a stream (see p.149), byelaws setting speed limits and those made under the Countryside Act, 1968, regulating forms of recreation (see below pp.132–133).

Fishing as a Nuisance to Navigation. Fishing activities which interefere with public navigation may be a public or private nuisance which may be restrained by the courts, or give rise to the payment of damages. Damages may only be claimed by an individual if he suffers "special and peculiar" injury clearly attributable to the nuisance.[1] In *Colchester Corp.* v. *Brooke* (above) the example given of how the exercise of fishing rights might interfere with navigation was the depositing of unreasonably large masses of oysters in the bed of a navigable channel so as to obstruct the passage of ships.

A person exercising his right to fish may not cut down the scope of the right of navigation, by, for example, forbidding anchoring, or requiring payment of a toll for anchoring without giving any service in return.[2]

Fishing weirs and obstructions. Chapter 8 deals with the legality of fishing weirs and other obstructions which hinder the migration of fish up and down rivers, and the position of the riparian owner is dealt with in Chapter 15.

The leading case on the obstruction of navigation by a weir attached to a fishery, is *Williams* v. *Wilcox*[3] in which Chief Justice Denman examined the historical and legal background to the problem.

The case involved an ancient weir placed in the River Severn under a royal grant made before the reign of Edward I. When the grant was made the weir did not obstruct navigation because it stood across a part of the river which was not used for navigation. Later, when the navigable channel became choked up, the defendant took it upon himself to demolish the fishing weir in order to free a new channel for navigation.

The judge settled the following points:

(1)   The public right of navigation is a right "to pass in all and every part of the channel".

(2)   A grant by the Crown of a right to raise a weir must be taken to be subject to the right of navigation, because navigation is a paramount right over rights of property.

(3)   But, the old statute of Edward III[4] in ordering weirs to be removed for the benefit of navigation, made an exception of pre-Edward I weirs and thereby made them legal for all purposes. He said:

---

[1] *Fraser* v. *Fear* (1912) 107 L.T. 423.
[2] *Gann* v. *Free Fishers of Whitstable* (1865) 11 H.L. Cas. 192.
[3] (1838) 8 A. & E. 314.
[4] 25 Ed. III c. 4, see Chapter 8.

" . . . a line was therefore drawn, which, preventing an increase of the nuisance for the future, and abating it in all the instances which commenced within a given period[1], impliedly legalised those which could be traced to an earlier period . . . The earlier weirs were not merely protected against the specific measures mentioned in the Act, but rendered absolutely legal."

The self-appointed weir demolisher was therefore guilty of trespass.

Water Skiing. In this respect, it has never been decided whether water skiing is part of the right of navigation, but it is suggested that it is not, because it is a recreation which is not concerned with the right of passage, and waterskis can hardly be called a craft or vessel. An argument could, however, be put up for the opposite point of view where waterskis are drawn by boats (as they usually are). In non-tidal waters, though, where the right of navigation will only have arisen by dedication or some other form of grant (express or implied) the right will be restricted to the use contemplated by the grant.[2] This alone would normally exclude water skiing. On many waters the sport is controlled by byelaws, either directly or indirectly.

Fishing and Other Forms of Recreation

No watery activities other than navigation prevail over fishing, and the angler's right to prevent interference with his pursuit will depend upon (a) whether the "offender" has the legal right to be where he is and do what he does; and (b) if so, whether he is practising his recreation in a reasonable manner. Water skiers, duck shooters, picnickers, bathers, bird watchers, otter hunters, and others may all be entitled to pursue their pastimes in the same places as anglers. The commonsense law of "live and let live" is then as good as any. If the navigator, with his paramount right, must avoid wanton or negligent interference with the angler, no less must others, and vice versa.

Where recreational interests conflict it is for leaders in each sport or pastime to seek equitable arrangements, if it is beyond the scope of individuals to do so. Angling, being especially vulnerable to disturbance, yet having long established rights on many waters, is in danger of losing out unless its leaders are active and vigilant in protecting angling interests — especially now that the recreational use of water space is to be put onto the desks of official planners.

The White Paper which preceded the Countryside Act, 1968[3], outlining coming legislation, stated: "Throughout full consideration will be given to the needs of anglers who on some rivers already have a clear priority." It would be unrealistic, however, to think that this "full consideration" will in fact be

---

[1] That is, from the accession of Edward I to the date of the Statute of Edward III (1273–1350).

[2] *Cf. Bourke* v. *Davis* (1889) 44 Ch. D. 110.

[3] *Leisure in the Countryside.* Cmnd. 2928 (February 1966).

given, or the "priority" recognised, unless anglers press their point of view strongly wherever organisation or regulation of countryside recreation takes place. Anglers may see a red light in the Transport Act, 1968, which chose the term "cruising waterways" to describe the class of inland waterway which included those where angling had "a clear priority", and imposed a duty on the British Waterways Board to keep them in a suitable condition for the use of powered cruisers (see below p.134).

The Countryside Act, 1968. By this Act a new body called the Countryside Commission stepped into the shoes of the National Parks Commission and were given wider responsibilities. It is outside the scope of this book to describe in full the role and powers of the new Commission, but broadly, as its name implies, its jurisdiction extends beyond National Parks to the countryside in general. In addition to functions to do with conservation of amenity it must keep under review and encourage the provision and improvement of facilities for the enjoyment of, and open-air recreation in, the countryside.[1]

By and large the Act seems to see the solution to conflicting activities to be regulation by byelaws.

Country parks. It also enables local authorities to establish *country parks* for planned public enjoyment of the countryside. Facilities and services are to be provided in country parks for open-air recreation and may include "sailing, boating, bathing and fishing" with all the trappings (car parks, lavatories, hot-dogs etc.).[2] Byelaws regulating the enjoyment of country parks may require the registration of boats, and may also require good neighbourliness by those resorting to the park.[3]

National Parks. National Park authorities may make similar provisions in National Parks and appoint wardens to enforce the byelaws. Facilities for watery recreation may be provided not only in National Parks but on waterways, or the sea, adjoining, or in the neighbourhood of them — provided the existing facilities are "inadequate or unsatisfactory".[4]

Byelaws may forbid or restrict "traffic of any description" on any lake in a National Park. The use of boats may be controlled by a system for registering them, imposing speed limits and requiring silencers to be fitted. Byelaws may also be made "for preventing nuisance or damage, and in particular nuisance from excessive noise".[5]

Reservoirs of water boards and water companies. Statutory water undertakers are also given powers to regulate recreation on their reservoirs and other waters. They too may require registration of boats and make byelaws "securing that persons resorting to the waterway or land will so

---

[1] Countryside Act, 1968, ss. 1(2) and 2(2).
[2] *Ibid.*, ss. 7 and 8.
[3] *Ibid.*, s. 41.
[4] *Ibid.*, s. 12, and see National Parks and Access to the Countryside Act, 1949, ss. 5–14.
[5] Countryside Act, 1968, s. 13.

behave themselves as to avoid undue interference with the enjoyment of the waterway or land by other persons".[1] It is proposed that the new Regional Water Authorities will take over these duties in the Government's water reorganisation plans.

Inland waters.[2] The new Regional Water Authorities are also earmarked to take over the present powers of river authorities to make byelaws prohibiting the use of inland waters in their areas for boating, swimming or other recreational purposes — or else to regulate these activities. This is a more restricted power to plan water recreation than others mentioned above, but a more hopeful one for anglers, because the byelaws can only be made for the purposes of the functions of river authorities relating to water conservation, land drainage or fisheries. It is also restricted to non-tidal waters which are not under navigation, or certain other, authorities, and land locked lakes, ponds and reservoirs are excluded.[3] Where such byelaws are made, facilities for any recreation allowed may be provided and charged for. The public may be permitted to make recreational use of reservoirs owned or managed by river authorities, and facilities may be provided and charged for this too.[4]

"Boat". Throughout the Countryside Act, 1968, a "boat" includes a hovercraft[5] so that these exotic craft can be controlled by byelaws and would come into any boat registration scheme.

Water Space Amenity Commission. In the Government's water reorganisation it is planned that the amenity use of water space will be overseen by a national body called the Water Space Amenity Commission, which will be linked with the Countryside Commission, the Sports Council and another new body to be called the National Water Council.

Inland Waterways.[6] The inland waterways at present governed by the British Waterways Board — mainly canals and canalised rivers — have been classified by the Transport Act, 1968, into (*a*) "commercial waterways"; (*b*) "cruising waterways"; and (*c*) "the remainder".[7] The plan is for these to be taken over under the Government's water reorganisation by the new Regional Water Authorities, and for the British Waterways Board to be abolished. Most of these waterways are "cruising waterways" (about 1,100 miles) and "commercial waterways" (340 miles). "The remainder" (about 600 miles) are wholly or partly un-navigable — but not necessarily un-fishable.

The unhappy term "cruising waterway" is supposed to describe the canals where fishing is to be fostered, along with other recreations. On many of these angling was the main form of recreation at the time the Transport

---

[1] Countryside Act, 1968, s. 22.
[2] See definition, p.10. Not to be confused with inland waterways (see below).
[3] Water Resources Act, 1963, s. 79(3) and (4).
[4] *Ibid.*, s. 80.
[5] Countryside Act, 1968, s. 49(2).
[6] Not to be confused with "inland waters" (see above).
[7] Transport Act, 1968, s. 104.

Act, 1968, was passed. Now the Act requires "cruising waterways" to be kept in a suitable condition to be used by powered cruisers of the same size as those customarily using the waterways in 1967.[1]

The hope of protection for angling interests lies in the Inland Waterways Amenity Advisory Council (IWAAC) whose membership must include persons who "appear to the Minister to have wide knowledge of, and interest in, the use of inland waterways for amenity or recreational purposes including fishing". As mentioned above (p.133) it is planned to create a body called the Water Space Amenity Commission. Among other duties it will take over the functions of the IWAAC which has been described by the Department of the Environment as "a central forum where all water space users representatives can meet and resolve their conflicting interests". The present function of the IWAAC is to advise the British Waterways Board on any proposals to add to or reduce the cruising waterways. They can also make recommendations on "any matter affecting the use or development for amenity or recreational purposes, including fishing, of the cruising water-ways" or the provision of services or facilities. The Council may appoint regional committees and sub-committees.[2]

Local authorities are empowered by the Transport Act, 1968, to assist "any person" in maintaining or improving amenities or recreational facilities, including fishing, on inland waterways.[3]

Angling interests would do well to press the new bodies responsible for inland waterways to appoint Fisheries Officers to see that valuable fishing rights are not swamped by the wash from cruisers, and that a fair measure of the authorities' resources are directed to the preservation of fisheries.

Opinions will differ as to whether angling is likely to gain or lose from the planning of countryside enjoyment. It has been shown in recent years that conflicting interests can come to workable arrangements for the joint use of water space, provided there is a genuine aim to co-operate and to understand the needs of each other. It will be important for angling interests to be adequately represented on the new bodies being created under the water reorganisation, and for anglers, clubs and their representative bodies to see that their interests forever pop up in the foreground of water use planning.

---

[1] Transport Act, 1968, s. 105.
[2] *Ibid.*, s. 110.
[3] *Ibid.*, s. 114.

CHAPTER 20

TACKLING POLLUTION

The fouling of the watercourses of the British Islands was such that it was openly said that there was no dirtier beast than man himself, and that Britain was "a pearl set in a sea of sewage" before the stench from the Thames at Westminster drove Parliament to legislate against river pollution with the Public Health Act, 1875. Since then various anti-pollution Acts have been tried. Some had little effect. Others furthered the evil they were supposed to be attacking by turning out in practice to be licences to pollute. Meanwhile hundreds of miles of rivers were having virtually all fish and vegetable life blotted out of them by poisonous discharges into them of sewage and trade effluents.

Common Law Rights. The extant statutes are examined below, but what has been most effective in attacking pollution and restoring befouled rivers to a state fit to support fish life and the food fish live on, has been the common law rights of riparian and fishery owners; and angling societies, notably of course the Anglers' Co-operative Association, have been a powerful force in using the common law to clean up rivers when the authorities holding the statutory powers have failed to do so.

At common law the riparian owner of land has a natural right to have the water flowing past or through his land in its natural state of purity.[1] The owner of fishing rights, whether or not he is a riparian owner, is entitled to take action against any person or body interfering with his use and enjoyment of his fishery, and he is also entitled to the free passage of fish in the river between the sea and its source. If these common law rights are infringed by polluters, normally the riparian owners and/or the owners of the fishing may have recourse to the courts to obtain an injunction to stop the pollution, and to obtain damages for the injury to their rights. An injunction carries with it the sanction that disobedience is a contempt of court for which the offender may be imprisoned.

Ironic Threat to Make Machiavellian History. This may be changed. Notwithstanding that history ancient and modern has demonstrated beyond doubt that the sharpest, and, frequently, the only effective, weapon against pollution has been the common law injunction, or threat of it, the Government have flighted a threat to do away with common law rights where polluters discharge effluent under a statutory consent. In its place would be a

---

[1] See Chapters 15 and 21.

claim for compensation from the consenting authority — but no means of stopping the pollution. Compensation will be little consolation to an angling club with unfishable waters. If this comes about, it must go down in history as a classic instance of Cinderella being fed to the Big Bad Wolf by an Administration which (aroused by public opinion) has vowed to convert the Wolf (namely, the polluter) into a Sheep. The irony is the more acute because the system will continue of reposing the responsibility for giving discharge consents and for controlling pollution in the same authorities, and those authorities must always, by law, be dominated by potential polluters (i.e. a majority of local authority members, plus representatives of industry and agriculture), and under the new law will themselves be sewage authorities.

What Is Pollution?

Criminal pollution. Pollution is a crime if the polluter offends against the statutes which are dealt with in the second part of this chapter, or if it amounts to a public nuisance. A public nuisance is an offensive activity or use of property which is so troublesome that it is an undue annoyance or inconvenience to the community in general, not a few individuals only. The Attorney-General, acting on behalf of the general public, can prosecute any person or body committing a public nuisance by pollution.[1]

Civil pollution. Pollution is a civil offence (a tort), if it infringes somebody's common law rights. As a riparian owner is entitled to have the water running through his land in its natural state, unchanged in quality or quantity, it is a wrong at common law substantially to alter the quality or temperature of water which flows through or past the land of another person.

The word "substantially" is used to indicate that the law will not take account of minimal or insignificant changes made to the water, or temporary changes which do no undue harm, such as a discharge of waste water which merely stirs up the mud in a river for a short time.[2] The riparian owner does not have to prove he has suffered any financial loss by the pollution in order to claim[3], but he must be able to show some damage to his rights.[4]

The angler is most concerned about pollution which poisons or deoxygenates the water so that the life or health of fish is affected, or their breeding or the food they live on. Typically this has come about from discharges of sewage by local authorities and others, trade effluents from factories, silage liquor and cowshed washings from farmers, and mineral wastes from mineral workings. It should also be noted, however, that discharges of hot water[5], though clean, may be actionable because of the deoxygenating effect of it. Likewise a discolouration of the water by a non-poisonous discharge could be actionable, if it destroyed vegetable or

---

[1] *R.* v. *Medley* (1834) 6 C. & P. 292: *R.* v. *Bradford Navigation Co.* (1865) 6 B. & S.631.
[2] *Taylor* v. *Bennett* (1836) 7 C. & P. 329.
[3] *Crossley & Sons* v. *Lightowler* (1867) 16 L.T. 438.
[4] *Elmhirst* v. *Spencer* (1849) 2 Mac. & G. 45.
[5] *Tipping* v. *Eckersley* (1855) 2 K. & J. 264.

animal life in the water by depriving it of light, and so would any discharge that made a material difference to the chemical content of the water — for example, the addition of hard water to a stream of soft water.[1]

It is important to note that a person discharging effluent into a watercourse is liable whenever it causes pollution, even though the effluent only becomes injurious due to factors beyond his control — for example, a hot summer or discharges by others.

Multiple pollution. Although in criminal proceedings the accused has sometimes been acquitted by shewing that others were polluting the water as well as himself, this is no defence to an action taken by a riparian owner for damages and an injunction.

This was decided in the important case of *Crossley & Sons* v. *Lightowler*[2] in which the claimant, with the object of preventing a river from being fouled by a dye-works, purchased a piece of riparian land from the dye-works itself, without disclosing his purpose. The Court held that he was entitled to an injunction as a riparian owner. In cases of multiple pollution a riparian owner may obtain an injunction against any single polluter, even if it cannot be proved that the individual pollution by itself would be injurious. Proceedings may be taken against all the polluters at the same time in a consolidated action, or cases may be taken against the polluters one at a time as long as the pollution lasts. It is possible, therefore, for the riparian owner to defeat pollution even where no individual discharge of effluent is sufficient to harm the fishery by itself, provided the combined effect of several is injurious. An example of this would be where an otherwise innocuous discharge from, say, a paper mill, is made deadly by a discharge of hot water from a factory raising the temperature of the stream. In such a case an injunction may be obtained to stop either or both discharges.

Water abstraction causing pollution. The abstraction of water from a stream may cause pollution by reducing the dilution of effluent in the water. Here again the polluter might escape conviction in a criminal court by pleading that it was someone else's abstraction that caused the trouble, but this plea is no defence to civil proceedings by a riparian owner — whether the flow is reduced by water abstraction, diversion of water or natural drought.

If the water abstraction which renders the effluent harmful is done unlawfully, then proceedings for damages and an injunction may be taken against the abstractor as well as, or instead of, the party who discharges the effluent. As appears in Chapter 21 river authority licences to abstract are now needed under the Water Resources Act, 1963, in nearly all cases. If the water abstraction is lawful, proceedings cannot be taken against the abstractor, but only against the partly discharging the effluent.[3]

---

[1] *John Younger & Co.* v. *Bankier Distillery Co.* [1893] A.C. 591.
[2] (1867) 16 L.T. 438.
[3] See Water Resources Act, 1963, s. 31(1).

Permissible Pollution

Action cannot always be taken under common law rights against pollution, because in some circumstances pollution is lawful and sometimes there is nobody with a right to take proceedings to stop it.

A man may pollute watercourses on his own property, provided that if the water flows from his land onto or through another's, it must leave his land unpolluted.[1] A further qualification is that the passage of migratory fish must not be prevented by pollution on one's own land. We have already noted in Chapter 15 the case of *Stockport Waterworks* v. *Potter*[2], where the claimants were powerless to tackle the polluters of the water which they were entitled to take from their waterworks. This was because they had no riparian or fishing rights, but only a right to take the water by way of "conduits and tunnels".

A legal right to pollute a watercourse may be acquired as against other users of the water. This can happen in the following ways:—

(i) *By an Act of Parliament,* authorising pollution notwithstanding the common law rights of riparian owners and owners of fisheries[3], or a statute might continue an already existing right to pollute.[4]

(ii) *By a grant or agreement* which gives the right to pollute expressly or by implication.[5]

(iii) *By custom.* This is not easy to prove, because it is necessary to prove that the custom has existed since time immemorial, and the courts will not recognise a custom which could only be illegal, such as gross pollution by sewage.[6] If a customary right is relied on, the customary use must not be exceeded, and the custom must be clear and reasonable — such as a custom of washing away sand and other impurities in a stream abutting a tin mine.[7]

(iv) *By prescription* (long use). The acquisition of rights by prescription is explained in Chapter 13, and just as fishing rights may be acquired by proving long enjoyment of them, a right to pollute a watercourse (called an easement to pollute) may be acquired by proving continuous acts of pollution over many years as if the right to pollute existed. A claim under the Prescription Act, 1832, must show perceptible pollution has continued for at least 20 years.[8] This claim has arisen typically by owners of mineral workings. In *Wright* v. *Williams*[9] for

---

[1] *Elmhirst* v. *Spencer* (1849) 14 L.T.O.S. 433.
[2] (1864) 10 L.T. 748.
[3] *Lea Conservancy Board* v. *Hertford Corpn.* (1884) 48 J.P. 628.
[4] *Somerset Drainage Commissioners* v. *Bridgwater Corpn.* (1899) 81 L.T. 729.
[5] *Hall* v. *Lund* (1863) 1 H. & C. 676.
[6] *Att.-Gen.* v. *Richmond* (1866) 14 L.T. 398.
[7] *Carlyon* v. *Lovering* (1857) 1 H. & N. 784.
[8] *Goldsmid* v. *Tunbridge Wells Commrs.* (1866) 1 Ch. App. 349.
[9] (1836) 1 M. & W. 77; [1835–1842] All E.R. Rep. 469.

example, it was held that a prescriptive right may arise to flush out water from a copper mine into a watercourse even though the discharge contained mineral substances which adulterated the stream flowing through neighbouring land.

Limits of prescriptive right. Here again strict limitations are placed upon the acquisition of pollution rights by long use. As we have seen elsewhere, *Goodman* v. *Saltash Corporation*[1] decided that there can be no prescriptive claim to a right that could not have a lawful origin. No right to pollute water could be claimed if it was a danger to public health[2], or was an act prohibited by statute. Furthermore, if a right to pollute water has been acquired by long continued use, no pollution is allowed beyond the strict limits of the use during the prescriptive period. There must therefore be no greater pollution than before[3], nor pollution caused by a business different from that carried on before even if it causes less pollution than the former business.[4] A change of the polluting substance, without a change in the business, might however be permissible, on the authority of *Baxendale* v. *McMurray.*[5] If the right has been acquired to extract water from a stream and return it polluted in a particular place, the right does not extend to doing so in a different manner and a different place.[6]

In *Liverpool Corporation* v. *Coghill*[7] it was held that an easement to pollute cannot be acquired by secret pollution over many years unknown and unsuspected by the owner of the servient tenement (that is, the land over which the easement is exercised). The defendant had unknown to the Corporation discharged poisonous matter from his factory into the sewers mainly at night. The Court decided that a prescriptive right could not be obtained in those circumstances.

No prescription where forbidden by statute. The right to pollute cannot be acquired by long use where the pollution is forbidden by an Act of Parliament. This has important practical implications for anglers, because the riparian owner may be lulled into the belief that no prescriptive right to pollute could now be acquired in view of the modern prohibitive legislation. This is not so. The Rivers (Prevention of Pollution) Acts of 1951 and 1961 do not ban pollution outright. Paradoxically, they enable river authorities to give licences to pollute. Where, therefore, discharges are permitted by these Acts it is possible for a right to pollute to be acquired, by continuous long use, against riparian owners and fishery owners. Conversely, where discharges are made illegal (that is, a crime) by these Acts, no prescriptive right can be obtained. Pollution was an offence from 1876 until the 1961 Act exonerated

---

[1](1882) 7 A.C. 633 (see p.99 above).
[2]*Blackburne* v. *Somers* (1879) 5 L.R. Ir. 1.
[3]*Millington* v. *Griffiths* (1874) 30 L.T. 65.
[4]*Clarke* v. *Somerset Drainage Commrs.* (1888) 58 L.T. 670.
[5](1867) 31 J.P. 821.
[6]*McIntyre Bros.* v. *McGavin* [1893] A.C. 268.
[7][1918] 1 Ch. 307.

licensed discharges[1] — so that today it is virtually impossible for a twenty years prescriptive period to have started running before 1961.

It is important to note that these Acts are not dealing with the legality of adulteration of streams as between the polluter and other persons who have rights over the water. The Acts make it a crime to discharge effluent into streams in contravention of the rules laid down by or under the Acts, and it is not a crime to discharge with permission or as authorised by the Acts. Whether or not a discharge is criminal, the riparian and fishery owners' right to clean water remains the same, and they may seek a remedy to restrain pollution even if the discharge is permitted by the Acts.[2]

The moral for riparian and fishery owners is to seek an injunction to restrain polluters even where there is no evidence of injury to fish life. Once an injunction has been obtained, no right to pollute by long-continued pollution could be obtained even if the discharge is permitted under the Acts. This was the practice before the Rivers Pollution Prevention Act, 1876, made it virtually impossible to acquire a prescriptive right to pollute.

Strict Liability for Escaping Matter

Another powerful rule of the common law which has not been relied on as much as it might have been to stop pollution of watercourses, is known as "The rule in *Rylands* v. *Fletcher*", or, as the older generation prefer it, more accurately, "The rule in *Fletcher* v. *Rylands*".[3] This is a rule of strict liability where anyone accumulates something on his land and allows it to escape to the detriment of others. By strict liability, is meant that hardly any excuse will exonerate the occupier who allows this to happen. The rule is in fact much older than the famous case of *Rylands* v. *Fletcher*. One hundred and sixty three years earlier Chief Justice Holt pithily expressed the rule thus:

"He whose filth it is must keep it in."[4]

Mr Justice Blackburn's statement of the rule was approved by the House of Lords in *Rylands* v. *Fletcher*, and remains enshrined as a crystal clear statement of the law:

" ... The true rule of law is, that the person who for his own purposes brings on his land and collects and keeps there anything likely to do mischief if it escapes, must keep it in at his peril, and, if he does not do so, is *prima facie* answerable for all the damage which is the natural consequence of its escape."

---

[1] Rivers (Prevention of Pollution) Act, 1961, s. 4.
[2] But see p.135 above, the Machievellion threat to change this.
[3] *Fletcher* v. *Rylands* (1866) L.R. 1 Ex. 265 in which the rule was stated became *Rylands* v. *Fletcher* on appeal to the House of Lords (1868) L.R. 3 H.L. 330.
[4] *Tenant* v. *Goldwin* (1703) Lord Raym. 1089.

The only excuses open to the occupier to avoid a claim, are:

(1) That the escape was due to the claimant's own fault; or

(2) That it was caused by an "Act of God" or other happening which is so unusual nobody could reasonably be expected to anticipate it — such as an earthquake; or

(3) That it was caused by a stranger over whom the occupier had no control.

The rule does not apply to a *natural use* of the land but only where something special is done which could be potentially harmful to others. As discharging effluent is not a natural use of land, it is unnecessary to discuss here this rather vague distinction in the rule.

Statutory authority. A polluter escapes liability under this rule if he has *statutory authority* for it, unless it is clear from the statute that he is not to be exonerated.[1] It should be noted, however, that the rule of strict liability makes the offender responsible for the damage whether or not the escape was due to his negligence. Where negligence can be proved, there is no need for the injured party to rely on the rule, and statutory authority is no defence.

Local authority sewage. The rule applies to discharges of sewage into watercourses, and local authorities are not exempt. As Mr Justice Vaisey said of the rule, in the case of *Haigh* v. *Deudraeth R.D.C.*[2] in which he restrained the R.D.C. from discharging crude sewage into a stream:

" . . . It lays down a familiar principle which has an almost universal application to cases in which anything deleterious is allowed to escape from the land of one onto the land of another."

Dumping toxic waste. The Deposit of Poisonous Waste Act, 1972, makes the dumping of toxic industrial waste a wrong "of absolute liability" — unless it accords with the Act.

Tidal Waters. The common law rule entitling the riparian owner to receive the water in its natural state unpolluted by others, applies equally to tidal rivers as to other streams.[3] Likewise the owner of a fishery can obtain an injunction to restrain pollution of tidal rivers or estuaries, if the pollution impedes or prevents the passage of migratory fish to and from the sea.[4]

Lakes, Ponds and Artificial Watercourses. Wherever there is an entitlement to riparian rights to water on or adjacent to property, the landowner can restrain pollution of the water. As appears in Chapter 13, riparian rights are enjoyed in respect of lakes and ponds, and this will also be so in the case of artificial watercourses if they have been constructed and

---

[1] *Smeaton* v. *Ilford Corpn.* [1954] 1 All E.R. 923.
[2] [1945] 2 All E.R. 661.
[3] *Lyon* v. *Fishmongers' Co.* (1876) 1 A.C. 677.
[4] *Myddleton* v. *John Summers & Sons Ltd* (1953) C.P.L. 719 (note), now fully reporte in *Water Pollution* by Newsom and Sherratt (John Sherratt Ltd).

used in such a way that owners of land abutting on them can be taken to have riparian rights.[1] The owner of the lake or pond or of a fishery in any such water has a remedy against polluters.

The Rivers (Prevention of Pollution) Acts, 1951 and 1961, do not apply to lakes and ponds which have no outfall into a stream.[2] The river authority therefore cannot act in these cases, but the owner of the land or the fishery can.

Likewise the owner of a canal, and any person owning fishing rights in a canal, has a remedy at common law against polluters.

Remedies at Common Law

The proper remedy for a riparian owner whose rights are injured by pollution is a permanent injunction, provided the pollution is not too trifling or temporary a nuisance. The claimant is also entitled to damages if he has suffered loss.

Damages. The amount of damages to be awarded to a person whose rights are injured by pollution is a sum equivalent to the actual loss suffered as the natural result of it.[3] The claim must not be stretched too far to include expense that is remote from the wrongful act of the polluter, but the depreciation in value of the fishing is to be assessed as best it can be, and other expenses necessarily incurred because of the pollution may also be recovered. Damages will not usually be awarded for loss of amenities as such[4], but in some cases this may be taken into account indirectly in assessing the loss in value of riparian or fishing rights.

Injunction. An injunction is a court order restraining a person or body from doing something. Disobeying the order is contempt of court for which the court may commit the offender to prison. The court may keep the offender in prison until he has "purged his contempt" which usually means until the judge is satisfied that he will obey the court order with no nonsense.

In an urgent case, the court will grant an interlocutory injunction before the hearing of the action providing proceedings have been started (e.g. a writ issued). This will be done (without prejudice to the ultimate decision in the case) if the court thinks it would be unduly harmful to allow the pollution to continue while the parties are waiting for the case to come to court. This was done by Mr Justice Buckley in *Swansea Corporation* v. *Redcliffe Holiday Properties (Caswell Bay) Ltd*[5], where he granted an interlocutory injunction restraining the defendants from discharging sewage onto the foreshore (except when the outfall was covered at high tide) in the interests of holidaymakers on the beach.

---

[1] *Sutcliffe* v. *Booth* (1863) 27 J.P. 613.
[2] Rivers (Prevention of Pollution) Act, 1951, s. 11(1).
[3] *Marquis of Granby* v. *Bakewell U.D.C.* (1923) 87 J.P. 105.
[4] *Earl of Harrington* v. *Derby Corpn.* [1905] 1 Ch. 205.
[5] *The Times*, April 29, 1966.

An interlocutory injunction is, however, unusual in pollution cases, but the court's ultimate order will normally be a permanent injunction, plus damages if the pollution is proved. An injunction may be refused if the court is satisfied that the pollution was temporary and will not occur again, and will be refused if damages is a sufficient remedy.[1] But damages are rarely a sufficient remedy in pollution cases.

Local Authority Sewage. As a local authority has a legal obligation to sewer its area under the Public Health Act, 1936, the court in granting an injunction to restrain them from polluting watercourses with sewage normally suspends the operation of the injunction for a stated period to give time for the alteration of the sewage works in order to comply with the court order. The injunction will, however, immediately restrain any new discharges. As we have seen above (p.141) local authorities are not exempt from the obligation to refrain from injuring the riparian and fishing rights of others, and s. 30 of the Public Health Act, 1936, provides as follows:

"30. Nothing in this Part of this Act[2] shall authorise a local authority to construct or use any public or other sewer, or any drain or outfall, for the purpose of conveying foul water into any natural or artificial stream, watercourse, canal, pond or lake, until the water has been so treated as not to affect prejudicially the purity and quality of the water in the stream, watercourse, canal, pond or lake."

It is not enough for the local authority after an injunction to attempt to purify the effluent and fail. If they are unable to make the effluent innocuous, they must stop discharging it into the watercourse.[3]

It has been held[4] that where a local authority was restrained by injunction from polluting a river with sewage, the injunction did not extend to restrain another authority which later took over its public health functions.

An injunction will be granted to restrain a local authority from discharging sewage into the sea, if fish are killed or oyster beds harmed.[5]

Injunction Will Be Granted However Onerous. The court will not withhold an injunction on the ground that compliance with it will be costly or inconvenient for the polluter. Once a person has established his right to have the pollution restrained, the court will make the order whatever the consequences of inconvenience or expense to the polluter. It will only be withheld if compliance would be impossible. The court may postpone the operation of the injunction for a stated period to give the defendant an

---

[1] For example, in *Chapman, Marsons & Co.* v. *Auckland Union* (1889) 23 Q.B.D. 294 damages only were awarded.
[2] I.e. the Part dealing with sewerage and sanitation.
[3] *Spokes* v. *Banbury* (1865) 13 L.T. 428.
[4] *Att.-Gen.* v. *Birmingham Corpn.* (1880) 15 Ch. D. 423.
[5] *Foster* v. *Warblington U.D.C.* [1906] 1 K.B. 648.

opportunity to change his ways, but the injunction will be made immediately.[1] Where the order is suspended in this way, the court usually gives both sides liberty to apply to have the period varied on shewing good cause.[2]

Injunction Against Threatened Pollution. A man does not have to wait until the nuisance starts before seeking protection from the courts. If he can show that it is coming, the court will restrain the threatened pollution. However, the court will not lightly make an injunction in advance, but only where a real danger of injury to rights is proved.[3]

Delay. Acquiescence in the pollution may prevent the riparian or fishery owner from obtaining an injunction[4], so that it is as well to take action as soon as the pollution is detected. Delay in taking proceedings does not necessarily imply acquiescence. People are expected to try to settle their disputes without recourse to law if possible, unless an urgent remedy is needed. The fact that pollution has been "put up with" after the local authority has given an assurance that it was being rectified, does not bar the injured party from seeking an injunction.[5] Furthermore, as it is in the national interest, as well as the angler's, that rivers should not be fouled, the courts are unlikely to refuse injunctions on the ground of delay, except in the clearest cases of acceptance by the riparian owners.

Discharge of Injunction. An injunction against pollution is usually perpetual, and because the courts will grant perpetual injunctions to riparian owners, even without proof of loss, there is hope that our dirty rivers will eventually be cleaned up. The court can, however, discharge a perpetual injunction, if the circumstances in which it was granted have materially changed.[6]

Who May Take Proceedings

As we have seen in Chapter 12 fishing rights are a legal property, so that any person who owns them may take proceedings against any person or body who interferes with these rights. Pollution is an interference with fishing rights if it does harm, and most of the points of law that arise in connection with a claim by the fishery owner against polluters have been dealt with in considering the *Ely Beet Sugar Factory* cases at pp.78–79.

Owners and Tenants. The following may therefore sue polluters: the owner of fishing rights, the tenant of fishing rights, the owner of the river bed, the tenant of the river bed, the owner of riparian land and the tenant of riparian land. *Mason* v. *Clarke*[7] (discussed on p.76) shews that the holder of

---

[1] *Att.-Gen.* v. *Colney Hatch Lunatic Asylum* (1868) 4 Ch. App. 146.
[2] See *Pride of Derby Angling Assn.* v. *British Celanese Ltd* [1953] 1 All E.R. 179.
[3] *Att.-Gen.* v. *Kingston-on-Thames Corpn.* (1865) 12 L.T. 665.
[4] *Wood* v. *Sutcliffe* (1851) 27 L.J. Ch. 253.
[5] *Att.-Gen.* v. *Birmingham Corpn.* (1858) 4 K. & J. 528.
[6] *Att.-Gen.* v. *Birmingham Drainage Board* [1912] A.C. 788.
[7] [1955] A.C. 778.

incorporeal fishing rights (that is rights not connected with the ownership of land) may take proceedings if the rights were granted by deed, and also if they were not granted by deed provided there has been "part performance" (see p.76).

A mere licensee (see p.88), having no property rights at law, cannot take proceedings against pollution.[1]

Riparian Owner in Stronger Position. The riparian owner, or tenant, is in the most powerful position to beat pollution, because he can obtain an injunction against a polluter without proving loss, and in cases of multiple pollution can tackle each polluter without having to prove that each discharge by itself would be damaging. Any significant degree of pollution enables the riparian owner to ask the Court for protection.

The owner or tenant of fishing rights who does not own riparian land can only claim an injunction and damages upon proof that the pollution is damaging the fishery or his use and enjoyment of it. If pollution in the river prevents the passage of migratory fish to and from the sea, the owner of a fishery in the river may take proceedings, because this inevitably injures his interest in the fishery.

The moral for angling clubs is to obtain, if possible, at least some land, however little, abutting on the rivers in which they have fishing rights. It is also desirable in leases of fishing from riparian owners to obtain, if possible, a covenant from the owner to join in any proceedings that may be taken by the club against polluters. If the club can give the owner an indemnity against his costs (which clubs belonging to the Anglers' Co-operative Association usually can) there is every incentive for him to give such a covenant. An example can be seen in the model fishing lease in Appendix B.

The Attorney-General. As we have seen above (p.136), where pollution amounts to a public nuisance, the Attorney-General acting on behalf of the public may prosecute the offender under the criminal law. He may also take civil proceedings on behalf of the public either on his own motion, or at the instance of a person or corporation (called a relator) who complains to him. If the offender is found guilty on a prosecution, he may be punished. If civil proceedings are taken the Attorney-General may obtain an injunction, and in a relator action damages as well.

When pollution is a public nuisance, any person whose rights are specially affected by it beyond the general detriment to the public, may take civil proceedings without the Attorney-General. A riparian or private fishery owner could therefore take proceedings, but not a member of the public without such particular rights.

Statutory Powers to Control Pollution

Statutory powers to control pollution of rivers and estuaries are given by four main Acts — the Salmon and Freshwater Fisheries Act, 1923

---

[1] *Whaley* v. *Laing* (1857) 2 H. & N. 476.

(amended by the 1965 Act); the Rivers (Prevention of Pollution) Acts, 1951 and 1961, and the Clean Rivers (Estuaries and Tidal Waters) Act, 1960. There are also a number of miscellaneous Acts dealing with particular types of pollution, referred to at the end of this chapter.

The power to control pollution under the main Acts is primarily in the hands of the river authorities.

The statutory control of effluents entering sewers[1] is not dealt with in this book, but it may be noted that no Act deprives fishing interests of their common law remedies. The discharger is liable for his trade effluent polluting a fishery even if it reaches the fishery through the sewers under a statutory consent.[2]

Protection of Fisheries. Section 8 of the Salmon and Freshwater Fisheries Act, 1923, makes it an offence for any person or body to:

> "Cause or knowingly permit to flow, or put or knowingly permit to be put, into any waters containing fish, or into any tributaries thereof, any liquid or solid matter to such an extent as to cause the waters to be poisonous or injurious to fish or the spawning grounds, spawn or food of fish."

This is a good start but the qualifications which follow have effectively blunted its teeth in practice. These are:

(1) A person shall not be penalised for doing any act in the exercise of a legal right, or for continuing a method of pollution in use in connection with the same premises before 1924, provided the Court is satisfied he has used the best practical means, within a reasonable cost, to prevent the matter from doing injury to fish or to the spawning grounds, spawn or food of fish.[3]

(2) The Act does not prevent anyone from acquiring a legal right in cases where he would have acquired it had the Act not been passed.[4]

The Salmon and Freshwater Fisheries Act, 1965, now adds a further qualification:[5]

(3) It is not an offence to use any substance in any waters for a scientific purpose, or for the purpose of protecting, improving or replacing stocks of fish, with the permission of the appropriate authority. Permission may only be given with the approval of the Minister.

---

[1] Public Health Acts 1936 to 1961.
[2] See Public Health (Drainage of Trade Premises) Act, 1937, s. 13. But see also the Machiavellian threat noted on p.135 above.
[3] Salmon and Freshwater Fisheries Act, 1923, s. 8(1)(*a*).
[4] *Ibid.*, s. 8(1)(*b*).
[5] See the new s. 9(5) of the 1923 Act, provided by s. 1 of the 1965 Act.

(4) No offence is committed under s. 8 of the 1923 Act if consent is given to the discharge under the Rivers (Prevention of Pollution) Acts, 1951 and 1961[1], which are dealt with below.

(5) On the other side of the picture the 1923 Act makes the proviso that the Act does not exempt anybody from any penalty to which he might otherwise be liable, nor does it make lawful any act or default which would but for the Act be a nuisance or otherwise contrary to law.[2]

Proceedings can only be taken by the river authority or a person who has first obtained a certificate from the Minister that "he has a material interest in the waters alleged to be affected".[3]

In practice the following considerations have made it difficult to obtain convictions for this offence:

(*a*) Accidental pollution is no offence under s. 8. Where creosote leaked into a watercourse from a railway truck, through nobody's negligence, it was held in *Moses* v. *Midland Railway*[4] that it had not been "caused to flow".

(*b*) No conviction can be obtained unless it can be proved that the water contained fish, and the defendant's pollution alone was injurious to the fish or spawn etc. This virtually rules out proceedings where there is multiple pollution, or where fish life has previously been blotted out by pollution.

(*c*) The defendant is not penalised where he has done his best at reasonable cost to eliminate pollution, but failed.

The 1972 Act has increased the previously ineffective penalties. The maximum on indictment is now a fine (no limit) or two years imprisonment, or both.[5]

Byelaws. The 1923 Act empowers river authorities to make byelaws regulating the deposit or discharge in any waters containing fish of any specified liquid or solid matter detrimental to fish, or the spawn or food of fish. Byelaws may not, however, prejudice any statutory powers of a sanitary or local authority to discharge sewage.[6]

Protection of Rivers

Abbreviations. The Rivers (Prevention of Pollution) Acts, 1951 and 1961, and the Clean Rivers (Estuaries and Tidal Waters) Act, 1960, are called

---

[1] Rivers (Prevention of Pollution) Act, 1961, s. 4(1).
[2] S. 8(1)(*b*). This prevents a prescriptive right accruing, see above p.139.
[3] 1923 Act, s. 8(3).
[4] (1915) 84 L.J.K.B. 2181, but cf. *Alphacell* v. *Woodward* [1972] 2 All E.R. 475 – see p.148 below.
[5] Salmon and Freshwater Fisheries Act, 1972, Sched. 2.
[6] Salmon and Freshwater Fisheries Act, 1923, s. 59(1)(*p*).

hereafter "the 1951 Act", "the 1961 Act" and "the 1960 Act", for short. The Minister concerned with these Acts is not the Minister of Agriculture but the Secretary of State for the Environment.

Preventing the pollution of streams. An offence is committed under the 1951 Act if a person (1) causes or knowingly permits to enter a stream any poisonous, noxious or polluting matter; or (2) causes or knowingly permits to enter a stream any matter so as to tend directly or in combination with similar acts (whether his own or another's) to impede the proper flow of the water of the stream in a manner leading or likely to lead to a substantial aggravation of pollution due to other causes or its consequences.[1]

"Causes." A person may be guilty of "causing" pollution even if there was no intention to do so and no negligence. Where, through nobody's negligence, leaves blocked the intake of a pump causing effluent to overflow a tank and enter a river, the owner of the premises was held to have "caused" the pollution.[2] But a person does not "cause" it, if it is due to the action of another unauthorised person, or an Act of God — such as where a trespasser at night opened the valve of a riverside fuel storage tank.[3]

The meaning of *"stream"* is given on p.151 below.

The penalty. The maximum penalty for any of these offences is a fine of £200, but if the offence is a repetition or continuation of an earlier offence for which the accused has previously been found guilty, he may be sent to prison for up to six months, or fined £50 for every day the earlier offence has continued up to a maximum of £500, or both.[4]

Effluent Discharged Through Sewers. Where poisonous, noxious or polluting matter passes into a stream from a sewer or sewage disposal works vested in a local authority, the local authority is deemed to be responsible, and not the person who discharges it into the sewer, provided the local authority was bound to receive the effluent, or consented to do so.[5]

Since June 1st, 1963, a penalty can no longer be avoided for discharging effluent from a local authority sewage works, or trade effluent into a stream, by shewing that no reasonable alternative was available and all reasonable steps had been taken to prevent unnecessary pollution.[6]

Discharges from Mines. The offences created by the 1951 Act are not committed where water from an underground mine is, without changing its condition, discharged into a stream — though the Secretary of State may lift this exemption for specified streams.[7] Nor is the offence committed if the solid refuse of a mine or quarry is deposited, with the consent of the river authority, on any land so that it falls or is carried into a stream, if no other site is reasonably practicable, and all reasonable steps are taken to prevent the

---

[1] 1951 Act, s. 2(1).
[2] *Alphacell* v. *Woodward* [1972] 2 All E.R. 475 (H.L.).
[3] *Impress (Worcester)* v. *Rees* [1971] 2 All E.R. 357 (D.C.).
[4] 1951 Act, s. 2(7).
[5] 1951 Act, s. 2(1).
[6] 1961 Act, s. 1, and S.I. 1963 No. 320.
[7] 1951 Act, s. 2(4).

refuse entering the stream. The river authority may not unreasonably withhold consent, and the Secretary of State decides any dispute about it.[1]

Application to County Court Before Pollution. If a river authority "apprehends" that an offence under the 1951 Act is likely to occur, it may apply to the County Court, and the court may prohibit the use or proposed use of a stream, land or vessel which causes the concern, or may lay down terms for using it which are designed to remove the cause of complaint.[2]

Cleansing River Bed and Cutting Vegetation. It is an offence if, without the consent of the river authority, any person (1) cleanses the channel or bed of a stream from a deposit accumulated by a dam, weir or sluice, and causes it to be carried away in suspension in the water; or (2) by his "wilful default" allows a substantial amount of cut or uprooted vegetation to remain in the stream. This does not apply to anyone exercising statutory land drainage, flood prevention or navigation powers. Where it does apply consent must not be unreasonably withheld. The penalty on conviction of the offence is a fine not exceeding £50.[3]

Byelaws. A river authority may make byelaws prohibiting or regulating (a) the washing or cleansing in a stream of anything of any description, or putting into a stream litter or other objectionable matter; or (b) the keeping or use on a stream of vessels provided with sanitary appliances from which polluting matter can pass into the stream.

In making byelaws the river authority must have regard to the character and flow of the stream, and the extent to which it is, or may in the future be, used for industrial purposes, fisheries, water supply, agriculture, transport or navigation.[4] The river authority must also first give reasonable notice of their intention to make byelaws:

> "To any body or persons designated to them for this purpose by the Minister as being representative of a class of persons having a material interest in the waters of the stream or of a part of it to which the byelaws are to relate."[5]

Some angling associations have been designated by the Minister in certain river authority areas. The procedure for making byelaws is now laid down in the Water Resources Act, 1963.[6]

Statutory Control of Effluent Disposal by Consents

Consents. The Rivers (Prevention of Pollution) Act, 1951, forbids the bringing into use of any new or altered outlet for the discharge of trade or

---

[1] 1951 Act, s. 2(5) and (6).
[2] *Ibid.*, s. 3.
[3] *Ibid.*, s. 4.
[4] *Ibid.*, s. 5(1).
[5] *Ibid.*, s. 5(6).
[6] Water Resources Act, 1963, s. 119 and Sched. 12.

sewage effluent to a stream, or to make a new discharge to a stream, without the consent of the river authority.[1] "New or altered" outlet means one wholly or partly constructed or substantially altered after October 1st, 1951.[2]

In the "excluded areas" outside river authority areas, the Thames Conservators, the Lea Conservancy or the Council of a London borough, as the case may be, is responsible for control and consents. References to a river authority in this part of this chapter are therefore to be taken as including these other authorities.

New Outlets and Discharges. Consent is not needed under the 1951 Act for a new or altered outlet for a sewage works of a local authority if ministerial approval has been given to the construction or alteration, or the raising of a loan to defray the cost[3], nor does the consent control of either the 1951 or 1961 Acts apply to discharges from a ship or vessel.[4] This is a wide gap in the river authority's armoury.

Conditions attached to consents. The river authority may attach reasonable conditions to any consent it grants, regarding:

    (*a*) The point of discharge into the stream;

    (*b*) The construction of the outlet;

    (*c*) The use of the outlet or any other outlet for effluent from the same land;

    (*d*) (For new discharges only) the nature, composition, temperature, volume or rate of discharge of effluent.[5]

The river authority must also see that it can taken samples of the effluent.[6]

Contraventions. Failure to obtain a necessary consent, or to comply with conditions attached to a consent, is an offence (maximum fine £200).[7] Where a new or altered outlet is brought into use, or a new discharge made, of trade or sewage effluent, without consent, the river authority may serve a notice on the persons concerned imposing any conditions it might have attached to a consent had an application for consent been made.[8]

What is "trade or sewage effluent"? River authority control by consents only applies to discharges of trade of sewage effluents into streams. The 1951 Act defines these effluents (to·some extent) as follows:[9]

---

[1] Rivers (Prevention of Pollution) Act, 1951, s. 7.
[2] *Ibid.,* s. 7(8). The 1961 Act now provides a like control for pre-October 1951 discharges.
[3] *Ibid.,* s. 7(9).
[4] 1961 Act, s. 13(3).
[5] 1951 Act, s. 7(2).
[6] *Ibid.,* s. 7(3).
[7] *Ibid.,* s. 7(13) amended by 1961 Act, s. 7(1).
[8] 1951 Act, s. 7(4).
[9] *Ibid.,* s. 11(1).

Trade effluent: " 'trade effluent' includes any liquid (either with or without particles in suspension herein) which is discharged from premises used for carrying on any trade or industry, other than surface water or domestic sewage, and for the purposes of this definition any land or premises wholly or mainly used (whether for profit or not) for agricultural or horticultural purposes or for scientific research or experiment shall be deemed to be premises used for carrying on a trade or industry."

Sewage effluent: " 'sewage effluent' includes any effluent from the sewage disposal or sewerage works of a local authority."

What is a "stream"? The definition of "stream" in the 1951 Act is important, because river authority consents are only required where the discharge is to a stream. The 1951 Act says:[1]

" 'stream' includes any river, stream, watercourse or inland water (whether natural or artificial) except that it does not include either:
(*a*) Any lake or pond which does not discharge to a stream; or
(*b*) Any sewer vested in a local authority;
or (save as otherwise provided by this Act) any tidal waters, but reference to a stream includes a reference to the channel or bed of a stream which is for the time being dry."

Tidal Waters. Although tidal waters are excluded from the definition of "stream" in the 1951 Act, certain tidal waters (in the "excluded areas", of the Thames, Lee and Metropolis) are included[2], and special rules are made for discharges of trade or sewage effluent into tidal waters in the 1951 Act. At least three months' notice must be given before bringing into use a new or altered outlet, or making a new discharge to any tidal waters or part of the sea included in a river authority's area for the purpose of the authority's fishery functions. New or altered outlets must comply with reasonable conditions imposed by the river authority to enable it to take samples. Failure to comply with these rules is an offence.[3]

In addition the Clean Rivers (Estuaries and Tidal Waters) Act, 1960, extends the rules about river authority consents for discharges (dealt with above) to the tidal waters and parts of the sea specified in the Act as "controlled waters". Ninety-five controlled waters are specified in the schedule to the Act. The Secretary of State may also make orders applying the 1951 and 1961 Acts to any tidal waters or parts of the sea, and in such areas river authority consents are required before effluent may be discharged.

In exercising its control the river authority must pay special regard to the interests of sea fisheries and the nature of the tidal action in diluting and

---

[1] *Ibid.*, s. 11(1).
[2] *Ibid.*, Sch. 2 para. 5(1).
[3] *Ibid.*, s. 7(16). These rules do not apply to "controlled waters" under the Clean Rivers (Estuaries and Tidal Waters) Act, 1960.

dispersing effluent.[1]

Pre-1951 Discharges

Since June 1st, 1963, it has been illegal to continue discharges of trade or sewage effluent to a stream without the river authority's consent, even if the discharge began before October 1st, 1951.[2] It is not illegal, however, to continue the discharge without consent pending the river authority's decision, if application for consent was made before June 1st, 1963. Similar rules about conditions and contraventions apply as for new outlets and discharges.

Tidal waters. Consent control by river authorities of pre-1951 discharges applies to those tidal waters which are subject to a ministerial order under s. 6 of the 1951 Act, but not to "controlled waters" specified in the Clean Rivers (Estuaries and Tidal Waters) Act, 1960.[3]

All Discharges

Appeals. River authorities must not withhold consent to discharges unreasonably, and must not impose unreasonable conditions. Aggrieved persons can appeal within three months of the river authority's decision, to the Secretary of State for the Environment.[4]

Protective effects of consents. A river authority consent to discharging effluent into watercourses may amount to an official licence to pollute, provided the consent and conditions are adhered to. If they are adhered to the discharge can be no pollution offence under any of the following laws:

(*a*) The Rivers (Prevention of Pollution) Act, 1951, s. 2(1) (p.147 above); or

(*b*) An order of the County Court made under the 1951 Act, s. 3 (see p.149 above); or

(*c*) The Salmon and Freshwater Fisheries Act, 1923, s. 8 (see p.146 above); or

(*d*) Any byelaw under the Sea Fisheries Regulation Act, 1966, (see Chapter 6); or

(*e*) The provisions against gas pollution in the Gas Act, 1972, and Public Health Act, 1875 (see p.154 below).

Official consent, however, as we have seen above, is no protection against an action for an injunction taken by riparian owners of fishing owners.[5]

---

[1] 1961 Act, s. 9(4).
[2] *Ibid.*, s. 1.
[3] *Ibid.*, s. 9.
[4] *Ibid.*, s. 6.
[5] But see Machiavellian threat noted on p.135 above.

Conditions attached to consents must be reviewed from time to time, and the Secretary of State for the Environment can require the river authority to vary or revoke conditions.[1]

Sampling and Analysing Effluents. The river authority is entitled to take away and analyse samples of any effluent passing from any land or vessel into any inland water in its area, or parts of the sea or "controlled waters" adjoining it area, and in granting consents to discharges can impose reasonable conditions to enable samples to be taken.

An analysis of an effluent sample is not, however, admissible in evidence in any legal proceedings unless the person taking the sample forthwith notifies the occupier of the land or master of the vessel from which the effluent came that he intends to have it analysed, and there and then divides the sample into three parts, seals up each part in a marked container and delivers one to the occupier, retains one for future comparison, and submits the third to an analyst if he thinks fit.[2] This does not apply to river samples — only effluent samples. An analysis includes "any test of whatever kind".[3]

The river authority may agree with the occupier on the point or points from which samples of the effluent are to be taken, and if agreement cannot be reached the Secretary of State for the Environment decides the issue. In legal proceedings it is to be presumed, until the contrary can be shown, that a sample taken at these sampling points, or at an inspection chamber or manhole, is a sample of what was passing from the land or premises into the waters.[4]

Any person who wilfully obstructs a river authority taking samples commits an offence and is liable to a fine not exceeding £20.[5]

Information to be Kept Confidential. The 1961 Act makes it an offence to disclose information obtained in connection with river authorities exercising their consent control under the 1951 and 1961 Acts, including the taking of samples of effluent, but not samples of water into which it is discharged.[6] No offence is committed, however, if the information obtained by the river authority is disclosed with the consent of the person giving the information, or, in the case of a sample, by the person making the discharge. Nor is the offence committed if the disclosure is made in connection with the execution of the Acts, or proceedings under the Acts.

The river authority is entitled to give reasonable directions to anyone discharging effluents, requiring him to give such information as the authority wants.[7]

---

[1] 1961 Act, s. 5.

[2] Water Resources Act, 1963, s. 113.

[3] *Ibid.*, s. 113(6), overruling *Trent River Board* v. *Wardle Ltd* (*The Times*, January 18, 1957) to some extent. Full judgments in *Water Pollution* by Newsom and Sherratt (John Sherratt & Son).

[4] 1961 Act, s. 10.

[5] Water Resources Act, 1963, s. 113(5).

[6] 1961 Act, s. 12.

[7] Water Resources Act, 1963, s. 114.

Proposed changes. At the time of writing, the Government are proposing to remove much of this confidentiality and to impose stronger duties on the authorities responsible for pollution control. Under their proposals the public will have access to analyses of effluents and waters, and also to registers of consents to discharge effluents. Applications for consents will be published and comments by objectors considered. Riparian owners damaged by a discharge may apply for a consent to be revoked or varied after a year, and the consent may be revoked or varied within two years. If discharges made without consent cause damage, the proposed regional water authorities will have power to remedy the damage and recover the cost of the work from the offender. The regional water authorities will have a duty to remedy damage done by their own discharges or by discharges to which they have consented.

These proposals would mitigate to some degree the retrograde step of abolishing common law rights (see above p.135), but they have the fatal flaw that once pollution has killed off all life in a watercourse no damage can be proved from further discharges, however filthy.

Miscellaneous Pollution Laws. In addition to the statutory provisions dealt with above, a number of statutes make it an offence to cause certain particular kinds of pollution. Examples of these with the statutes concerned are briefly as follows:

The British Gas Corporation and manufacturers of gas must not pollute waters with gas or gas waste (Gas Act, 1972, and Public Health Act, 1875);

Oil must not be discharged from a ship into navigable waters (Oil in Navigable Waters Act, 1955);

The Radioactive Substances Act, 1960, controls disposal of radioactive waste;

Harbours Acts of 1814 and 1847[1] forbid the dumping of ballast, stone, earth, wreck, filth and other kinds of litter into harbours;

Diseased carcases of animals must not be thrown into inland waters or in the sea within three miles of the shore (Diseases of Animals Act, 1950);

Alkali waste must be safely disposed of without causing a nuisance (Alkali etc. Works Regulation Act, 1906);

Offensive matter from cemeteries must not be allowed to enter any stream, canal, reservoir, aqueduct, pond or watering place (Cemeteries Clauses Act, 1847).

By s. 38 of the Countryside Act, 1968, the Countryside Commission,

---
[1] Harbours, Docks and Piers Clauses Act, 1847.

Forestry Commission and local authorities in exercising functions under the Act must have due regard to protecting from pollution the water sources of water undertakers.

Protecting Waters and Removing Polluting Matter. Statutory water undertakers are given power to acquire land and carry out works to protect water supplies from pollution[1], and river authorities are given like powers.[2] Where polluting matter gets into waters in its area due to an accident or other unforeseen happening, the river authority is empowered to do anything it considers necessary to remove and dispose of the polluting matter, and to remedy or mitigate the pollution.[3]

---

[1]Water Act, 1945, s. 22.
[2]Water Resources Act, 1963, s. 68.
[3]*Ibid.*, s. 76.

CHAPTER 21

WATER ABSTRACTION

An adequate flow of water is essential to a river fishery in order to maintain the life and health of fish and their food, and to dilute and carry away polluting matter that enters the river. A good run of water is also important on the more general grounds of public health and amenity. One of the great dangers to angling at the present time is the massive extraction of water from rivers for water supplies, industry and irrigation at times when it cannot be spared. Not all large or multiple abstractions are harmful to fishing, of course, and in many cases sufficient water is returned in good quality to prevent injury to the watercourse – but the abstractions from certain waters have been mortal. The Water Resources Act, 1963, imposes upon river authorities a water conservation duty and powers to control abstraction. In exercising certain of their duties the river authorities have a statutory admonition to pay due regard to the interests of anglers.

Common Law Rights to Water. Nobody owns the water flowing in a river. Riparian owners, however, have rights to take and use the water (see Chapter 15) and also are entitled to have the water flowing through or past their land undiminished in quantity or quality so long as it is consistent with the legitimate rights of other riparian owners.

At common law the riparian owner's right to abstract water from watercourses is therefore qualified. He is entitled to take it for his domestic purposes and for his livestock, even if in so doing he deprives lower riparian owners of sufficient water for these purposes. The lower riparian owners have no redress in this case, but if they are prejudiced by an upper riparian owner abstracting water for other purposes (and not returning it in sufficient quantity and quality), they can claim damages and an injunction.[1] In *Rugby Joint Water Board* v. *Walters*[2] an injunction was made to restrain spray irrigation, which was held not to be a riparian right.

Statutory Control of Abstractions

Licensing abstractions. The Water Resources Act, 1963, controls water abstraction, by prohibiting the abstraction of water from a source of supply "in a river authority area" "except in pursuance of a licence under this Act

---

[1] *Chasemore* v. *Richards* (1859) 7 H.L. Cas. 349 – but see the protective effect of statutory licences noted below, p.158.
[2] [1966] 3 All E.R. 497.

granted by the river authority and in accordance with the provisions of that licence".[1] In certain circumstances no licence is required, in others a licence could not be refused provided an application for the licence was made before June 30, 1965, and in the remaining cases the grant of a licence is at the discretion of the river authority.

A licence of right was obtainable if the applicant had abstracted water for spray irrigation in the five years before July 31, 1963, or for other purposes in the five years before April 1, 1965. He is entitled to a licence for the same amount of water as he was taking in the five-year period, or, if he abstracted under a statutory authorisation (e.g. an order under the Water Act, 1945) for the quantity he could take under the authorisation.[2]

What is a "source of supply"? The meaning given by the Water Resources Act, 1963, to "source of supply" can be found from the combined effect of its elaborate definitions of this term and "inland water".[3] In short it means all or any part of a river, stream, or watercourse (whether natural or artificial, or tidal or non-tidal), or of a lake, pond, reservoir or dock, within any river authority area, and so much of any channel, creek, bay, estuary or arm of the sea as falls within a river authority area. It also includes any underground strata in the area. But a lake, pond or reservoir which does not discharge into any other inland water, or a group of these only discharging into each other, are not a source of supply.

Applications for Abstraction Licences (and Objections). Licences of right can no longer be applied for, and so the granting of all new licences is now in the discretion of the river authority and must be applied for under the procedure laid down in the Water Resources Act, 1963. A notice of the application has to be published in two successive weeks in at least one local newspaper, and notice must also be sent to certain authorities. The public notice must state where a copy of the application, with its maps and plans etc., can be inspected. The public must be allowed to inspect them free of charge at any reasonable hour during a period of at least twenty-eight days, and the notice must state:

"that any person may make representations in writing to the river authority with respect to the application at any time before the end of that period."[4]

The river authority must not determine the application until the twenty-eight days are up[4], and before making a decision must "have regard to" any representations made to them before the end of that period, and also to the reasonable requirements of the applicant.[5]

---

[1] Water Resources Act, 1963, s. 23(1).
[2] *Ibid.*, ss. 33–35.
[3] *Ibid.*, s. 135(1) and s. 2.
[4] *Ibid.*, s. 28.
[5] *Ibid.*, s. 29.

Committees of angling clubs are advised to ensure that all applications for licences which might affect their waters are examined in good time, so that representations can be made to the river authority if necessary to protect the fishing. An angling club might oppose the granting of a licence altogether — e.g. on the ground that the river flow was already too low, or that pollution would be brought to a deadly level by abstraction — or, for instance, might make representations about the quantity of water applied for, or the need to have the water returned to the river in good quality and quantity, or about alternative sources of supply, or about periods when abstraction should be prohibited or reduced.

The Licence. If an abstraction licence is granted, it must specify, among other things, how much water can be taken and when and how; where it is to be used, and for what purpose; and whether the licence may authorise the abstraction of different amounts at different periods, or at different points, or for different purposes.[1]

The Protective Effect of the Licence. It is important for angling interests to ensure as far as they can that abstractions are not authorised to an extent or in a manner which prejudices the fishing, because the Water Resources Act, 1963, enacts that:

> "In any action brought against a person in respect of the abstraction of water from a source of supply, it shall be a defence for him to prove that the water was abstracted in pursuance of a licence under this Act, and that the provisions of the licence were complied with."[2]

This, however, does not exonerate anybody from an action for negligence or breach of contract.[3]

Obtaining Information. As with polluters, a river authority is empowered to give directions to anyone who is abstracting water from a source of supply in their area, requiring them to give such information about the abstraction as the river authority wants.[4]

Minimum Acceptable Flows. In order to have a proper yardstick for determining applications for abstraction licences, the river authority must fix "the minimum acceptable flow" for each water in the area that abstraction licences are needed for.[5] In deciding whether to grant a licence, or how much water to allow to be abstracted the river authority must pay regard to the need to secure that the flow will not be reduced below the minimum that has been fixed, if a minimum has been fixed. If fixed too low, obviously fishing interests in a river can be seriously affected. Especially if polluting matter is being discharged into it. After nine years it is believed that no "minimum acceptable flows" have yet been fixed. Until this is done, the river authority

---

[1] Water Resources Act, 1963, s. 30.
[2] *Ibid.*, s. 31(1).
[3] *Ibid.*, s. 31(3).
[4] *Ibid.*, s. 114.
[5] *Ibid.*, s. 19.

must have regard to the considerations which they must take into account when fixing "minimum acceptable flows".[1]

These considerations include the requirements of fisheries, and also the character both of the water concerned and its surroundings, in particular any natural beauty, the safeguarding of public health, the needs of existing lawful uses of the water, including those of agriculture, industry, and water supply, and also the requirements of land drainage and navigation.[2]

Anybody whose interest may be affected by the standard of flow may object to the draft statement of the river authority's proposals, and may be heard either at a local inquiry or at a private hearing.[3]

This is discussed further in Chapter 10.

River Authority Discharging Water

Under the Water Resources Act, 1971, the Secretary of State for the Environment can make orders authorising river authorities to discharge water into any inland water or underground strata. This enables water supply rivers to be recharged in dry seasons from balancing reservoirs or underground sources. Anyone who suffers damage attributable to the discharge is entitled to compensation.

Fishing Owner's Application to Revoke or Vary Licences

Where no minimum acceptable flow has been fixed by the river authority, any owner of fishing rights in an inland water may apply to the Secretary of State for the Environment to revoke or vary licences to abstract water from the inland water, except for licences of right.[4] An "inland water"[5] means virtually the same as a "source of supply", explained above (except that underground strata are not included) and so, oddly enough, parts of the sea are brought in. The owner of fishing rights can apply on the ground that in his capacity of owner of those rights, he has sustained loss or damage directly arising from abstraction of water under the licence in question. He may not apply until at least one year after the licence was granted.

The Water Resources Act, 1963, also provides for revocation or variation of licences upon proposals by the river authority, and if the Secretary of State is persuaded that a licence should be reviewed he can direct the river authority to make proposals.[6] Where, therefore, a minimum acceptable flow has been determined, it is still open to owners of fishing rights to make representations to the river authority, or the Secretary of State, to review licences with a view to varying or revoking them. The Act

---

[1] Water Resources Act, 1963, s. 29.
[2] *Ibid.*, s. 19(5).
[3] *Ibid.*, Sched. 7, para. 8.
[4] *Ibid.*, s. 47.
[5] See definition p.10.
[6] *Ibid.*, s. 42.

lays down procedures for review, which enables the licence-holder and others to object or make representations.

The Act also provides for temporarily suspending or restricting spray irrigation at times of "exceptional shortage of rains or other emergency".[1]

Exemptions from Licensing. As we have seen above from the definition of "source of supply" no licence is required to abstract from certain self-contained waters, because they are not a "source of supply" so far as the Water Resources Act is concerned. In addition, riparian occupiers do not need a licence to exercise their riparian rights to take water for domestic or agricultural purposes on the riparian land and any land held with it. A licence is always needed, however, for spray irrigation.[2]

There are a number of other special exemptions, but the most important one is that the Secretary of State may make orders excepting whole areas from licensing requirements, on the ground that they are not necessary for the protection of water resources.[3] So far no such orders have been made.

Penalties. Any person contravening the abstraction licence requirements of the Water Resources Act, 1963, or who does not comply with conditions or requirements in a current abstraction licence held by him, commits an offence, and may be fined up to £100.

---

[1] Water Resources Act, 1963, ss. 45 and 129.
[2] *Ibid.*, s. 24(2).
[3] *Ibid.*, s. 25.

CHAPTER 22

WATER REORGANISATION AND THE AUTHORITIES

Water Reorganisation

At the time of writing the Government has announced proposals for water reorganisation. The general scheme is to create nine all-purpose Regional Water Authorities (RWAs) for England and a Welsh National Development Authority to be responsible for all things wet and watery. The RWAs will replace the 27 river authorities, the Thames Conservancy and the Lee Conservancy Catchment Board. Some of the proposals are referred to in other parts of this book. Only a broad outline is given in this chapter, because the measures to implement them have yet to hazard the rough and tumble of Parliament, and in some respects the sniping of informed opinion, before becoming law.

The Minister of Agriculture, Fisheries and Food

The Minister of Agriculture, Fisheries and Food is the Minister responsible for fisheries in England and Wales. It is proposed that he shall continue to be when the water reorganisation takes place – in consultation, where appropriate, with the Secretary of State for Wales. He features in many chapters of this book, having for example, powers and duties concerning obstructions in watercourses, the approval and certification of fish passes and free gaps; the approval of gratings; confirmation of byelaws; approval of amounts to be charged for licences to fish; control of diseases of fish; and many other fishing matters.

Regulation of fisheries – Part IV Orders. Part IV of the 1923 Act gives the Minister power to make orders for the regulation of fisheries, with a view to the maintenance, improvement and development of the salmon, trout, freshwater or eel fisheries within any area[1], upon the application of any of the following:

(1) A river authority; (2) county council; (3) the owners of at least one-fourth in value of the several (that is, private) fisheries proposed to be regulated; (4) the majority of the persons holding licences to fish in public waters in the area of the proposed order; or (5) any association which in

---

[1] Salmon and Freshwater Fisheries Act, 1923, s. 37, as amended by the 1935 Act, s. 1. and the 1972 Act, Sched. 3.

the opinion of the Minister is sufficiently representative of fishing interests within such area.[1]

The 1923 Act states what may be contained in an order[2], and among other things, orders may:

(1) Enable river authorities to purchase or take leases of fisheries, land or foreshore in order to erect or work fixed engines for catching salmon or migratory trout for a limited period; (2) modify the rules laid down by the 1923 Act, or a local Act, in relation to fisheries in a specified area; (3) provide for compensation to be paid to anyone injuriously affected by the order; (4) require contributions to be paid by owners or occupiers of several fisheries[3] regulated by the order.

Since the Water Resources Act, 1963[4], the Minister has not had power to set up by order a fishery board in a river authority area. Fishery boards, once principal actors, have now left the stage.

A procedure for making orders is laid down in the 1923 Act[5] requiring publication of a notice of intention to make the order, notice to owners, lessees or occupiers of any fishery, land, foreshore or easement (e.g. rights of way) to be compulsorily acquired, and giving opportunities for objection. If an order goes through it has the same force as an Act of Parliament.

Licences to rear salmon or trout. Orders for the regulation of fisheries do not apply to any waters in which the business of artificially propagating or rearing salmon or trout is carried on under a licence granted by the Minister. The Minister can grant such licences subject to any conditions he thinks fit, and may revoke licences if he believes that any condition imposed has not been observed.[6]

River Authorities and Regional Water Authorities

These are taken together because when the water reorganisation becomes law the proposed regional water authorities (RWAs) will take over the functions of the river authorities on a date appointed by the legislation. Thereafter, in all likelihood, "regional water authority" can be read for "river authority" in practically every place it appears in this book.

When the 1923 Act was passed local responsibility for administration of fishery functions was mainly in the hands of fishery boards in fishery districts, and this continued until the River Boards Act, 1948, transferred

---

[1] 1923 Act, s. 39.
[2] *Ibid.*, s. 38 — but see amendments and repeals made by the Water Resources Act, 1963, Sch. 3, para. 8, and the Salmon and Freshwater Fisheries Act, 1972, Sch. 3.
[3] For definition see above p.72.
[4] Sched. 3, para. 8.
[5] Salmon and Freshwater Fisheries Act, 1923, s. 40.
[6] *Ibid.*, s. 38(3).

their functions to river boards where a fishery district was in a river board area. The Water Resources Act, 1963, substituted river authorities for river boards. There are twenty-seven river authorities covering the whole of England and Wales except for the Thames and Lee catchment areas and the Metropolitan area (known as the "excluded areas").

In river authority areas, river authorities are responsible for fisheries, land drainage, pollution prevention and water conservation.

It is proposed that RWAs will not only take over these functions, but also responsibility for bulk sewage, inland navigation and water-based recreation.

Constitution. At least one member of each river authority must be appointed by the Minister to represent fishery interests.[1] A majority of the members are appointed by the County Councils and County Borough Councils in the area, and certain other interests must be represented, such as agriculture, land drainage, industry and public water supply.[2]

When RWAs are set up, it is proposed that the Minister of Agriculture will be required to appoint to each authority only two members who between them will be qualified in agriculture, land drainage and fisheries.

Fishery functions. Fishery functions of river authorities appear in various chapters of this book. To summarise, they include:

(*a*) granting and charging for licences to fish;[3]
(*b*) dealing with illegal obstructions and fixed engines;[4]
(*c*) construction and maintenance of fish passes and free gaps;[5]
(*d*) placing and maintaining gratings;[6]
(*e*) purchasing or leasing fisheries for artificial propagation or rearing of fish;[7]
(*f*) purchasing or leasing dams, fishing weirs, fixed engines and other obstructions and removing, altering or working them;[8]
(*g*) making and enforcing byelaws for protection and improvement of fisheries;[9]
(*h*) fixing minimum acceptable flows;[10] and
(*i*) taking legal proceedings where offences are committed.[7]

River authorities also have the general power "to expend any moneys in their hands in any manner which they think most conducive to the maintenance, improvement, or development of the fisheries within their

---

[1] Water Resources Act, 1963, s. 6(3)(*b*).
[2] *Ibid.*, s. 6.
[3] Salmon and Freshwater Fisheries Act, 1972, s. 6 and Sched. 1.
[4] Salmon and Freshwater Fisheries Act, 1923, s. 11.
[5] *Ibid.*, s. 20,
[6] *Ibid.*, s. 24.
[7] *Ibid.*, s. 54(1).
[8] *Ibid.*, s. 16.
[9] *Ibid.*, s. 59.
[10] Water Resources Act, 1963, s. 19 – and see Chapter 21.

area", and "to execute such works, do such acts, and incur such expenses as
they deem expedient" for the purpose of carrying out their functions.[1] They
must not however, do anything that injuriously affects a navigable river, canal
or inland navigation.[2]

When the coming RWAs take over these fishery functions it is proposed
to impose a duty on them to maintain, improve and develop salmon and
freshwater fisheries. Even so, they will not be required to have fisheries
committees, but the Minister "intends to recommend" that each should have
a regional fisheries committee and small local advisory committees, serviced
by the fisheries staff of the RWAs, for at least each of the previous river
authority areas.

Dredging watercourses. River authorities may dredge watercourses and
remove the spoil, and in doing so are permitted to spread the spoil over the
river bank so that it can be removed in one further operation. In doing so,
however, they must not create a nuisance, and must pay compensation if they
cause negligent damage. In the absence of negligence the payment of
compensation is discretionary.[3]

Acquisition of land. For the purpose of performing any of their
functions, river authorities have powers to acquire land, or any interest in or
right over land, either by agreement or compulsorily, and to carry out
building, engineering and other works, subject to certain conditions. They
may sell, exchange or let any of their land not required for their functions.[4]

Default of river authorities. The Secretary of State for the Environment
and the Minister of Agriculture, may order an inquiry, on receiving
representations from the Water Resources Board or anyone else, to see if any
river authority has failed to perform any function it ought to have performed.
If it is found that the river authority has defaulted, it may be directed to
perform its duties as specified in the direction. If it still fails, the Ministers
may carry out the duties themselves or transfer the function to the Water
Resources Board or another river authority.[5]

Water Resources Board

This Board has duties of overseeing, advising on and researching into
water resources and conservation. It has proved singularly useful. Yet it is
intended to abolish the Board in the water reorganisation. The members are
appointed by the Secretary of State for the Environment, and must not
exceed eight.[6] One of their specific tasks is to draw the attention of river
authorities to any cases where the quality of the water could and should be

---

[1] Salmon and Freshwater Fisheries Act, 1923, s. 54(1).
[2] *Ibid.*, s. 54(3)(*b*).
[3] Land Drainage Act, 1961, s. 29, and see Chapter 12.
[4] Water Resources Act, 1963, ss. 65 to 71. For powers of entry see below pp.167–168.
[5] *Ibid.*, s. 108.
[6] *Ibid.*, s. 13.

improved by exercising powers under the Rivers (Prevention of Pollution) Acts.[1]

Drainage Authorities

In addition to river authorities there are numerous internal drainage boards with a more local jurisdiction, administering internal drainage districts. Anglers should know of them principally because they have powers to make byelaws affecting fishing, and also because they have powers to deal with obstructions to watercourses, dredging, and the disposal of spoil similar to river authorities. Internal drainage boards, however, must carry out their land drainage functions with due regard to fisheries[2], including sea fisheries[3], and are liable to compensate the owners of fishing for damage to their interests (see Chapter 12).

The penalty for contravention of the byelaws is a fine up to £50 and a further £5 for every day that the contravention continues. The internal drainage board may also take any action needed to remedy the effect of the contravention and recover the cost of doing so from the offender.[4]

It is planned to retain internal drainage boards in the water reorganisation with the same responsibilities as now, and to make it compulsory for each of the proposed Regional Water Authorities to have a land drainage committee.

Local Authorities

Fishermen are not much concerned with local authorities, except that sewage disposal has blotted out fishing on many miles of river. Local authorities may make byelaws and also frequently have obtained local Acts of Parliament, which may impinge on the activities of anglers. A local authority may be yet another drainage authority, and may carry out works to facilitate land drainage or prevent flooding. No change is proposed in these functions in the water reorganisation, and local authorities will continue to deal with local sewage disposal.

Other Bodies

The Department of the Environment will have overall responsibility for water when the reorganisation takes place (though the Minister of Agriculture, Fisheries and Food will have fishery and land drainage duties).

The Sports Council will remain an official adviser to the Government

---

[1] Water Resources Act, 1963, s. 12(3)(*f*).
[2] Land Drainage Act, 1930, s. 62.
[3] Land Drainage Act, 1961, s. 32 and Sched. 1, para. 23.
[4] Land Drainage Act, 1930, s. 47(8), as amended by Land Drainage Act, 1961.

on sporting affairs through the *Minister for Sport.*[1] It has 10 regional councils in England and Wales.

The Countryside Commission, the *British Waterways Board* and the *Inland Waterways Amenity Advisory Council* (the latter two being under sentence of death) are referred to in Chapter 19, along with the proposed *National Water Council* and *Water Space Amenity Commission* (both advisory, rather than executive, bodies).

Grants for Angling

Angling clubs and associations should note that grants to aid the provision of facilities for sport and recreation intended mainly for adults, are obtainable under the Physical Training and Recreation Acts, 1937 and 1958. Angling qualifies for these grants. The grants are available towards such things as the cost of acquiring fishing rights, the improvement and maintenance of fisheries and angling facilities, the stocking of new fisheries, and the provision of changing rooms, lockers etc. for anglers. Up to 50% of the approved capital cost as assessed by the Distrct Valuer may be paid within high and low limits set by the Department of Education and Science.

To qualify for grant aid clubs must be open to anyone to join — but they will not be disqualified by imposing reasonable restrictions or by limiting membership numbers to prevent over-fishing. The Department lays down various other criteria to justify the grant of public money.[2]

It is essential to apply for grant *before* entering into contracts and before any work is started. In practice Regional Sports Councils advise the Department on applications for grants, and the National Anglers Council is consulted where the grant is for fishing.

Water Bailiffs and Other Law Enforcers

Official Water Bailiffs. Water bailiffs may be appointed by river authorities under the Water Resources Act, 1963[3] or by the Minister under the 1923 Act[4], in either case the water bailiffs have the same powers, and are referred to in this chapter as "official water bailiffs". They are deemed to be constables for the purposes of enforcing the 1923 Act or byelaws.[5]

Checking licences to fish. Official water bailiffs, members of river authorities, constables and holders of fishing licences can demand the production of fishing licences as described in Chapter 4.[6]

---

[1] Now less conveniently called the Parliamentary Under-Secretary with special responsibility for sport.

[2] Full particulars are given in *All For Fishing* by Gregory and Seymour, (London, Charles Knight, 1970).

[3] See Water Resources Act, 1963, Sch. 3, para. 10, and Sch. 4, para. 20.

[4] Salmon and Freshwater Fisheries Act, 1923, s. 72.

[5] *Ibid.*, s. 67(3).

[6] Salmon and Freshwater Fisheries Act, 1972, s. 9.

Examination of obstructions etc. An official water bailiff may examine any dam, fishing weir, fishing mill dam, fixed engine, or obstruction, or any artificial watercourse, and may enter on any land for the purpose.[1]

Examination of tackle, receptacles, vehicles, boats and bait. An official water bailiff may examine any "instrument" or bait he reasonably suspects is being, has been, or is likely to be used in taking fish in contravention of the 1923 or 1972 Acts, and he may examine any container he reasonably suspects is being, has been, or is likely to be used for holding any such instruments, bait or fish. He may stop and search (*a*) any boat or other vessel used in fishing in a river authority area; or (*b*) any vessel or vehicle he reasonably suspects contains fish, instruments, bait or containers which he has a right to examine.[2]

Seizure of fish, vehicles etc. He may seize any fish, instrument, vessel, vehicle or other thing liable to be forfeited under the 1923 Act[3] or the Sea Fish (Conservation) Act, 1967.[4]

Obstructing water bailiffs in their duties. It is an offence to refuse to allow an official water bailiff to make an entry, search, examination or seizure under any of his powers mentioned above, or to resist or obstruct him.[5] A water bailiff is "deemed to be a constable" when exercising his official duties, and has the same powers and privileges, and is subject to the same liabilities as a constable.[6]

Apprehension of offenders at night. Any water bailiff with any assistants may without a warrant seize and apprehend and deliver to a police officer any offender who at night illegally takes or kills salmon, trout or freshwater fish, or is found on or near any waters with such illegal intent, or having in his possession an illegal instrument for the capture of salmon, trout or freshwater fish. Night means here the period "between the expiration of the first hour after sunset on any day and the beginning of the last hour before sunrise on the following morning".[7]

See Chapter 9 for powers of "any person" to arrest for offences under the Theft Act, 1968.

Powers of entry. An official water bailiff needs no warrant to exercise any of the powers set out above, production of his written appointment being sufficient warrant.[8] Armed with a special order in writing from the river

---

[1] Salmon and Freshwater Fisheries Act, 1923, s. 67(1)(*a*). For meaning of terms see Section 92(1) and Chapter 8.

[2] *Ibid.*, s. 67(1)(*b*) and (*c*) as substituted by 1972 Act, s. 11(1).

[3] Salmon and Freshwater Fisheries Act, 1923, s. 67(1)(*d*) as amended by Salmon and Freshwater Fisheries Act, 1965; see Chapter 7 for forfeiture.

[4] Ss. 4–6 and 18(1)(*b*).

[5] 1923 Act, s. 67(2) as amended by 1972 Act, s. 11(2).

[6] *Ibid.*, s. 67(3); and see *Heseltine* v. *Myers* (1894) 58 J.P. 689.

[7] Salmon and Freshwater Fisheries Act, 1923, s. 71.

[8] *Ibid.*, s. 67(4). Although production of his warrant is a condition precedent to exercising powers (*Barnacott* v. *Passmore* (1887) 19 Q.B.D. 75) failure to produce is no defence to a charge of assaulting a constable where poachers scuffle with a bailiff before he can produce his instrument of appointment (*Edwards* v. *Morgan* [1967] Crim. L.R. 40).

authority, he or any other officer or servant of the river authority has more extensive powers, being allowed to:

> "enter remain upon and traverse any lands ... adjoining or near to any waters within the [river authority area] for the purpose of preventing any offence"

against the 1923 Act or 1972 Act.[1] The order must be signed by the Chairman or Clerk of the river authority and two members, shall not remain in force for more than twelve months, and it will not apply to decoys or lands used exclusively for the preservation of wild fowl. Nor will it authorise entry of a dwelling-house or the curtilage of a dwelling-house, a magistrate's warrant being necessary for this.[1]

If a water bailiff or member or any other officer or servant of a river authority has good reason to suspect that an offence under the 1923 Act or 1972 Act is being or is likely to be committed on any land situated on or near any waters, a justice of the peace may authorise him by written order, during a period of not more than twenty-four hours, to go and remain on the land by night or day for the purpose of detecting the offence.[2]

A justice may also, upon a sworn information that there is probable cause to suspect that an offence has been committed against the 1923 Act or 1972 Act or that fish[3] have been illegally taken or that illegal nets or other instruments are upon some premises, issue a warrant authorising a water bailiff, member or any other officer or servant of a river authority or a constable to enter the premises by day or night for the purpose of detecting the offence or the fish, nets or instruments. They may be authorised to seize any illegal nets or instruments found on the premises and any fish suspected to have been illegally taken. The warrant may remain in force for no more than one week.[4]

The Water Resources Act, 1963, gives any person authorised in writing by a river authority or an appropriate Minister general powers to enter land to exercise statutory functions, or to determine whether or how they are to be exercised. An application can be made to a magistrate for a warrant if difficulty is encountered — e.g. if entry is refused or the land is unoccupied. Vessels may be entered for anti-pollution functions. The Act lays down some safeguards for owners and occupiers, and in certain cases seven days notice must be given before entry.[5]

Private Water Bailiffs. A water bailiff appointed by the owner of a private fishery can, of course, only act as a bailiff on his employer's property. He can turn trespassers off the land using no more force than is reasonably necessary, and if he finds someone fishing unlawfully on the property, he

---

[1] 1923 Act, s. 68, as amended by 1972 Act, s. 11(3).
[2] *Ibid.*, s. 69, as amended by 1972 Act, s. 11(3).
[3] Including eels — 1972 Act, s. 11(5).
[4] 1923 Act, s. 70, as amended by 1972 Act, s. 11(3).
[5] Water Resources Act, 1963, ss. 111 and 112; Sea Fish (Conservation) Act, 1967, s.18.

may exercise the right of arrest and seizure of tackle given by the Theft Act, 1968, described in Chapter 9. Before using force to remove an offender, or to seize his tackle, he should make a reasonable demand to him to comply.[1] If he holds an official fishing licence he may demand production of fishing licences as described above, p.166.

The Magistrates' Court

Penalties under the 1923 Act. A person committing any of the numerous offences against the 1923 Act or 1972 Act may be taken before a Magistrates' Court. This is the court often, but misleadingly, referred to as the "Police Court". It is also called a court of summary jurisdiction. All these terms mean the court in which Magistrates sit. They also are variously described as Justices of the Peace (or "J.P.s"), Justices, or perhaps, by less respectful anglers, "Beaks". For some offences the accused may go for trial by jury.

The maximum penalties specified for various offences under the Acts are conveniently tabulated in Schedule 2 of the 1972 Act. Where no penalty is mentioned the maximum is a fine of £50, or in the case of a second or subsequent conviction, £100.[2] On conviction the court may also order forfeiture of (*a*) any fish illegally taken or in the offender's possession at the time of the offence; (*b*) any "instrument, bait or other thing used in the commission of the offence"; (*c*) "in the case of an offence of unlawful possession of any substance or device in contravention of section 9 of the 1923 Act, that substance or device." If the offender goes for trial by jury the court can order forfeiture of "any vessel or vehicle used in or in connection with the commission of the offence or in which any substance or device unlawfully in his possession was contained at the time of the offence".[3]

Disqualifications. If a person convicted of an offence under the 1923 Act or 1972 Act, on again being convicted the court may direct the forfeiture of his fishing licence, and disqualification from holding a licence or from fishing under a general licence for up to one year.[4] Anyone prosecuted must deliver any fishing licence or general licence he holds to the clerk of the court, by hand or post, before the hearing, or bring it with him to the hearing. If on conviction he is ordered to surrender the licence, he commits a further offence should he not have so delivered the licence and he does not surrender it as required.[5]

Convictions and Fines. Fines imposed go to the Secretary of State[6], and not, as of old, to the fishery authorities. If an offence is committed in a

---

[1] *Hughes* v. *Buckland* (1846) 15 M. & W. 346.
[2] Salmon and Freshwater Fisheries Act, 1972, s. 12(4).
[3] *Ibid.,* s. 12(5).
[4] *Ibid.,* s. 12(7).
[5] *Ibid.,* s. 13(1).
[6] See Salmon and Freshwater Fisheries Act, 1923, s. 73, and Magistrates' Court Act, 1952, s. 131.

river authority area, upon conviction the clerk of the court must forward a certificate of the conviction and notice of any fishing licence surrender or disqualification order to the clerk of the river authority. The certificate shall be receivable in evidence in all legal proceedings.[1]

Jurisdiction of Magistrates. A Magistrate must not try any case regarding an offence committed on his own land, or in respect of a fishery of which he is the owner or occupier. He is not disqualified from sitting by reason of being a subscriber to a society for the protection of fish.[2] He may not sit, however, if he was present at a meeting of a society which decided to authorise the prosecution, unless he took no part in the decision of the meeting.[3]

Offences committed at sea, or on the sea-coast beyond the ordinary jurisdiction of the Magistrates' Court, are taken as being within the jurisdiction of the court that covers the land abutting on the sea or the sea-coast where it happened.[4]

Disposal of forfeited fish etc. Where fish or any other perishable thing is seized as being liable to forfeiture, the person seizing it may sell it, and the net proceeds of sale may be forfeited. If the Magistrates do not order forfeiture the net proceeds are payable to the owner on demand. Other things forfeited are "to be disposed of as the court thinks fit", except that there are special provisions for forfeited vessels and vehicles.[5]

Fishery Byelaws

When duly made, byelaws have the same force as Acts of Parliament. Most important for the angler are the byelaws of river authorities and river conservators. Examples of byelaws affecting angling are given in Appendix C.

The public are entitled to inspect river authority byelaws at the river authority office without charge, and are entitled to copies on payment of a reasonable sum.[6] Byelaws must be both reasonable and certain in their terms, otherwise they can be set aside on application to the Court[7] – but the Court will only interfere if they are patently oppressive.[8]

Procedure for making river authority byelaws. The Water Resources Act, 1963, lays down a procedure for making river authority byelaws, and no byelaws can have effect before they are confirmed by the Minister.[9] Any proposed byelaws must be published and open to inspection free of charge to

---

[1] Salmon and Freshwater Fisheries Act, 1923, s. 77, and 1972 Act, s. 13(2).
[2] 1923 Act, s. 76.
[3] *R. v. Pwhelli Justices, ex p. Soane* [1948] 2 All E.R. 815.
[4] Salmon and Freshwater Fisheries Act, 1923, s. 75(1); and see the "pirate" radio case *R. v. St. Augustine, Kent, Justices (The Times*, December 14, 1966).
[5] 1923 Act, s. 79 and 1972 Act, s. 12(5) and (6).
[6] Water Resources Act, 1963, Sched. 12, para. 6.
[7] *Kruse v. Johnson* [1898] 2 Q.B. 91.
[8] *Denithorne v. Davies* [1967] 2 Lloyds Rep. 489, see p.28 above.
[9] Water Resources Act, 1963, s. 119 and Sched. 12.

the public. Any interested person is entitled to a free copy of proposed byelaws, and as they require confirmation, there is nothing to prevent any person opposed to them objecting to the Minister. The Minister may make byelaws where there is no river authority[1], and also if river authorities default in making close season byelaws by June 29, 1975.[2]

Compensation to owners and occupiers of fisheries. If any byelaw injuriously affects the value of a fishery, the owner or occupier may within twelve months after the confirmation of the byelaw claim compensation by giving written notice to the clerk of the river authority. Compensation for damage to the fishery may be made in a lump sum or by annual payments. If agreement cannot be reached about compensation, it is to be settled by an arbitrator appointed by the Minister. If compensation is paid by way of an annual payment, either the river authority, or the person entitled to receive it may have the amount reviewed at five-year intervals.[3]

Contents of byelaws. The 1923 Act specifies the purposes for which river authorities may make byelaws relating to fishing. Where there is no river authority the Minister may make byelaws for the same purposes.[1] These are briefly as follows:

(1)   To fix or alter the annual close seasons and weekly close time for salmon and trout and annual close season for freshwater fish and rainbow trout;

(2)   To designate the specifications of nets and other instruments (not fixed engines) which may be used for taking salmon, trout, freshwater fish and eels; and the manner in which they may be used. A byelaw prohibiting altogether specified kinds of net may be made;[4]

(3)   To require or regulate the marking of licensed nets and instruments or of boats and other vessels used for fishing; and to prohibit the carrying of any net which is not licensed or properly marked in any boat whilst being used in fishing for salmon or trout (not freshwater fish). The fisherman need not actually be in the boat for it to be in use for fishing;[5]

(4)   To prohibit or regulate the carrying in a boat during the annual close season for salmon of nets capable of taking salmon — other than one commonly used in the district for sea-fishing in a boat commonly used for sea-fishing;

(5)   To prohibit the use of specified instruments (not fixed engines) for taking salmon, trout or freshwater fish; and regulate what lure or bait may be used with rod and line; and to specify when a gaff

---

[1] Salmon and Freshwater Fisheries Act, 1923, s. 59(1); amended by 1972 Act, ss. 3, 4 and 5.
[2] 1972 Act, s. 3(2) and see p.9 above.
[3] 1923 Act, s. 59(4).
[4] *Clayton v. Peirse* [1904] 1 K.B. 424.
[5] *Moses v. Raywood* [1911] 2 K.B. 271.

may be used in fishing for salmon or migratory trout with rod
and line;

(6)   To prohibit the taking of fish, live or dead, from specified waters;
(7)   To specify the sizes of trout or freshwater fish that may be taken;
(8)   To prohibit night fishing by rod and line (i.e. "between the
       expiration of the first hour after sunset on any day and the
       beginning of the last hour before sunrise on the following
       morning");
(9)   To lay down the annual period when gratings need not be
       maintained;
(10)   To specify the distance above or below obstructions within which
       fish may be taken;
(11)   To regulate the discharge of polluting matter in any waters, but
       not so as to prejudice a sanitary or local authority's statutory
       sewage disposal;
(12)   To require returns of salmon, trout or freshwater fish taken,
       including nil returns;
(13)   To authorise fishing with rod and line for eels during the close
       season for freshwater fish;
(14)   Generally for the better execution of the Salmon and Freshwater
       Fisheries Acts, and the better protection, preservation, and
       improvement of fisheries in the area.

Extent. Any byelaw may be made to apply to the whole or any part of
the river authority area, or to the whole or any part of the year.[1]

Penalties. Failure to comply with a byelaw is an offence under the 1923
Act and may be dealt with as described above (p.169).

---

[1] Salmon and Freshwater Fisheries Act, 1923, s. 59(2).

APPENDICES

APPENDIX A

MODEL ANGLING CLUB RULES AND BYELAWS

1. **Name**

   The name of the Club shall be the . . . .

2. **Objects**

   The general objects of the Club shall be to provide the facilities of an angling club for its members, including the organisation and provision of angling, and to promote the interests of angling and anglers.

3. **Trustees**
   (*a*) There shall be not less than two nor more than three Trustees of the Club, save that a corporate body may be a sole Trustee. The first Trustees shall be . . . . [name them]. Subsequent appointment of Trustees shall be by the Committee.
   (*b*) Trustees shall hold office until death or resignation, or until removed from office by a resolution of the Committee.
   (*c*) All property of the Club (except cash, which shall be under the control of the Hon. Treasurer) including leases and fishing leases shall be vested in the Trustees to be dealt with by them as the Committee shall from time to time by resolution direct.
   (*d*) The Trustees shall be indemnified out of the assets of the Club against any risk and expense incurred by them in pursuance of their office.

4. **Membership**
   (*a*) The Club shall consist of the following classes of members, viz.:
      (i) Ordinary Members;
      (ii) Temporary Members;
      (iii) Honorary Members.
   (*b*) Membership in any class may be limited by the Committee subject to confirmation at the next General Meeting.

5. **Ordinary Membership**
   (*a*) Every candidate for Ordinary Membership shall be proposed and seconded by two members of the Club in good standing who as well as the candidate shall sign the application form. Admission

to Ordinary Membership shall be by election of the Committee who may refuse any application without stating a reason.

(b)   Every candidate elected to Ordinary Membership shall be notified of his election by the Hon. Secretary and upon paying [the entrance fee and] the first annual subscription (which shall be paid within [two] weeks of the said notification or the election shall be void) he shall be a member of the Club and shall be deemed to have agreed to be bound by the Rules and Byelaws of the Club.

6.   Temporary Membership

The Committee shall have power to elect Temporary Members on such terms as they may determine.

7.   Honorary Membership

Honorary Members may be elected at any General Meeting of the Club for such period as the meeting shall determine upon a two-thirds majority vote of members present and voting.

8.   Subscription

The annual subscription payable by Ordinary Members shall be such sum as the members shall determine from time to time in General Meeting. It shall be payable on election to Ordinary Membership and thereafter annually on the . . . . day of . . . .

(N.B. Special rules can be made if desired for temporary subscriptions, for members joining late in the year, for juveniles and for entrance fees.)

9.   Resignations

A member may resign his membership at any time by notice in writing to the Hon. Secretary, but a member whose written resignation is received by the Hon. Secretary after his subscription for the current year has become due shall be liable for his subscription for that year.

10.   Expulsion

(a)   The Committee shall expel from the Club any member for conduct which in their opinion is injurious or tends to be injurious to the interests of the Club or its objects or its members or angling, but before expelling a member the Committee shall inquire into his conduct and he shall be given a reasonable opportunity to defend and justify himself either in writing or by appearing before the Committee as he shall elect, and the Committee's power to expel shall be on a majority vote of those present at the inquiry.

(b)   An expelled member shall forfeit all rights and privileges of membership but shall remain liable for any dues or debts to the

Club which became payable or were incurred before the date of expulsion.

11.   Management

The management of the Club shall be vested in the Committee (except as otherwise provided by these Rules).

12.   Officers

A President, Vice-President, Honorary Secretary, and Honorary Treasurer shall be elected annually at the Annual General Meeting of the Club after being proposed and seconded and indicating their consent, and shall be ex officio members of the Committee.

13.   The Committee

(a)   The Committee shall consist of the President, Vice-President, Hon. Secretary, Hon. Treasurer and not less than [5] or more than [10] Ordinary Members of the Club elected at an Annual General Meeting, and shall have power to co-opt up to two members, and may in their discretion invite any persons, whether members of the Club or not, to attend any Committee meeting.

(b)   At the Annual General Meeting each year one-third of the Committee for the time being (or the number nearest to one-third) being those longest on the Committee since last elected shall retire from office, but shall be eligible for re-election, when every Ordinary and Honorary Member shall be entitled to vote for as many candidates as there are vacancies to be filled, and in the case of two or more candidates for a vacancy receiving an equal number of votes the Chairman of the meeting shall have a second or casting vote.

(c)   The Committee shall have power to fill any casual vacancy on the Committee, and any member so appointed shall retire at the next Annual General Meeting but shall be eligible for re-election.

(d)   The Committee shall meet in at least [8] months of each year to examine the accounts and to arrange the affairs of the Club, and minutes shall be taken of every meeting.

14.   Byelaws

(a)   The Byelaws set out in the Appendix to these Rules and any byelaws made under para. (b) of this Rule shall be binding upon the members until repealed by the Committee or by a resolution of a General Meeting, subject to any amendment made under para. (b) of this Rule.

(b)   The Committee shall from time to time make, repeal or amend all such byelaws as they deem expedient (provided that they shall not be inconsistent with these Rules) to take effect unless set aside at a General Meeting.

15.   Annual General Meetings

The Annual General Meeting of the Club shall be held in the month of........................in each year to receive and consider the audited accounts and annual balance sheet prepared by the Hon. Treasurer; to appoint officers and auditors; to fill vacancies on the Committee; and to decide on any resolution submitted by the Committee or under Rule 17.

16.   Special General Meetings

A Special General Meeting may be held at any time that the Committee shall determine, and the Committee shall call a Special General Meeting upon the requisition in writing of any [20] members for a purpose stated in the requisition, and upon receipt of such a requisition, unless they shall determine the purpose to be frivolous, the Committee shall call the meeting within 40 days of the receipt by the Hon. Secretary of the requisition.

17.   Notices of General Meetings and Resolutions

(*a*)   Notice of the date and time and place of every General Meeting, stating the last date for submitting resolutions, shall be sent to each member of the Club at his last known address at least 30 days before the date of the meeting.

(*b*)   Notice of any resolution to be moved at a General Meeting unless recommended by the Committee shall be submitted in writing to the Hon. Secretary at least 21 days before the meeting and signed by the proposer and seconder. Any such resolution, unless withdrawn, shall be included in the business of the meeting and notice of it shall be sent to each member of the Club at his last known address at least 10 days before the date of the meeting.

(*c*)   Accidental omission to give notice to, or non-receipt of notice by, any member under paragraphs (*a*) and (*b*) of this Rule shall not invalidate any of the proceedings of the meeting.

18.   Proceedings at General Meetings

(*a*)   [6] members (not including temporary members) shall form a quorum at any General Meeting.

(*b*)   At every General Meeting the President, or in his absence the Vice-President, or, in the absence of both, a member elected by the members present, shall take the Chair. The Chairman and all Ordinary and Honorary Members present shall be entitled to vote and in the event of an equality of votes the Chairman shall have a second or casting vote.

(*c*)   Except as otherwise provided by these Rules, a majority vote of the Ordinary and Honorary Members present and voting shall carry any motion or resolution, save that no Rule of the Club may be made, repealed or amended on a vote of less than two-thirds of the members present and voting.

19. Interpretation

  (*a*) The Committee shall be the sole authority for the interpretation of the Club Rules and Byelaws, and the decision of the Committee upon any question of interpretation or any matter affecting the Club not provided for by the Rules or Byelaws shall be final and binding upon the members.

  (*b*) In the Club Rules and Byelaws, where the context permits, words importing the masculine shall include the feminine, and words importing the singular shall include the plural, and vice versa.

APPENDIX.   CLUB BYELAWS

N.B. It will be convenient to include in byelaws detailed rules concerning the fishing and use of Club waters and property. These could be printed on membership cards, and for example:

  (*a*) Require compliance with the byelaws of the river authority.
  (*b*) Require fair and lawful fishing.
  (*c*) Prohibit trespass, digging for bait and cutting or damaging trees, vegetation and other property.
  (*d*) Prohibit leaving litter, particularly monofil line, and polythene scrap.
  (*e*) Specify size limits and numbers of fish that may be retained from each Club water.
  (*f*) Specify the number of rods that may be used and tackled up at any time.
  (*g*) Specify means of access, parking places etc. for each Club water, and require closing of gates.
  (*h*) Regulate use of boats.

APPENDIX B

MODEL LEASE OF FISHING

This form is framed for a lease of fishing for a term of years between a riparian owner and an angling club by way of its trustees. It should be adapted according to the circumstances of the case and the agreement of the parties.

THIS DEED is made the   day of   19
BETWEEN   of
(hereinafter called "the owner") of the one part and
                    of
                    [name and addresses of Trustees]
(hereinafter called "the tenants", which expression shall include the Trustees
for the time being of the   Angling Club)
of the other part

WHEREAS
(1) The owner is the owner in fee simple [or as the case may be] of
                    [recite ownership
of soil and fishing rights]
(2) The owner has agreed for the consideration stated below to let the
fishing in part of the River   for the benefit
of the members of the   Angling Club

NOW THIS DEED WITNESSES AS FOLLOWS:
1. In consideration of the rent reserved and the covenants of the tenants
hereinafter contained the owner hereby grants and demises to the Trustees
and members of the   Angling Club (hereinafter called
"the Club") the exclusive right to fish in and take and carry away fish from
so much of the River   as is situated between
the points marked "A" and "B" on the plan attached hereto being
                    [yards or miles] of the said River   between
                    and
[describe terminal points of letting] (hereinafter called "the river") in the
parish of   in the County of

TOGETHER WITH the right of access and egress between
                    [public road] and the river along the path running

180

[describe the route as precisely as possible] and marked red on the attached plan and the right of entering on and passing and repassing along and angling from the banks of the river for the purposes of the right of fishing hereby granted and for no other purpose whatsoever TO HOLD the premises unto the tenants for the term of   years from the   day of
            19   the tenants paying therefor an annual rent of £   in advance the first payment to be made on the execution hereof and subsequent payments on the   day of
in each year of the tenancy.

2. The tenants hereby covenant with the owner that they and every member of the Club for the time being shall observe and perform the provisions and stipulations set out in the Schedule hereto.

3. AND IT IS HEREBY AGREED AND DECLARED

(i)   The owner shall permit the tenants to use his name in any proceedings taken during the term of this lease against any third parties for the protection of the fishing rights in the river or of any of the rights granted and demised herein or of the enjoyment of any such rights, provided that the tenants shall keep the owner indemnified against any reasonable costs or expenses incurred by him and any costs awarded against him in any such proceedings.

(ii) The owner may exclude from the exercise or enjoyment of any of the rights granted or demised herein any member of the Club who shall fail to produce to the owner or his water bailiff [or his gamekeeper] on request his current membership card or who shall commit a breach of or fail to observe any of the provisions or stipulations set out in the·Schedule hereto, save that no exclusion shall continue for more than
[e.g. six weeks] in respect of any one such breach or failure.

(iii) The tenants shall keep the owner indemnified against all actions claims or demands arising by reason of the exercise of the rights hereby granted and demised (except any such actions claims or demands caused by the wrongful act or default of the owner his servants or agents) or by reason of any act or omission by the tenants or members of the Club on the premises or on any land or property of the owner, provided that the owner shall not settle or compromise any such action claim or demand here referred to without the consent of the tenants

(iv) If any question between the owner and the tenants and/or the members of the Club shall arise from the terms or provisions of this Deed or as to the rights or liabilities of the parties hereto or the members of the Club the same shall be referred to a single arbitrator for determination pursuant to the Arbitration Acts or any statutory enactment substituted therefor.

4. PROVIDED ALWAYS and this Lease is made upon this express condition — Upon the happening of any of the following events, namely:

    (*a*)   The rent reserved herein being 21 days in arrear and unpaid after the same shall have become due, whether demanded or not;

    (*b*)   Any breach or non-observance of any of the provisions or stipulations set out in the Schedule hereto;

    (*c*)   The Club going into liquidation, or being wound up or ceasing to exist;

    (*d*)   The Club its Trustees or Committee making any composition with or assignment for the benefit of the creditors of the Club;

the owner may by written notice delivered to or sent by post to the tenants or any Trustee of the Club determine the aforesaid grant and demise and thereupon the rights granted herein shall cease absolutely and determine without prejudice to any right of action which shall have accrued to the owner by reason of any of the said events.

5. The owner hereby covenants with the tenants that the tenants paying the rent hereby reserved and the tenants and members of the Club observing and performing the provisions and stipulations set out in the Schedule hereto the tenants and members of the Club shall peaceably enjoy the rights herein granted and demised without interruption by the owner his servants or agents or any person lawfully claiming under or in trust for him.

6. The owner further covenants that he shall not run, or permit or suffer to be run, any bull, bullock or dangerous animal in any field or on any part of the banks of the river or means of access thereto which the Club are permitted by this Deed to enter, at times when the Club are permitted to enter the same, save with the prior agreement of the Honorary Secretary or the Committee of the Club.

In witness etc.

THE SCHEDULE ABOVE REFERRED TO

(Tenants' covenants)

(1) To pay the rent reserved on the days and in the manner aforesaid.

(2) To pay all rates and taxes and any other lawful assessments whatsoever in respect of the aforesaid rights.

(3) Not to assign sub-let or transfer the aforesaid rights or any part thereof.

(4) To comply with the byelaws of the river authority and any other authorised laws and byelaws relating to the premises or aforesaid rights, and before angling to obtain any fishing licence required by law.

(5) To fish in a fair and sportsmanlike manner by rod and line angling

only and only at times and seasons not prohibited by law.

(6) To exercise the aforesaid rights so as to do as little injury as possible to the banks of the river, and to make compensation to the owner for any damage not made good.

(7) Not to permit the rights granted and demised to be exercised by any persons other than members of the Club, and to issue to each member of the Club and to no other person a membership card to be produced if and whenever required by the owner or his water bailiff [or gamekeeper] and not to permit more than   rods to angle in the river at any time.

(8) To keep the river free from nets (other than landing nets used auxiliary to angling with rod and line) and any unlawful fixed engines apparatus or devices for taking fish, and as far as reasonably possible to prevent unlawful taking of fish, or unlawful attempts to take fish, and to give immediate notice to the owner of any unauthorised person, under a claim of right or otherwise, attempting to take fish from the river, and, if requested, to join the owner in proceeding against offenders.

(9) Not to trespass on adjoining or any other land or property of the owner, nor to do any damage to the same, leave litter, dig for bait, or light fires on the same.

(10) Not to cut or break any trees, bushes, hedges or fences on any land of the owner, save that trees or bushes may be cut, lopped or trimmed in a husbandlike manner with the prior permission in writing of the owner.

(11) To keep all gates used by the tenants or members of the Club closed, and to do nothing which would enable stock poultry or any animals kept on the premises or adjoining land to escape.

(12) To keep any dogs brought onto the premises under control.

(13) Not to take any vehicles onto the land of the owner except [state where vehicles may be taken and parked].

(14) Not to introduce any obstruction whatsoever into the river or to divert the flow of the water without the prior written consent of the owner.

[Covenants for salmon and trout waters]

(15) To keep an accurate record of all fish taken and to permit the owner or his water bailiff [or gamekeeper] to inspect the record at any reasonable time.

(16) [if not undertaken by owner] To employ at all times [a] competent keeper(s) to maintain and protect the fishing and to supervise the river and to expel all trespassers.

(17) Not to kill or take away from the river any kelts or samlets, or any trout measuring less than   inches from the snout to the fork of the tail, but to return immediately to the water any such fish taken from the river.

(18) Not to angle by means of worming, spinning, float fishing, minnowing or wet fly fishing, except that between the   day of   [specify what kind of fishing may be carried out when].

(19) Not to kill or take from the river more than   salmon or trout per person per day.

[Covenants for coarse fishing waters]

(20) Not to kill or take away from the river but to return immediately to the water any fish of the following species measuring less from the snout to the tip of the tail than the number of inches stated in each case as follows:

(21) Not to use any hemp seed, live bait or gorge bait in the river, except that between the   day of   [specify what may be done when].

(22) Not to kill or take from the river more than   in total per person per day of the species of fish referred to in paragraph 20 above.

(23) [If desired] Not to permit or carry out match fishing in the river.

(24) [If desired] Not to permit or carry out fishing for pike before the   day of   in any season.

APPENDIX C

FISHERY BYELAWS

The following are byelaws of the Avon and Dorset River Authority, reproduced here, with the Authority's kind permission, to indicate the kind of byelaws that are made where there is both coarse and game fishing.

1. **Annual Close Season for Netting for Salmon**
   The annual close season for netting for salmon shall be:—
   (i)   in that part of the River Board Area[1] which includes the Rivers Avon and Stour and their tributaries the period between the 31st day of July and the 1st day of February following; and
   (ii) in that part of the River Board Area which includes so much of the River Frome and its tributaries as lies above a line drawn true south-west from Swineham Point to Turners Cove the period between the 31st day of August and the 1st day of March following; and
   (iii) in all other parts of the River Board Area the period between the 31st day of July and the 1st day of April following.

2. **Rod Close Season for Salmon**
   The annual close season for fishing for salmon with rod and line shall be:—
   (i)   in that part of the River Board Area which includes the Rivers Avon and Stour and their tributaries the period between the 30th day of September and the 1st day of February following; and
   (ii) in all other parts of the River Board Area the period between the 30th day of September and the 1st day of March following.

3. **Annual Close Season for Netting for Trout**
   The annual close season for netting for trout shall be the period between the 31st day of July and the 1st day of April following.

4. **Rod Close Season for Migratory Trout**
   The annual close season for fishing for migratory trout with rod and

---

[1] Throughout these byelaws River Board Area now means River Authority Area, and references to the River Board or Board are to the River Authority (Water Resources Act, 1963, s. 5, Sch. 3, para. 4).

line shall be the period between the 31st day of October and the 16th day of April following.

5. **Rod Close Season for Trout Other Than Migratory Trout**
   The annual close season for fishing for trout other than migratory trout with rod and line shall be the period between the 30th day of September and the 1st day of April following provided that with the exception of the part of the River Nadder which lies above the road bridge at Barford St. Martin this byelaw shall not apply to so much of the River Avon and its tributaries as lies above Bickton Mill.

The following byelaw of the former Hampshire Rivers Board of Conservators Fishery District remains operative in the Avon and Dorset River Board Area:

6. **Close Season for Trout**
   The period during which it shall be illegal to take or kill trout or char, is hereby altered, so that in that part of the said district which includes so much of the River Avon as lies above the Mill Dam at Bickton Mill and the tributaries flowing into it above such Mill Dam, such period shall commence on the 15th day of October and terminate on the 15th day of April following, both days inclusive, provided that this byelaw shall not apply to that part of the River Nadder which lies above the road bridge at Barford St. Martin.

7. **Electrical Fishing Instruments**
   No person shall in any waters within the Avon and Doreset River Board Area take kill or injure or attempt to take kill or injure any salmon trout freshwater fish eels or elvers by means of any instrument or device which passes an electric current through or into the water without the written permission of the Board (or any of its officials duly authorised to give such permission) and subject to such conditions as the Board in giving permission may impose.

8. **Removal of Coarse Fish During the Close Season**
   No person being the owner or occupier of any several fishery where salmon or trout are specially preserved shall, during the statutory annual close season for coarse fish, fish for with rod and line any freshwater fish within such fishery or authorise any other person so to do except with the previous permission in writing of the Board or any of its officials duly authorised to give such permission.

9. **Prohibition of Night Netting**
   Between the hour of nine on each of the evenings of Wednesday, Thursday and Friday and the hour of five on each of the respective following mornings no person shall in any part of the River Board Area

use any net except a landing net used as auxiliary to angling with rod
and line.

10. **Use of Nets**
    (i)   The kind of net not being a landing net used as auxiliary to
angling with rod and line which may lawfully be used for taking
salmon and trout within the River Board Area shall be draft or
seine nets which shall be unarmoured nets without bags or
pockets and consisting of a single sheet of netting measuring not
more than 200 yards in length and not more than 8 yards in
depth at any part; all such measurements to be made when the
net is wet.
    (ii) The manner of using such nets shall be by holding one end of the
net on the shore or bank and the net shall be shot or paid out
from a boat which shall start from such shore or bank and shall
return thereto without pause or delay and the net shall thereupon
forthwith be drawn into and landed on the shore or bank from
which it started.
    (iii) Such net shall not be used by more than four persons in all at one
time.
    (iv) The use during the weekly close time for salmon of nets for
taking freshwater fish is hereby prohibited, except where there is
a several right of fishery, in so much of the Rivers Avon and
Stour as lie above a straight line drawn from the South Eastern
corner of Beacon Lodge to the seaward end of Long Rocks.

11. **Marking and Numbering of Nets and Boats**
Every licence for a net shall be distinguished by a number. A label
bearing the number of the licence shall be issued by the River Board
with every licence and such label shall be attached and shall always be
maintained attached to the head rope of the net for the use of which
the licence is granted. The same number shall be conspicuously painted
and maintained on the outside of any boat or vessel from or in
connection with which the net is used, near the centre of the gunwale
on each side in white letters not less than six inches high on a black
background, each stroke of such letters to be not less than one inch
broad.

12. **Carrying of Unlicensed Nets**
The carrying in a boat or vessel whilst being used in fishing for salmon
or trout of any net which is not licensed and has not attached thereto
the label prescribed by Byelaw No. 11 is hereby prohibited.

13. **Prohibition of Netting in Non-Tidal Waters**
The use of any net whatsoever, not being a landing net used as auxiliary
to rod and line, in non-tidal waters for the taking of salmon, trout or

freshwater fish is hereby prohibited; provided that nobody shall be guilty of an offence against this Byelaw who does any act for the following purposes, namely:—

    (i)   for the purpose of the artificial propagation of salmon, trout or freshwater fish, or for some scientific purpose, or for the purpose of the preservation or development of a private fishery and has obtained the previous permission in writing of the Board or any of its officials duly authorised to give such permission.

   (ii)   for the purpose of taking freshwater fish only, for use as bait in conjunction with rod and line and has obtained the previous permission in writing of the Board or any of its officials duly authorised to give such permission.

14.   Prohibition of Nets at Mouth of Frome

The use of nets is hereby prohibited in that part of the River Frome (not being a several fishery) which lies between the bridge across the said River Frome known as Holme Bridge and the bridges across the said river on the branch line of the British Railways from Wareham to Swanage.

15.   Return of Salmon and Migratory Trout Taken

Any person by whom salmon or migratory trout or both such fish are taken within the River Board Area or any General Licensee shall, not later than the 15th day of November in each year make a full and true return to the River Board on a form provided by the Board of the number and aggregate weight of all such salmon or migratory trout taken by him or his agents or servants, or in the case of a general licence by any person whatsoever who fishes in pursuance of such licence, within the River Board Area during the year; provided that no person shall be guilty of an offence againt this Byelaw unless he has been supplied by the River Board at the time of the issue of a licence to him with a form of return for this purpose.

16.   Use of Night Lines

No person shall within the River Board Area take or attempt to take salmon, trout or freshwater fish by means of any night-line or set-line whatsoever and any such night-line or set-line shall be deemed to be an illegal instrument within the meaning of the Act; provided that nobody shall be guilty of an offence against this Byelaw who does any act for the purpose of the preservation or development of a private fishery or for some scientific purpose and has obtained the previous permission in writing of the Board or any of its officials duly authorised to give such permission.

17.   Taking of Undersized Trout and Freshwater Fish

    (1) No person shall take fish of any kind hereinafter mentioned

which is of less than the minimum size prescribed hereunder:—

(*a*)   In all waters within the River Board Area.

		Inches
Gudgeon	- - - -	4
Roach	- - - -	8
Perch	- - - -	8
Dace	- - - -	8
Rudd	- - - -	8
Carp	- - - -	12
Bream	- - - -	8
Barbel	- - - -	16
Tench	- - - -	9

(*b*)   (i)   In the main River Stour (excluding tributaries) and
(ii)   In the River Avon below Town Bridge, Fordingbridge.

		Inches
Grayling	- - - -	12

(*c*)   In all such rivers (including tributaries) within the River Board Area as enter the sea to the East of a line drawn due North and South through the Coast Guard Station at West Bay, Bridport.

		Inches
Trout	- - - -	10

(*d*)   In all such rivers (including tributaries) within the River Board Area as enter the sea to the West of a line drawn due North and South through the Coast Guard Station at West Bay, Bridport.

		Inches
Trout	- - - -	9

(2) The minimum size prescribed by this Byelaw for any fish shall be ascertained by measuring from the tip of the snout to the fork or cleft of the tail.

(3) Provided that nobody shall be guilty of an offence against this Byelaw who:—

(*a*)   Takes any undersized fish unintentionally if he at once returns the same to the water with as little injury as possible.

(*b*)   Takes any undersized fish during a *bona fide* fishing match if he keeps the same alive in a proper Keep Net during such match and returns such fish to the water with as little injury as possible immediately on the conclusion of the weighing in after the match, such weighing in to take place on the river bank.

(*c*)   Takes any undersized fish for use as bait.

(*d*)   Does any act for the purpose of the preservation or development of a private fishery or for some scientific purpose and with the previous permission in writing of the Board or any of its officials duly authorised to give such permission.

18.   **Use of Lures or Baits with Rod and Line**
       No person shall use in connection with fishing with rod and line for
       salmon in any waters within the River Board Area any prawn shrimp
       worm or plug before the 15th day of May in any year.

19.   **Use of Gaff**
       It shall be not lawful to use a gaff in connection with fishing with rod
       and line for salmon or migratory trout in any waters within the River
       Board Area between the 31st day of August and the 1st day of
       November following.

20.   **Removal of Fish**
       No person (other than a member or bailiff of the Board, or in the case
       of a private fishery the owner or lessee (or his authorised agent)
       concerned) shall take or remove any live fish or any dead fish from any
       waters within the River Board Area unless acting by written permission
       of the Board or any of its officials duly authorised to give such
       permission, or otherwise lawfully authorised so to do.

21.   **Stocking**
       No salmon, trout or freshwater fish, nor any spawn thereof, may be
       introduced from any source into any waters within the River Board
       Area, without the previous permission in writing of the Board or any of
       its officials duly authorised to give such permission.

INDEX

Angling and the Law

1976 SUPPLEMENT AND NOTER-UP
TO THE SECOND EDITION

MICHAEL GREGORY, LL.B., Barrister

Published by Charles Knight & Company Limited
25 New Street Square, London, EC4A 3JA
& Sovereign Way, Tonbridge, Kent, TN9 1RW

First published 1976

This supplement and noter-up is intended for
use in conjunction with the Second Edition of
Angling and the Law by Michael Gregory,
published by Charles Knight & Company
Limited in 1974.

Printed in Great Britain

ISBN 0 85314–283–1

WATER REORGANISATION AND CONSOLIDATION OF SALMON & FRESHWATER FISHERIES ACTS

The water reorganisation previewed in Chapter 22 has taken place pretty much as envisaged. The changes are mainly to be found in the Water Act, 1973. This Act transferred to nine new regional water authorities and a Welsh National Water Development Authority the functions and duties of the river authorities. The new authorities are also made responsible for water supply and sewage disposal. The river authorities have followed the sometime river boards and fishery boards to the grave. Throughout the book for "river authority" now read "water authority".

All the extant law in the sundry Salmon and Freshwater Fisheries Acts has been consolidated into one statute, the Salmon and Freshwater Fisheries Act, 1975, which is supposed not to have changed the law. The previous Acts are repealed. The 1975 Act contains some law derived from other sources. A Table is given below showing where the law in the repealed fishery Acts has got to in the 1975 Act. This is done by taking each of the repealed Acts section by section.

The Noter-Up does not refer to the changes shewn in the Table but does indicate the modifications needed to the text of the second Edition by reason of other changes or developments of the law. It should be noted that much of the Water Resources Act, 1963 has been repealed or amended by the Water Act, 1973 and significant changes are being made by the Control of Pollution Act, 1974.

Life being like that, even more changes are contemplated in a recent Consultative Document of the Government, "Review of the Water Industry in England and Wales".

Abbreviations. The following abbreviations are used in this Supplement.
"the text" = the text of the Second Edition of *Angling and the Law*
"The 1923 Act" = The Salmon and Freshwater Fisheries Act, 1923
"The 1963 Act" = The Water Resources Act, 1963
"The 1972 Act" = The Salmon and Freshwater Fisheries Act, 1972
"The 1975 Act" = The Salmon and Freshwater Fisheries Act, 1975
"s." = section   "ss." = sections   "Sch." = schedule

THE SALMON AND FRESHWATER FISHERIES ACT, 1975

Table of Derivations and Destinations

Note. In many instances the section of the repealed Act had been amended or repealed in part before the 1975 Act. In these instances, of course, the 1975 Act re-enacted the law as it found it. The invaluable help of Miss D. E. Sawyer of the Fisheries Department of the Ministry of Agriculture, Fisheries & Food (always a helpful Department) in providing an analyses of derivations and destinations, is acknowledged.

Section of Repealed Act	Now in 1975 Act, Section:	Section of Repealed Act	Now in 1975 Act, Section:	Section of Repealed Act	Now in 1975 Act, Section:
Salmon and Freshwater Fisheries Act, 1923		21	11(4), (5)	38(1) (f)	Sch.3, para. 1(c)
		22	12	38(1)(g)–(i)	Repealed
1(1)	1(1)	23(1)	14(1); 41(1)	38(1) (j)	28(5)
1(2)	1(2)	23(2)–(6)	14(2)–(7); 41(1)	38(1) (k)	28(3)
1(3)	1(3)	24(1)	15(1), (4); 41(1)	38(1) (1) & proviso	Repealed
1(4)	1(4)	24(2)	41(1)	38(2)	Obsolete
2	2(1)	24(3)	15(1); 41(1)	38(3)	28(4); 29
3	2(2), (3)	24(4)	15(3), (4)	38(4)	Repealed
4	2(4)	24(5)	15(2); 18(1); 41(1)	39(1)	Sch.3, para. 5
5	2(5)	24(6)	18(2)–(4)	39(2)	Sch.3, para. 6
6	3(1)	25	18(5)	40(1)	Sch.3, para. 7
7	3(2)–(4)	26(1)	19(2)	40(2)	Sch.3, para. 8
8(1)	4(1), (2)	26(2)	19(2), (3)	40(3)	Sch.3, para. 9
8(2)	Repealed	26(3)–(5)	Sch.1, para. 6	40(4)	Sch.3, para. 10
8(3)	4(3)	27(1)	19(2)	40(5), (6)	Sch.3, paras. 11, 12
9	Substituted	27(2)	19(2)	41	Obsolete
9(1)	5(1), (2)	27(3)	Sch.1, para. 6	42–53	Sch.3, para. 13
9(2)	5(3)	28	20	54	36(3); Sch.3, paras. 37–39
9(3)	5(4)	29	20	55	Repealed
9(4)	Repealed	30(1), (2)	22(1)	56–58	Obsolete
9(5)	5(5), (6)	30(3)	22(2)	59(1)	Sch.1; Sch.3, para. 15
10	Repealed	30(4)	22(4)	59(1) (a)–(e)	Sch.1, para. 3; Sch.3, para. 20
11(1)	6(1)	31(1)	19(4)	59(1) (f)	Sch.3, para. 21
11(2)	6(2)	31(2)	19(4), (5)	59(1) (g)–(p)	Sch.3, paras. 22–31
11(3)	6(1)	31(3)–(5)	Sch.1, para. 6	59(1) (q)	Sch.3, para. 32
11(4)	6(3)	31(6)	20	59(1) (r)–(u)	Sch.3, paras. 33–36
12(1)	7(1), (5); 8(1), (5)	31(7)	20(6)	59(2)	Sch.3, para. 16
12(2)	7(4); 8(3) (a)	32(1)	22(1), (3)	59(3)	28(7)
13	7(2)–(4)	32(1A)	22(2)	59(4)	Sch.3, paras. 17, 18
14(1)	8(2)	32(1B)	22(4)	60	Obsolete
14(2)	8(3) (b)	32(2)	22(1)	61–65	Repealed
14(3)	8(4)	33(1)	23(1)	66	Obsolete
15	16	33(2)	23(5)	67(1)	31(1)
16(1)	Sch.3, paras. 37, 38	33(3)	23(2)	67(1) (a)	31(1) (a)
16(2)–(6)	Obsolete	33(4)	23(3)	67(1) (b), (c)	31(1) (b), (c)
17(1), (2)	17(1)	33(5)	23(4)	67(1) (d)	31(1) (d)
17(3)	17(2)	34(1)	24(1)	67(2)	31(2)
17(4)	17(3); 18(4)	34(2)	24(2)–(5); 41(1)	67(3)	36(1)
18	13	34(3)	24(1), (6)	67(4)	36(2)
19(1)	9(1)	34(4)	41(1)	68	32
19(2)	9(2)	35	19; Sch.1	69	33(1)
19(3)	9(3)	36(1), (2)	21(1)	70	33(2), (3)
19(4)	18(1)	36(3)	21(2)	71	34
19(5)	9(4)	37	28(3)	72	31–34
19(6)	Repealed	38(1)	Sch. 3, para 4		
20(1)–(3)	10	38(1) (a)	28(3)		
20(4)	18(1)	38(1) (b), (c)	Repealed		
20(5)	18(3), (4)	38(1) (d)	Sch.3, para. 1(a)		
20(6)	18(2)	38(1) (e)	Sch.3, paras. 1(b), 2, 3, 37(c)		
20(7)	Sch. 3, paras. 37, 38				

Section of Repealed Act	Now in 1975 Act, Section:	Section of Repealed Act	Now in 1975 Act, Section:	Section of Repealed Act	Now in 1975 Act, Section:
73(1)	Sch.4, para. 1(2)	*Salmon and Freshwater Fisheries Act, 1935*		6(1)–(9)	25(1)–(8)
73(2), 74	Repealed			7	26(1)–(7)
75(1)	Sch.4, para. 2	1	28(3)	8	27
75(2)	Repealed	2	Repealed	9(1)	35(1)
76	Sch.4, para. 4			9(2), (3)	35(2), (3)
77(1)	Sch.4, para. 12	*Salmon and Freshwater Fisheries Act, 1965*		10	30
77(2)	Sch.4, para. 13			11(1)	31(1) (b), (c)
78	41(1); Sch.4, para. 7	1	5	11(2)	31(2)
		2(1)	Obsolete	11(3)	Repealed
79	Sch.4, para. 8	2(2)	31(1) (d)	11(4)	33(2), (3)
80	42(5)			11(5)	33(2), (3); 34
81	Obsolete	*Salmon and Freshwater Fisheries Act, 1972*		12(1), (2)	37; Sch.4, para. 1(1)
82	39(1)			12(3)	Sch.4, para. 1(3)
83	39(1)	1(1)	1(1)	12(4)	Sch. 4, para. 1(2)
84	Obsolete	1(2)	1(3)		
85(1)	39(2)	1(3)	1(4)	12(5), (6)	Sch.4, para. (5), (6)
85(2)	39(3)	2(1)–(3)	11(1)–(3)	12(7)	Sch.4, para. 9
86	40	2(4)	11(5)	13	Sch. 4, paras. 10, 11
87	Repealed	3(1)	Sch.1, para. 1		
88	Obsolete	3(2)	Sch.1, para. 2	14(1)	41(1)
89	42(8)	3(3)	Sch.1, para. 6	14(2)	Obsolete
90	41(3)	3(4)	Sch.1, paras. 1, 3	14(3)	41(1)
91(1)	38(1)			14(4)	Obsolete
91(2)–(4)	38(2)–(4)	3(5)	Obsolete	15(1), (2)	Obsolete
92(1)	41(1)	4(1)	Sch.1, para. 3; Sch.3, para. 20	15(3)	Sch. 4, para. 3
92(2)	41(1)	4(2)	Obsolete	16(1)–(3)	Obsolete
93(1)	Repealed	4(3)	19(6), (7)	16(4)	25(9); 26(8)
93(2)	42(3); 41(4)	4(4)	19(8)	16(5), (6)	Obsolete
94 & Schedules	Obsolete & repealed	4(5)	Sch.1, para. 4	Sch.1, paras. 1–18	Sch.2, paras. 1–18
		4(6)	Sch.1, para. 5	Sch.2	Sch.4, para. 1; Table
Salmon and Freshwater Fisheries (Amendment) Act, 1929		5(1)	Obsolete	Sch.3	Obsolete
		5(2)	Sch.3, para. 21		
1	22(2), (4)	5(3)	Sch.3, para. 32		

NOTER-UP

Page of
Second Edition

CHAPTER 1

p.3 The Salmon and Freshwater Fisheries Acts. See note at the beginning of this Supplement for the consolidation of the Acts in the 1975 Act. The transfer from the repealed Acts to the 1975 Act is shown in the Table above.

CHAPTER 3

pp.8–9 Duty to make byelaws. The 1975 Act repeats the duty of every water authority to make byelaws but without specifying the time limit and says if a water authority had not done so before the commencement of the 1975 Act the Minister may (Sch. 1, paras. 1 & 2).

p.10 Close Seasons for Freshwater Fish. The transmogrification of the Thames and Lee Conservancies into a water authority (the Thames Water Authority) made (from April 1, 1974) all "inland waters" in their areas subject to the coarse fish close season, even if landlocked, in uniformity with the rest of the country.

p.13 Close Season for Trout. See note to pp.8–9 above on the duty to make byelaws.

CHAPTER 4

p.17 Fishing Licences for Freshwater Fish and Eels. Licences are now needed in the Lee, Thames and London areas, now governed by the Thames Water Authority (Water Act, 1973, Sch.1).

pp.20–21 Production of Licence. The right of a member of a river authority (now water authority) to require production of a licence was deleted by the Water Act, 1973. The 1975 Act,s.35, unlike former Acts, does not state a bailiff must first produce evidence of his authority before requiring the production of a licence, but he must—see p. 167 of the text.

CHAPTER 6

p.31 Accidents on Pier. Where an exoneration clause is exceptionally wide it is ineffective if explicit attention is not drawn to it (*Thornton v. Shoe Lane Parking Ltd.* [1971] 1 All E.R. 31). See also *Burnett v. British Waterways Board* [1973] 2 All E.R. 631 noted to p.64 below.

CHAPTER 7

p.34 Previous Permission of Minister where no River Authority exists. In all cases consent must be from the water authority now there is full coverage by water authorities.

p.37 Poison, Explosives and Electric Fishing. In the Thames, Lee and London areas permission must now be obtained from the Thames Water Authority.

p.38 Size Limits. The Ministry no longer have the power to make size limit byelaws now all areas are covered by water authorities.

CHAPTER 8

p.40 Fixed Engines. The Minister's power to take over or destroy is gone now all areas are covered by water authorities. In reproducing the definition of "fixed engine" the 1975 Act, s.41(1) omits from (c) the words "not being a fishing weir or fishing mill dam."

p.46 Fish Passes Needed for New Dam Works since 1873. The duty to make and maintain a fish pass now only arises "if so required by notice given by the water authority". No default powers are exercisable by the Minister now all areas are covered by water authorities.

p.47 Supply of Water to Dams and Fish Passes. The Minister has no power to excuse now all areas are covered by water authorities. All notices to let off water for cleaning or repairing must be to the water authority.

p.48 Compulsory Purchase of Bank. The compulsory purchase procedures in the 1923 Act have been allowed to lapse. They are not in the 1975 Act, so Part VI of the 1963 Act applies and the general power of water authorities "to do anything" to discharge their functions (Water Act, 1973, Sch.3, para. 2; 1975 Act, Sch.3, para.37).

p.49 Presumed Guilt of Owner or Occupier. The Minister can no longer serve a notice to repair etc. now all areas are covered by water authorities.

p.51 Application to River Authority Areas Only. This paragraph no longer applies. The 1975 Act, s.17 is of universal application.

Compulsory Purchase. See note to p. 48 above.

p.52 Confirmation by Minister is Conclusive. This unfair rule has lapsed with the 1923 procedures.

p.53 Compulsory Hiring. See note to p.48 above. "Grating" is now defined in 1975 Act, s.41(1) as "a device approved by the Minister for preventing the passage of salmon or trout through a conduit or channel in which it is placed".

p.54 Installation of Gratings by River Authority. The former s.24(3) of the 1923 Act is now simplified to provide that the water authority may place the grating "at any suitable place" in the watercourse, etc. (1975 Act, s.15(1) (a)).

CHAPTER 9

p.64 Occupiers Liability Act 1957. In *Burnett v. British Waterways Board* [1973] 2 All E.R. 631 a notice disclaiming liability for any injury or damage caused to persons entering a dock was ineffective to protect the Board from their common law duty of care to a lighterman who had no choice as to the terms on which he entered the dock.

p.65 Bulls. In the Scottish case of *Lanarkshire Water Board v. Gilchrist* [1973] S.L.T. 58, an interdict was granted to stop a farmer keeping a bull on land where the Board had a right of way to their reservoir.

CHAPTER 10

p.69 Regulation of Fisheries. Byelaw making powers and procedures are now in the Water Act, 1973, s.36 and Sch.7 and the 1975 Act, s.25 and Sch.3. The 1963 Act, s.119 and Sch.12 repealed.

CHAPTER 12

p.80 Compensation for Statutory Works. For the valuation of fishing rights on compulsory purchase see *Davies v. Welsh National Water Development Authority* (1976) R.V.R. 97.

Land Drainage Works. *Burgess v. Gwynedd River Authority* (1972) was

7

upheld on appeal under the new name of *Welsh National Water Development Authority v. Burgess* (1974) R.V.R. 395.

A new Land Drainage Bill is before Parliament at the time of writing, consolidating the Land Drainage Acts, and see Land Drainage (Amendment) Act 1976, which makes some amendments to the law in preparation for the consolidation.

CHAPTER 13

p.85 **Meaning of "Premises".** The plot thickens. In *Maunsell v. Olins* [1974] 2 All E.R. 250, a let farm was held not to be "premises" within the Rent Act, 1968, s. 18(5). This confirms *Hobhouse v. Wall* [1963] 1 All E.R. 701 where Upjohn LJ said, "I think Parliament is here thinking of something in the nature of buildings".

Note printing error: First sentence of third para should read, 'What is more important is that the House of Lords included fishing rights within the term "premises", on the same principle, in the case of *Whitley v. Stumbles.*'

pp.87–8 **Fishing Let with Cottages.** The protection of the Rent Acts has been extended to furnished lettings by the Rent Act, 1974. The holiday letting exception remains, and out-of-season lettings of holiday accommodation are not protected if let for a fixed term of not more than 8 months after a notice given under Rent Act, 1968, Sch.3, Case 10B.

p.88 **Licence.** *Heslop v. Burns* [1974] 3 All E.R. 406 held exclusive occupation denotes a licence rather than a tenancy where it is granted as a personal benefit or act of generosity.

p.91 **Fishing Rights in Ponds and Large Lakes.** Though planning permission may not be needed an impounding licence may be under 1963 Act, ss. 36 & 37.

CHAPTER 14

pp.96–7 **Ownership of Riparian Land to Middle of River.** Further reference to the elasticity of the middle line in practice was made by Ormrod LJ in *Welsh National Water Development Authority v. Burgess* (1974) R.V.R. 395 where he referred to "the good sense of fishermen and their legal advisers"!

CHAPTER 15

p.104 **Generally.** See note to p.48 on compulsory purchase of bank.

Footnote 2. *Peach v. Best* should be *Peech v. Best*.

CHAPTER 17

p.117 **Exemption of Agricultural Land.** In *Jones v. Bateman* (1974) 232 E.G. 1392 a trout farm with 5 acres, rearing trout for eating, was held by the Lands Tribunal to be agricultural and exempt from rating, the trout being "livestock" within the Rating Act 1971. The Scottish case of *Wallace v. Assessor for Perth & Kinross* [1975] S.L.T. 118 is to the contrary, holding that "livestock" does not mean fish.

CHAPTER 18

p.122 **Footnote 3.** The Diseases of Fish Order, 1973 (S.I. 1973, No. 2093) extended the Act to IPN, VHS, whirling disease, IHN, UDN and IDC or IAD in any of its forms.

p.125 **Penalties.** Water authorities are empowered by the Water Act, 1973, Sch.8, para.43 to take proceedings to enforce the Diseases of Fish Act, 1937 in their areas. A new s.8(2) has been substituted.

CHAPTER 19

p.126 **Scope of Public Navigation.** In *Trustees of Hamilton Wills Settlement v. Cairngorm Canoeing & Sailing School Ltd.* (*Times*, 4 March 1976) the House of Lords shed light on the nature of the public right of navigation. It depended on the capacity of the river, could not be lost by non-use, did not extend to "revolutionary new types of craft", but did include canoeing.

Evans v. Godber (*Times*, 9 July 1974) held that "right of way" in the National Parks and Access to the Countryside Act, 1949, s.20 meant a right on land, not a right of navigation; and mooring had no fixed meaning, it was a question of fact, not law.

p.130 **Byelaws must be observed.** For control of pollution see also Water Act, 1973, Control of Pollution Act, 1974 and note below to p. 145.

p.131 **Water Skiing.** In *Trustees of Hamilton Wills Settlement v. Cairngorm Canoeing & Sailing School* (*Times*, 4 March 1976) Lord Fraser considered the right of public navigation would not include "operations which would be more like acrobatic feats than navigation".

Fishing and Other Forms of Recreation. Water Act, 1973 provides for recreational use of water and associated land (s.20), places duties on water authorities and the Minister to have regard to conservation of amenity (s.22), sets up the Water Space Amenity Commission (s.23) and provides for recreation and amenity in and around London (s.25).

p.133 **Reservoirs.** The water authorities have taken over the duties as envisaged in the text. Countryside Act, 1968 s.22(1) is repealed and minor amendments made to s.22(2)–(5) (Water Act, 1973, Sch.9 & Sch.8, para.92).

Inland Water. Water Act, 1973, s.36 & Sch.7 lay down byelaw powers and procedures for the Minister, water authorities, other water undertakers and internal drainage boards. The 1963 Act s. 79(4) is amended and s.80 repealed (Water Act, 1973, Sch.8, para.82 & Sch.9).

Water Space Amenity Commission. The Government's Consultation Document "Review of the Water Industry in England & Wales" (1976) proposes the replacement of the National Water Council by a new body, the National Water Authority, merger of British Waterways Board with the new Authority, and comments there would then "clearly not be room for" the WSAC and the IWAAC.

p.133-4 **Inland Waterways.** In the reorganisation the water authorities did not take over inland waterways, nor did WSAC take over IWAAC, but death sentences have been renewed—see preceding note.

CHAPTER 20

p.135-6 **Ironic Threat to Make Machiavellian History.** The envisaged clause to remove the common law injunction was included in a bill called, believe it or not, the Protection of the Environment Bill, but the House of Lords magnificently booted out the clause. The bill fell with the dissolution of Parliament in 1974. After the General Election the same bill under a new name was introduced without the evil clause, now the Control of Pollution Act, 1974.

pp.139-40 **No Prescription where Forbidden by Statute.** See note below to p.145 for the replacement of the 1951 and 1961 Acts by the Control of Pollution Act, 1974.

p.141 **Dumping Toxic Waste.** The 1972 Act is replaced by the Control of Pollution Act, 1974.

pp.141-2 **Lakes, Ponds and Artificial Watercourses.** See note below to p.145 on Control of Pollution Act, 1974. The exception for land-locked lakes, etc. is continued.

9

p.145 The Attorney-General. See *Att.-Gen. v. Wellingborough UDC* (*Times*, 29 March 1974) (injunction against UDC); and *Att.-Gen. v. Chaudry* [1971] 3 All E.R. 938 (injunction against hotel).

Statutory Powers to Control Pollution. The Control of Pollution Act, 1974 (when in force) repeals the Rivers (Prevention of Pollution) Acts, 1951 & 1961 (except ss.10, 12, 13(1) and 15(1) & (3) of the 1961 Act), Clean Rivers (Estuaries & Tidal Waters) Act, 1960, Noise Abatement Act, 1960, Deposit of Poisonous Waste Act, 1972 and sundry miscellaneous pieces of other Acts, replacing them with a new code which re-enacts much of what is repealed and introduces new laws to tackle Waste on Land (Part I), Pollution of Water (Part II), Noise (Part III) and Pollution of the Atmosphere (Part IV). The snag is that the Act only comes into force as and when the Secretary of State decides (s.109(2)) and after two years, for all the Governmental boasting, most of the improved law against water pollution is not yet in force, including laws for public registers of consents to discharge trade and sewage effluent, publication of applications for consents and opportunities for objectors (ss.34–42), duties on water authorities to remedy or forestall pollution injurious to fauna and flora of streams (s.46), and powers to stop harmful agricultural practices (s.51). Sections 33, 47 and 48 deal with waste from vessels.

pp.147–8 Protection of Rivers. See previous note.

p.148 "Causes". *Price v. Cromack* [1975] 2 All E.R. 113 held the accused not guilty of "causing" pollution when industrial effluent escaped to pollute a stream through no positive act of the accused.

The Penalty. Maximum penalties for similar offences in the Control of Pollution Act, 1974 are (a) on summary conviction—3 months imprisonment and/or £400 fine; (b) on indictment—2 years imprisonment and/or unlimited fine (s.31).

Discharges from Mine. See Control of Pollution Act, 1974, s.31(3) (permissible deposits) and s.50 (investigation of problems).

p.149 Cleansing River Bed and Cutting Vegetation. Maximum penalty for similar offences in Control of Pollution Act, 1974 is a £200 fine (s.49).

Byelaws. See note above to p.69.

pp.149–55 Statutory Control of Effluent Disposal by Consents. See note above to p.145.

p.150 Contraventions. False statements in applications for consents will be punishable by a fine not exceeding £400, or, on indictment, up to 2 years imprisonment and/or an unlimited fine (Control of Pollution Act, 1974, s.34(5)).

pp.151–2 Tidal Waters. See Control of Pollution Act, 1974, s.32 and Dumping at Sea Act, 1974. The 1960 Act is repealed by the Control of Pollution Act, 1974 on a day to be appointed.

p.152 Protective Effects of Consents. See also Control of Pollution Act, 1974, ss.31(2) & 54.

p.154 Proposed Changes. See Control of Pollution Act, 1974 and notes above to pp.135–6 and 145.

Miscellaneous Pollution Laws. Oil in Navigable Waters Act, 1955 repealed and replaced by Prevention of Oil Pollution Act, 1971.

p.155 Protecting Waters and Removing Polluting Matter. Water Act, 1945, s.22 amended by Water Act, 1973, Sch.8, para.51. The 1963 Act, s.76(3) repealed by Water Act, 1973 and the rest of s.76 repealed on a day to be appointed by the Control of Pollution Act, 1974.

CHAPTER 21

p.156 Statutory Control of Abstractions. New powers to protect water resources are given by the Drought Act, 1976.

75p *net*

ISBN 0 85314–283–1

Printed in Great Britain by Tonbridge Printers Ltd., Tonbridge, Kent